BBC

DOCTOR WHO

THE ROAD TO THE THIRTEENTH DOCTOR

"A tremendous sense of pace and energy... innovatively clever script work... feels like pure joy dropped onto the page!"
BLOGTOR WHO

"A good old-fashioned *Doctor Who* adventure!"
CBR

"By looking to *Doctor Who's* past to tease its future, *The Road to the Thirteenth Doctor* is a path worth taking!"
NEWSARAMA

"The Tenth Doctor encounters lost, ghostly spaceships, the Eleventh Doctor and Alice visit a robot-infested 19th-century San Francisco, and the Twelfth Doctor finds London's Piccadilly Circus transformed into a wasteland of emptiness and pterodactyls!"
ENTERTAINMENT WEEKLY

"A wonderful little story, which will have you wondering what the writers and artists will do next! "
SCI FI PULSE

"The humor and the mystery are so good. It feels like an episode of the series!"
POP CULTURE UNCOVERED

"Entertaining – and always great to see the Matt Smith version of the Doctor back in action!"
CHUCK'S COMIC OF THE DAY

"If you need your *Doctor Who* fix before Jodie Whittaker's season begins, this is a fine choice!"
MULTIVERSITY COMICS

"An enjoyable adventure – the pacing is breakneck!"
BLEEDING COOL

Editor
Jessica Burton

Senior Designer
Andrew Leung

Titan Comics

Managing and Launch Editor
Andrew James

Production Assistant
Rhiannon Roy

Production Controller
Peter James

Senior Production Controller
Jackie Flook

Art Director
Oz Browne

Circulation Executive
Frances Hallam

Sales & Circulation Manager
Steve Tothill

Press Officer
William O'Mullane

Publicist
Imogen Harris

Brand Manager
Chris Thompson

Ads & Marketing Assistant
Bella Hoy

Direct Sales & Marketing Manager
Ricky Claydon

Commercial Manager
Michelle Fairlamb

Head Of Rights
Jenny Boyce

Publishing Manager
Darryl Tothill

Publishing Director
Chris Teather

Operations Director
Leigh Baulch

Executive Director
Vivian Cheung

Publisher
Nick Landau

For rights information contact Jenny Boyce
jenny.boyce@titanemail.com

Special thanks to Chris Chibnall, Matt Strevens, Sam Hoyle, Mandy Thwaites,
Gabby De Matteis, Ross McGlinchey, David Wilson-Nunn, Kirsty Mullan, Kate Bush,
and Ed Casey for their invaluable assistance.

BBC Worldwide

Director Of Editorial Governance
Nicolas Brett

Director Of Consumer Products And Publishing
Andrew Moultrie

Head Of UK Publishing
Chris Kerwin

Publisher
Mandy Thwaites

Publishing Co-Ordinator
Eva Abramik

DOCTOR WHO: THE ROAD TO THE THIRTEENTH DOCTOR
ISBN: 9781785869310

Published by Titan Comics, a division of Titan Publishing Group, Ltd. 144 Southwark Street, London, SE1 0UP.
Titan Comics is a registered trademark. All rights reserved.

A CIP catalogue record for this title is available from the British Library.
First edition: January 2019.

10 9 8 7 6 5 4 3 2 1

Printed in Spain.

BBC

DOCTOR WHO

THE ROAD TO THE THIRTEENTH DOCTOR

THE GHOST SHIP
THE STEAMPUNK CONUNDRUM
TULPA

WRITER
JAMES PEATY

ARTISTS
IOLANDA ZANFARDINO
PASQUALE QUALANO
BRIAN WILLIAMSON

COLORIST
DIJJO LIMA

THE ROAD TO...

WRITER
JODY HOUSER

ARTIST
RACHAEL STOTT

COLORIST
ENRICA EREN ANGIOLINI

LETTERER
RICHARD STARKINGS
AND COMICRAFT'S JIMMY BETANCOURT

TITAN
COMICS

BBC

BBC

DOCTOR WHO

THE ROAD TO THE THIRTEENTH DOCTOR

Character Bios

TENTH DOCTOR

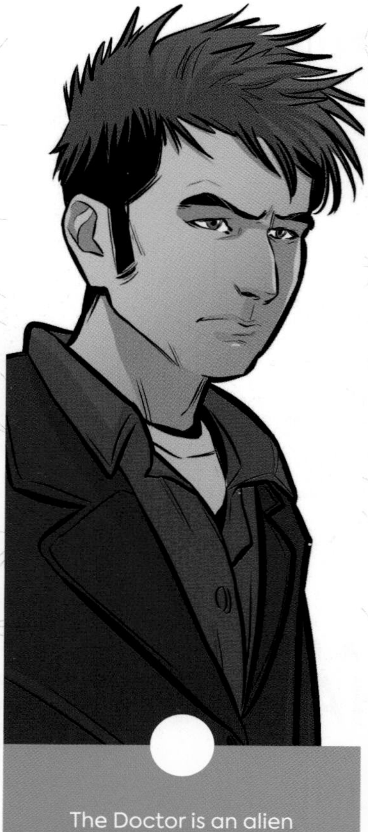

The Doctor is an alien who walks like a man. His Tenth incarnation still hides his post-Time War guilt beneath a happy-go-lucky guise.

Never cruel or cowardly, he champions the oppressed across time and space!

ELEVENTH DOCTOR

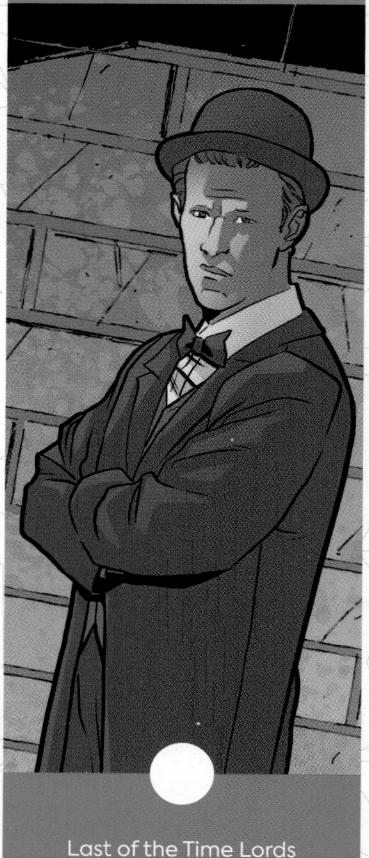

Last of the Time Lords of Gallifrey, the Doctor's Eleventh incarnation is a gangly boy professor with an old, old soul.

He has made many mistakes in his time – some enormous! – but owns each and every one of them.

TWELFTH DOCTOR

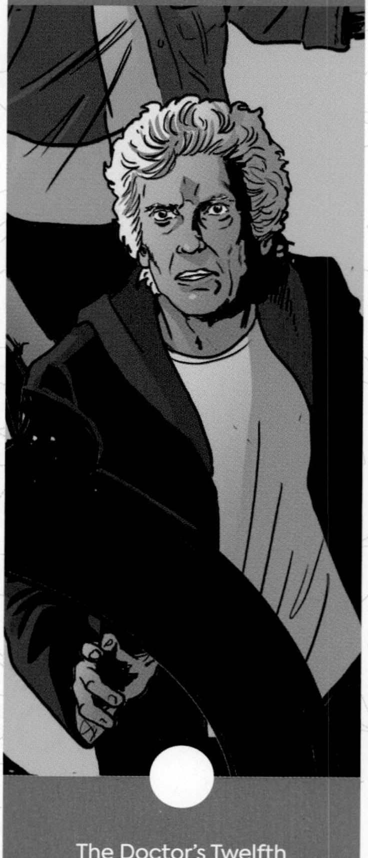

The Doctor's Twelfth incarnation is done with guilt, wants to fix things, and now he feels he has licence to!

Wanting to find the good in an often cruel universe, he manages to find adventure – and danger – wherever he goes!

The Doctor has had many adventures – all of them putting his wits to the test! Join the Doctor's Tenth, Eleventh, and Twelfth incarnations as they battle previously unseen foes and fight for the future, across time and space.

And in moments of stolen time, in the middle of familiar adventures, a mysterious figure reaches out from beyond... Who could they be?!

GABBY GONZALEZ

Gabriella Gonzalez is a young artist from Brooklyn, New York, who has had many adventures alongside the Tenth Doctor, shining a light on what he misses. Gabby has even gained time-related powers on her travels!

CINDY WU

Gabby's best friend, travelling with her in the TARDIS. Cindy has learned first-hand of the dangers and joys that time and space can bring, but she never shies from what's right — or from telling the Doctor just how wrong he is!

ALICE OBIEFUNE

Former Library Assistant Alice Obiefune is among the bravest of the Doctor's friends. She has saved the Eleventh Doctor from himself and others on multiple occasions, and the two trust each other implicitly!

BILL POTTS

First encountered the Twelfth Doctor while working at the university where he was teaching. Warm-hearted and full of wonder, Bill is keen for adventure —but she also knows when to put the Doctor in his place!

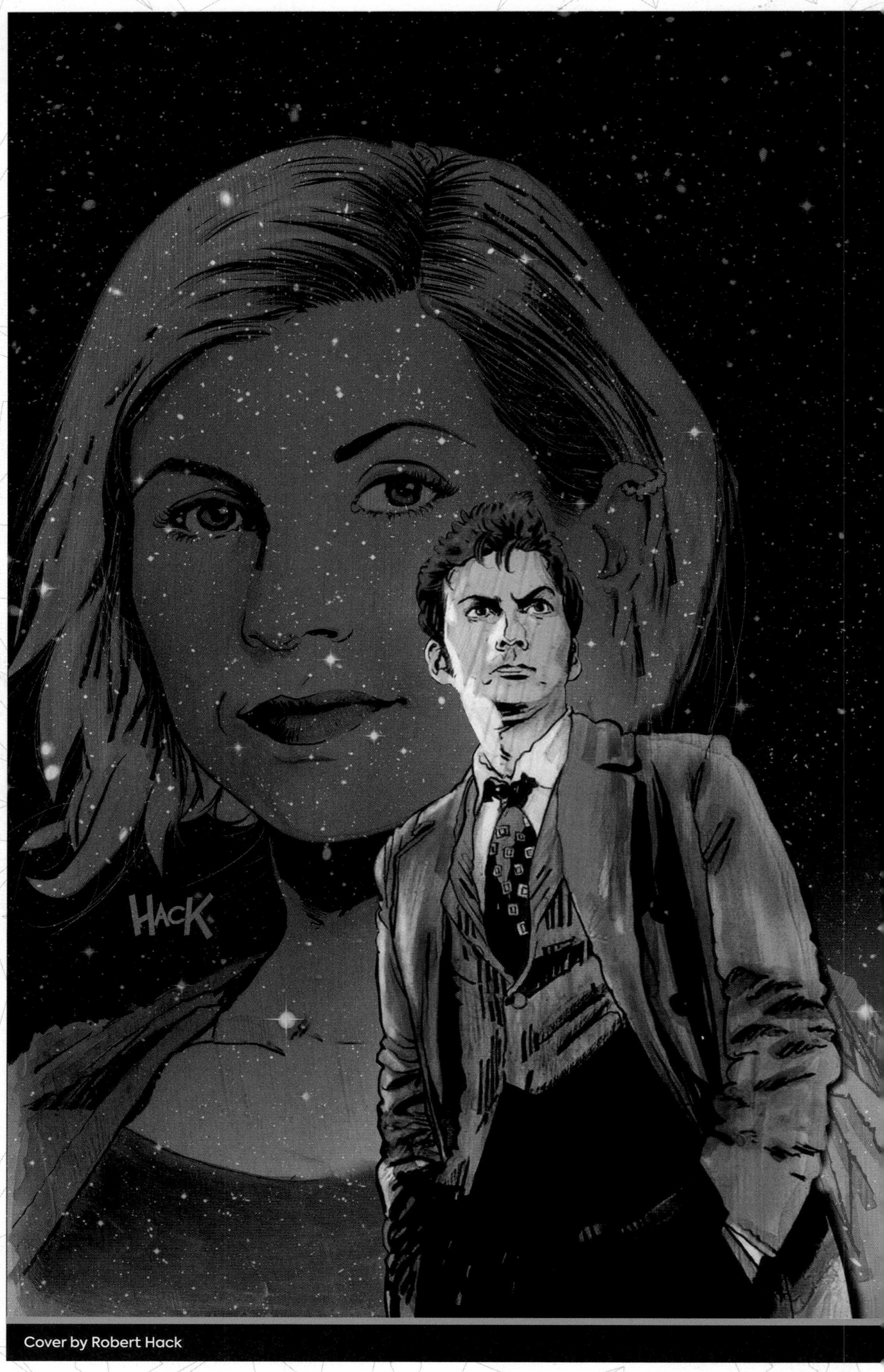
HACK

Cover by Robert Hack

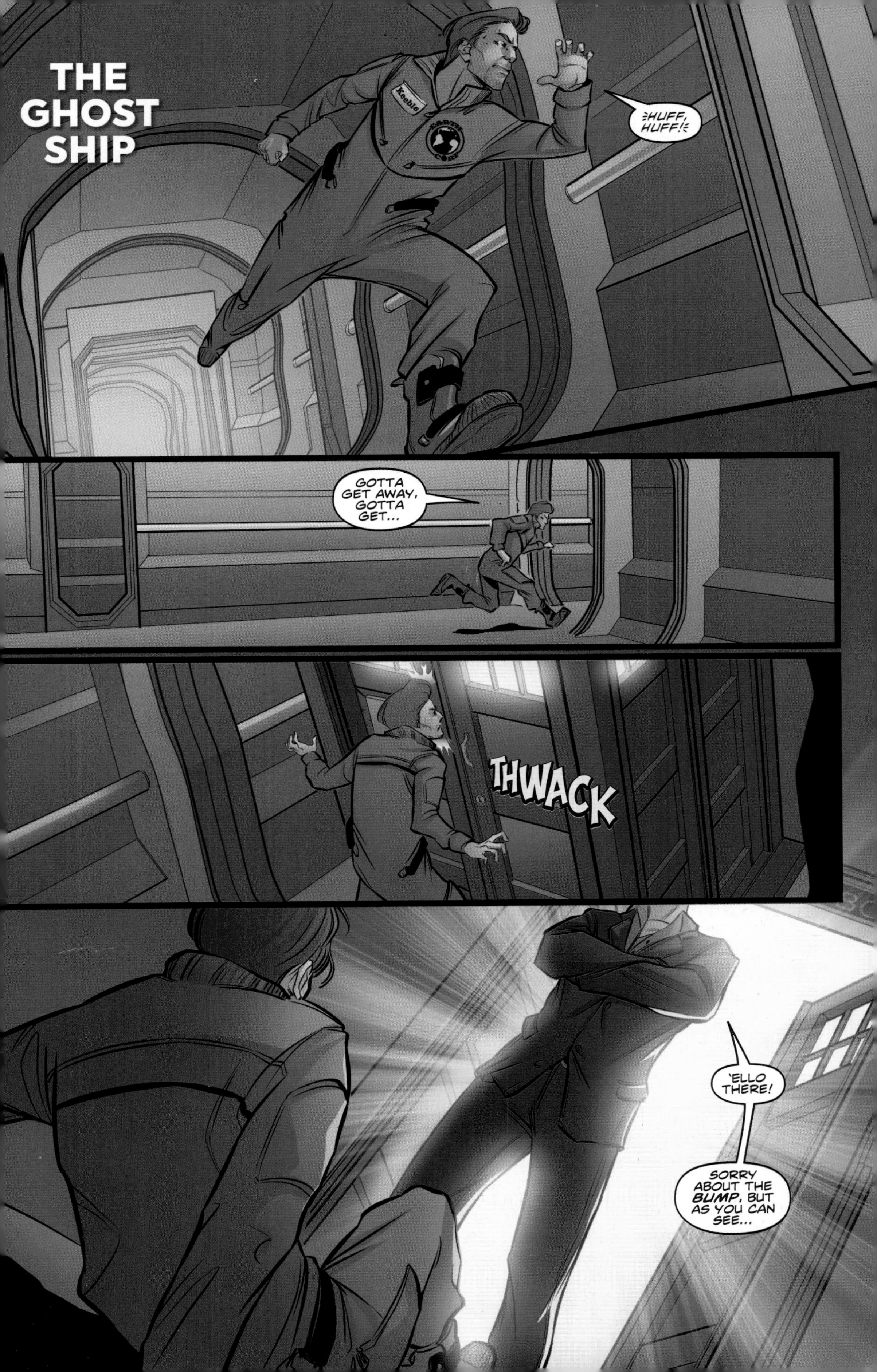
THE GHOST SHIP
Keeble
EARTH CORP
HUFF, HUFF!
GOTTA GET AWAY, GOTTA GET...
THWACK
'ELLO THERE!
SORRY ABOUT THE *BUMP*, BUT AS YOU CAN SEE...

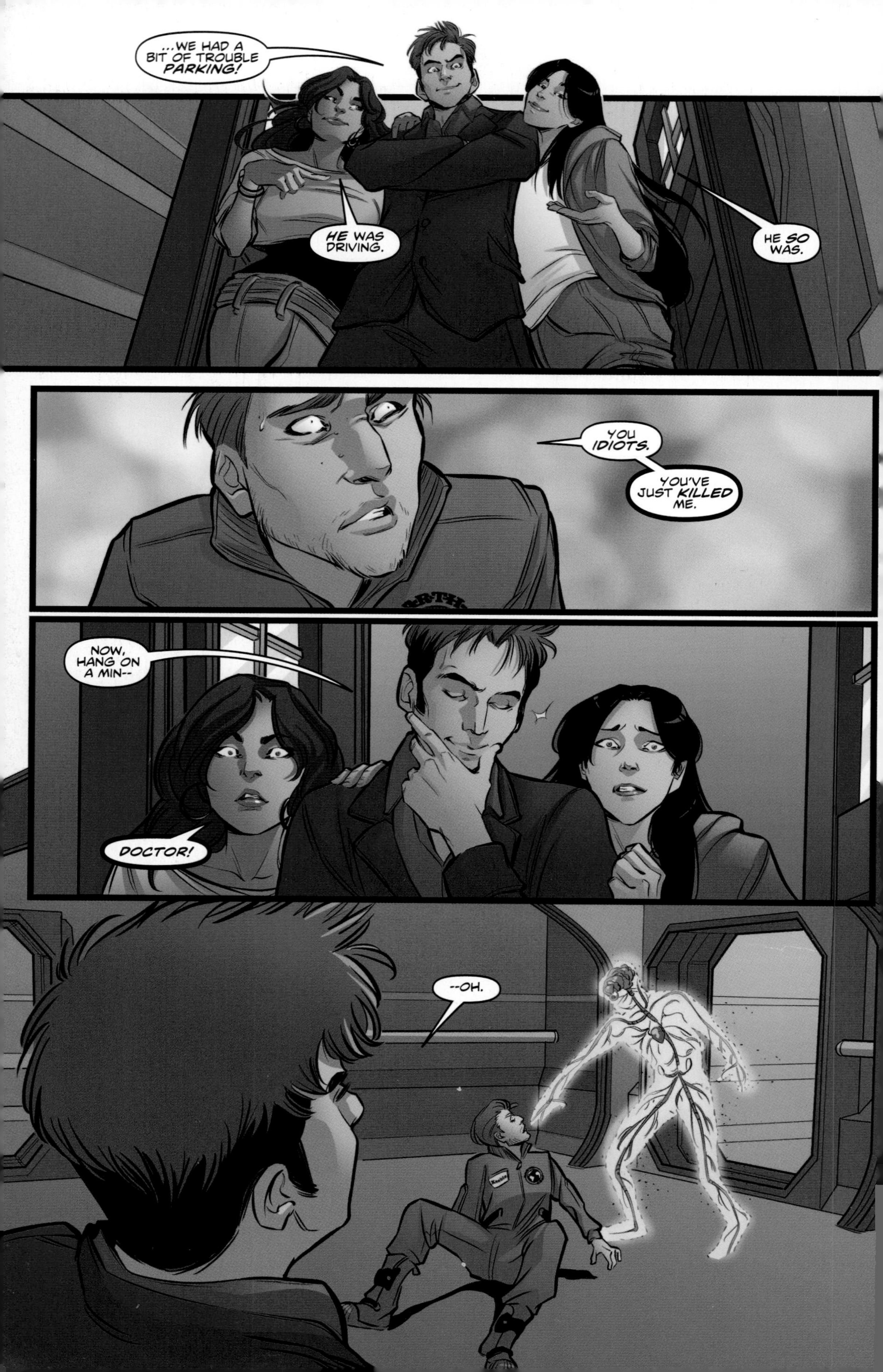
...WE HAD A BIT OF TROUBLE PARKING!
HE WAS DRIVING.
HE SO WAS.
YOU IDIOTS.
YOU'VE JUST KILLED ME.
NOW, HANG ON A MIN--
DOCTOR!
--OH.

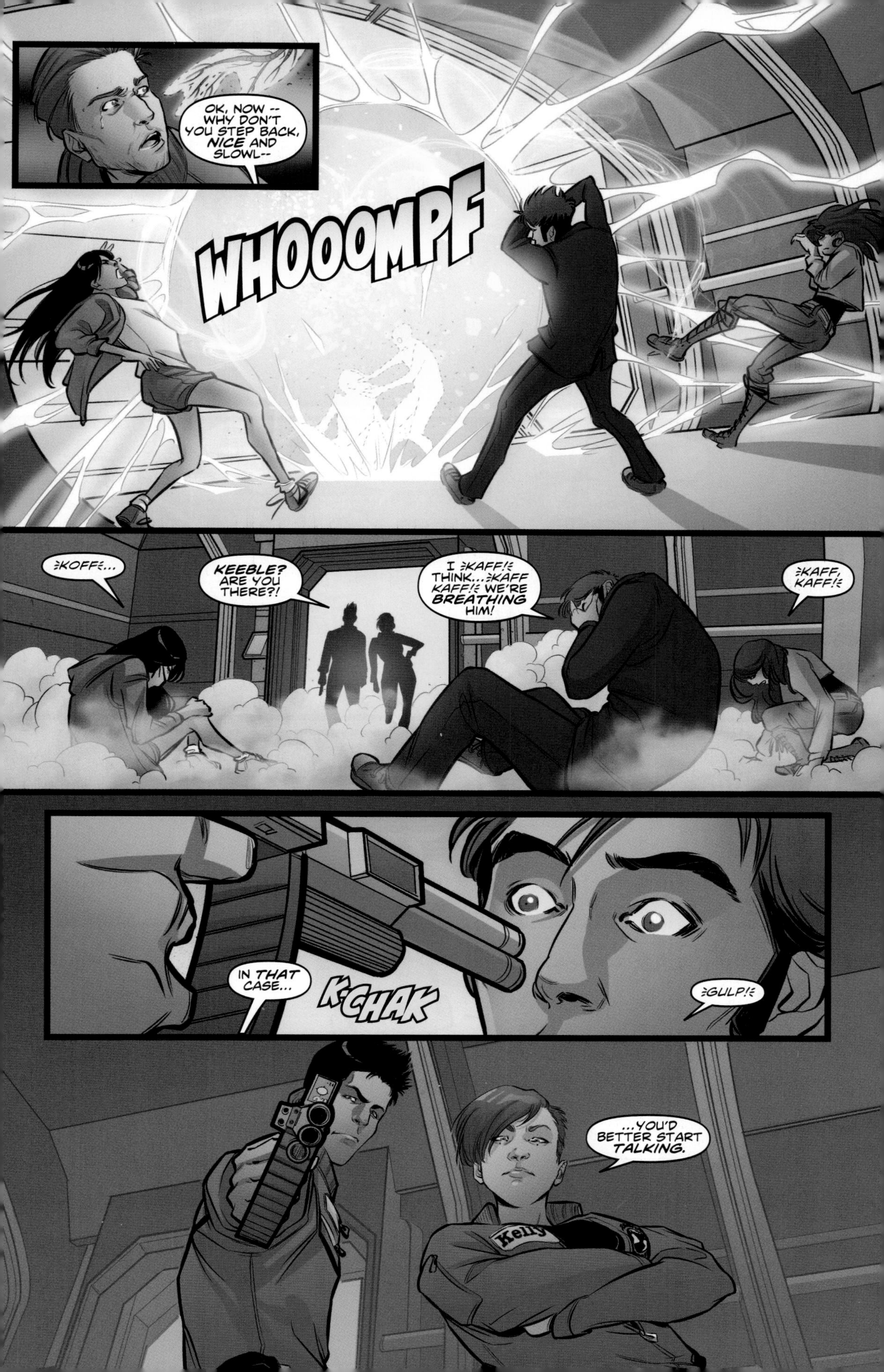
OK, NOW -- WHY DON'T YOU STEP BACK, NICE AND SLOWL--
WHOOOOMPF
⁝KOFF⁝...
KEEBLE? ARE YOU THERE?!
I ⁝KAFF!⁝ THINK... ⁝KAFF KAFF!⁝ WE'RE BREATHING HIM!
⁝KAFF, KAFF!⁝
IN THAT CASE...
K-CHAK
⁝GULP!⁝
...YOU'D BETTER START TALKING.
Kelly

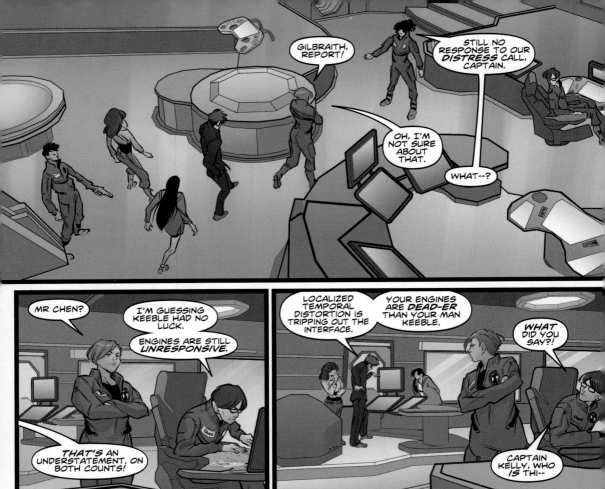

GILBRAITH, REPORT!

STILL NO RESPONSE TO OUR *DISTRESS* CALL, CAPTAIN.

OH, I'M NOT SURE ABOUT THAT.

WHAT--?

MR CHEN?

I'M GUESSING KEEBLE HAD NO LUCK. ENGINES ARE STILL *UNRESPONSIVE.*

THAT'S AN UNDERSTATEMENT. ON BOTH COUNTS!

LOCALIZED TEMPORAL DISTORTION IS TRIPPING OUT THE INTERFACE.

YOUR ENGINES ARE *DEAD-ER* THAN YOUR MAN KEEBLE.

WHAT DID YOU SAY?!

CAPTAIN KELLY, WHO *IS* THI--

"EARTH CORPS: SPECIAL OPS.

"RESCUE DIVISION."

DO THEY *HAVE* ONE?

THEY DO *NOW!* I'M THE *DOCTOR* AND THESE ARE MY ASSOCIATES, *ARTOO* AND *THREEPIO.* I'LL LET YOU WORK OUT WHICH IS WHICH.

HEY!

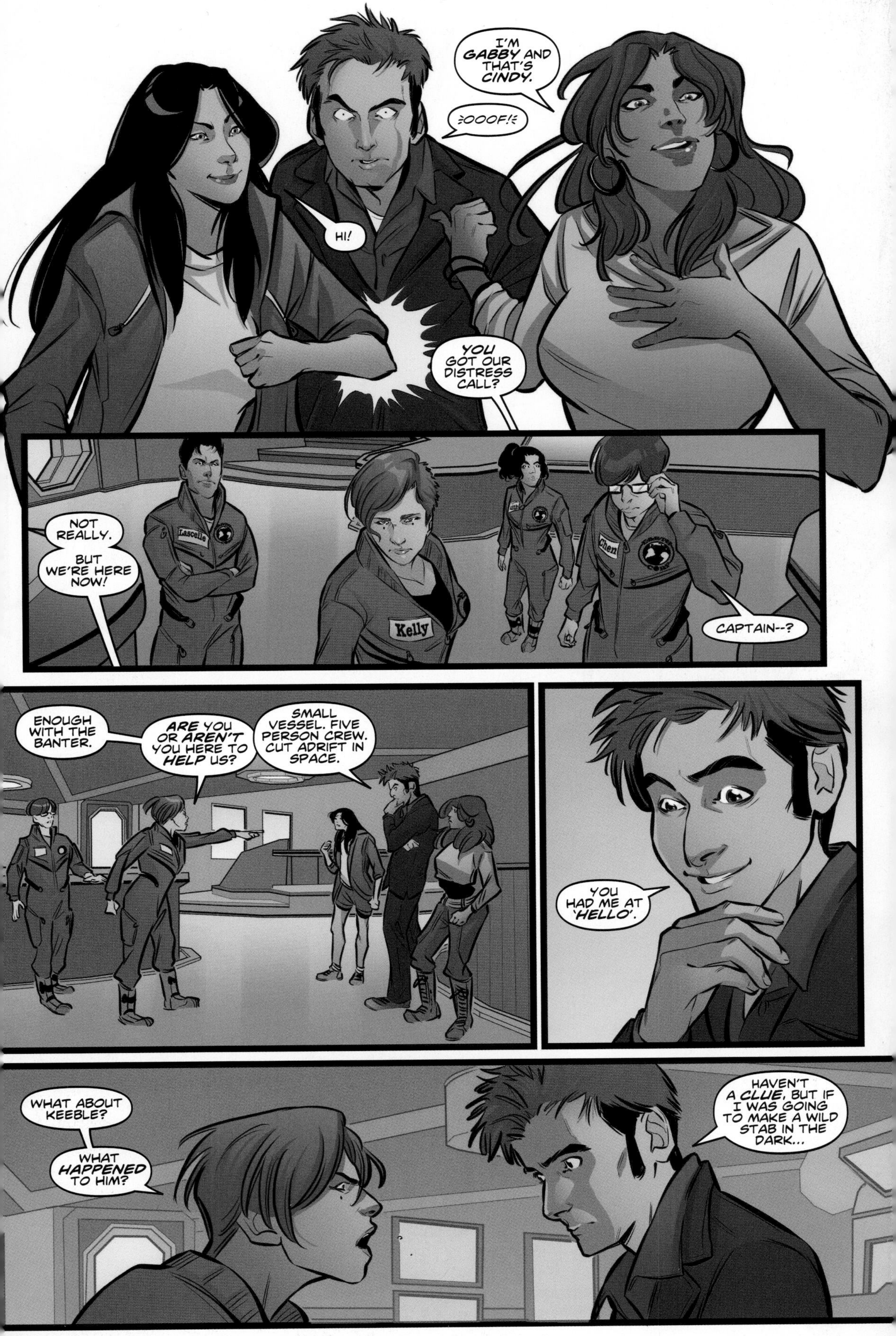
I'M GABBY AND THAT'S CINDY.
OOOF!
HI!
YOU GOT OUR DISTRESS CALL?
Lascelle
Chen
Kelly
NOT REALLY.
BUT WE'RE HERE NOW!
CAPTAIN--?
ENOUGH WITH THE BANTER.
ARE YOU OR AREN'T YOU HERE TO HELP US?
SMALL VESSEL. FIVE PERSON CREW. CUT ADRIFT IN SPACE.
YOU HAD ME AT 'HELLO'.
WHAT ABOUT KEEBLE?
WHAT HAPPENED TO HIM?
HAVEN'T A CLUE, BUT IF I WAS GOING TO MAKE A WILD STAB IN THE DARK...

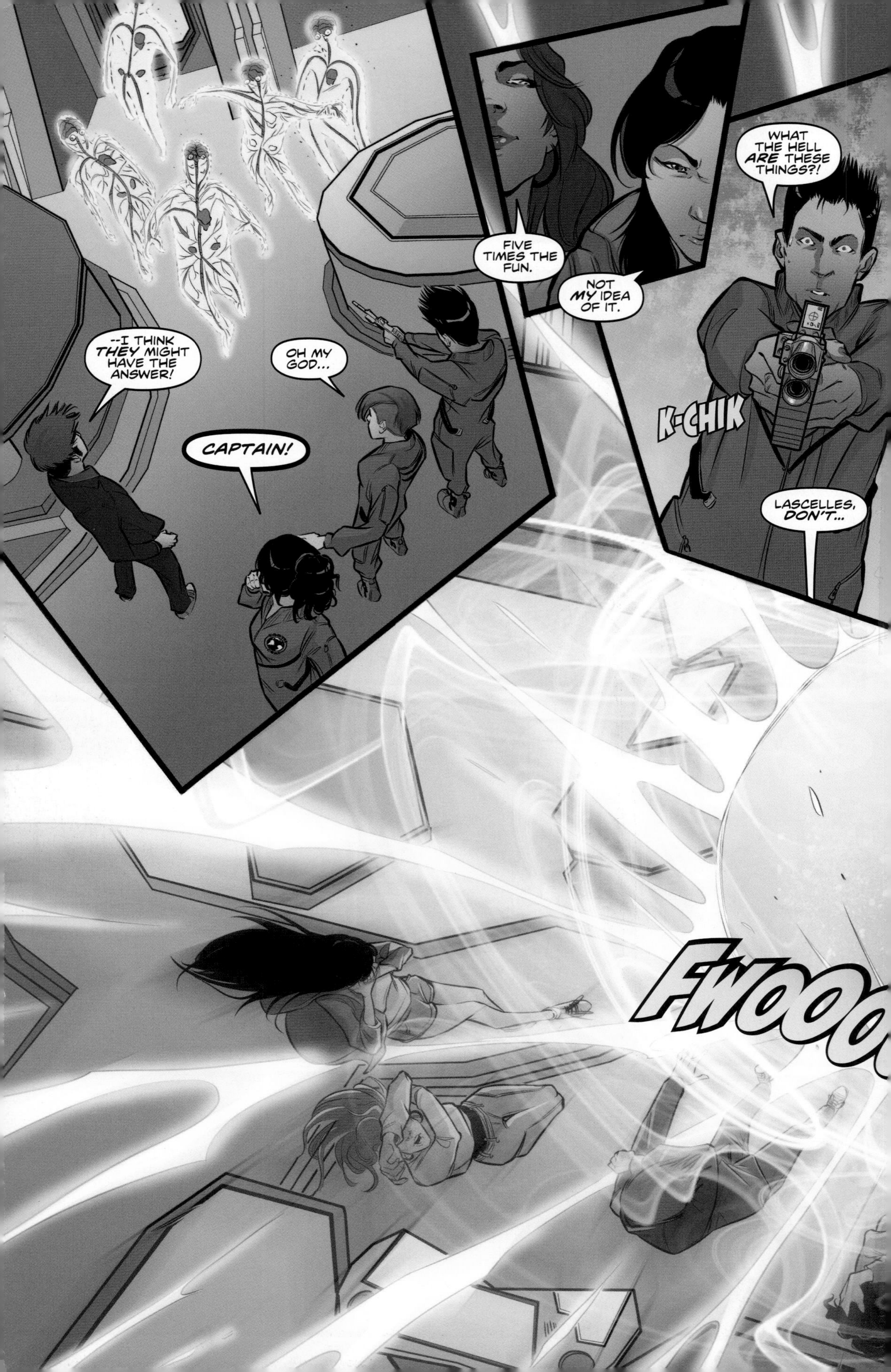
--I THINK THEY MIGHT HAVE THE ANSWER!
OH MY GOD...
CAPTAIN!
FIVE TIMES THE FUN.
NOT MY IDEA OF IT.
WHAT THE HELL ARE THESE THINGS?!
K-CHIK
LASCELLES, DON'T...
FWOOO

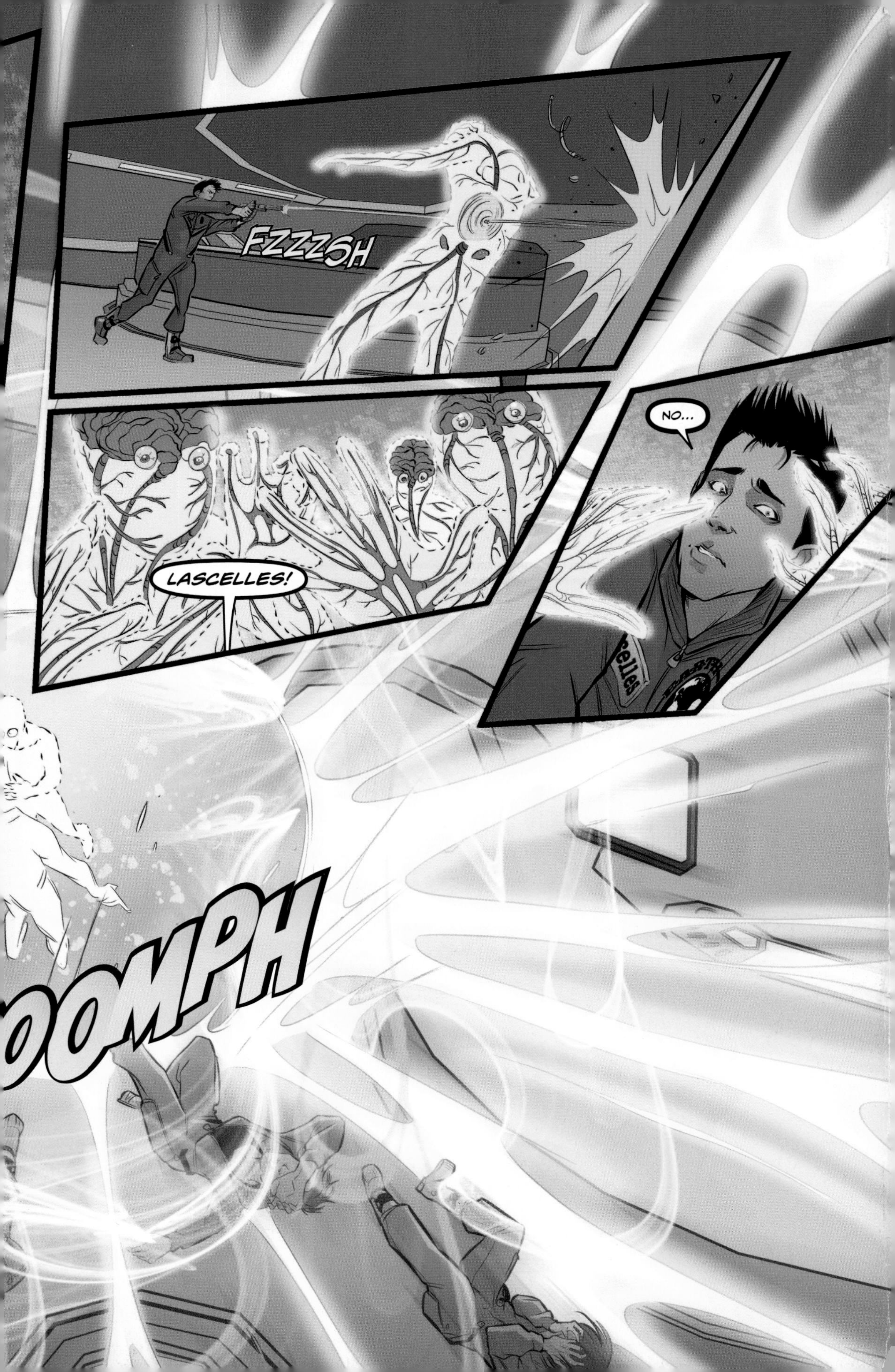
FZZZSH
LASCELLES!
NO...
OOMPH

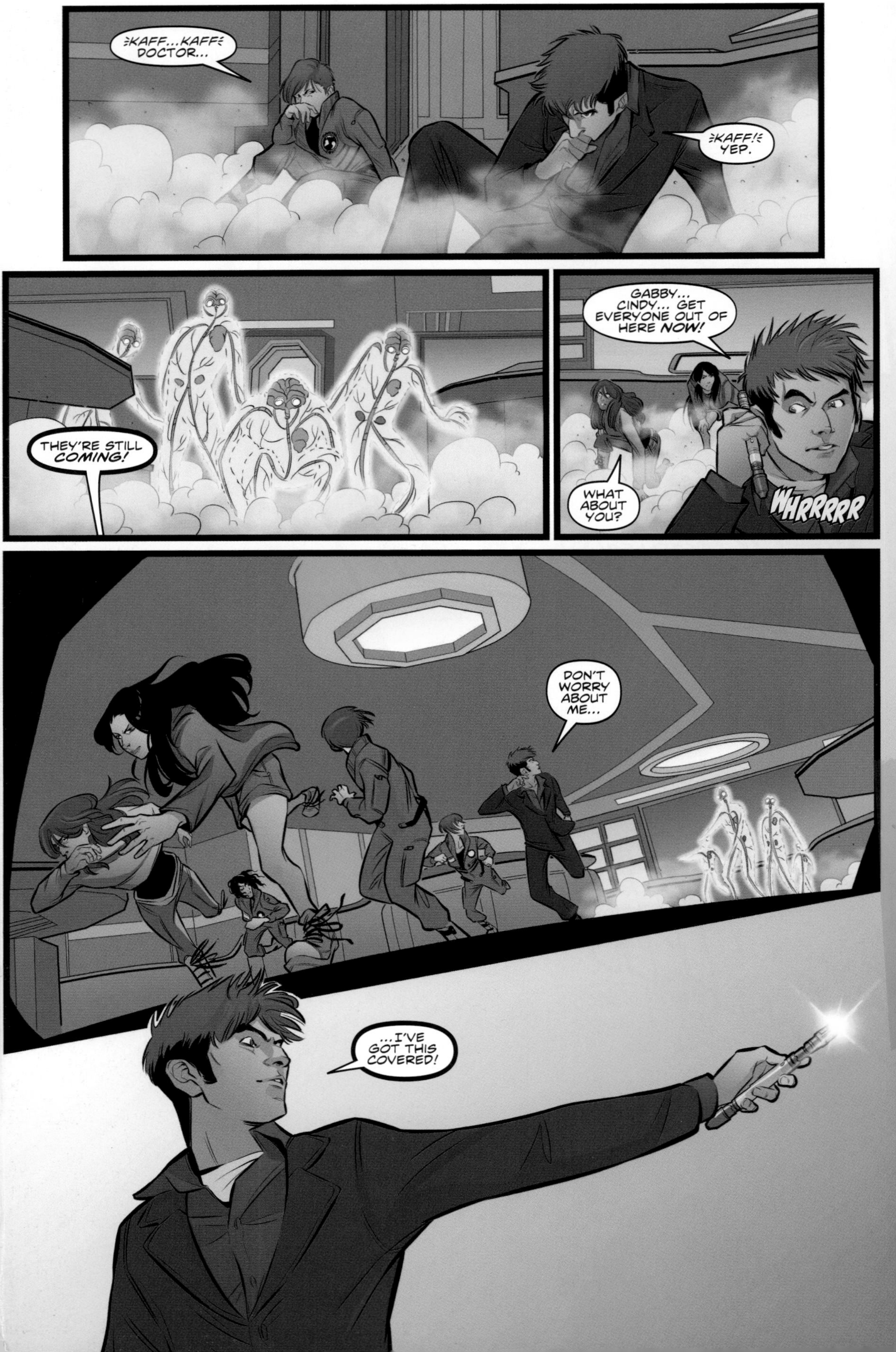

KAFF...KAFF
DOCTOR...
KAFF!
YEP.
THEY'RE STILL COMING!
GABBY... CINDY... GET EVERYONE OUT OF HERE NOW!
WHAT ABOUT YOU?
WHRRRRR
DON'T WORRY ABOUT ME...
...I'VE GOT THIS COVERED!

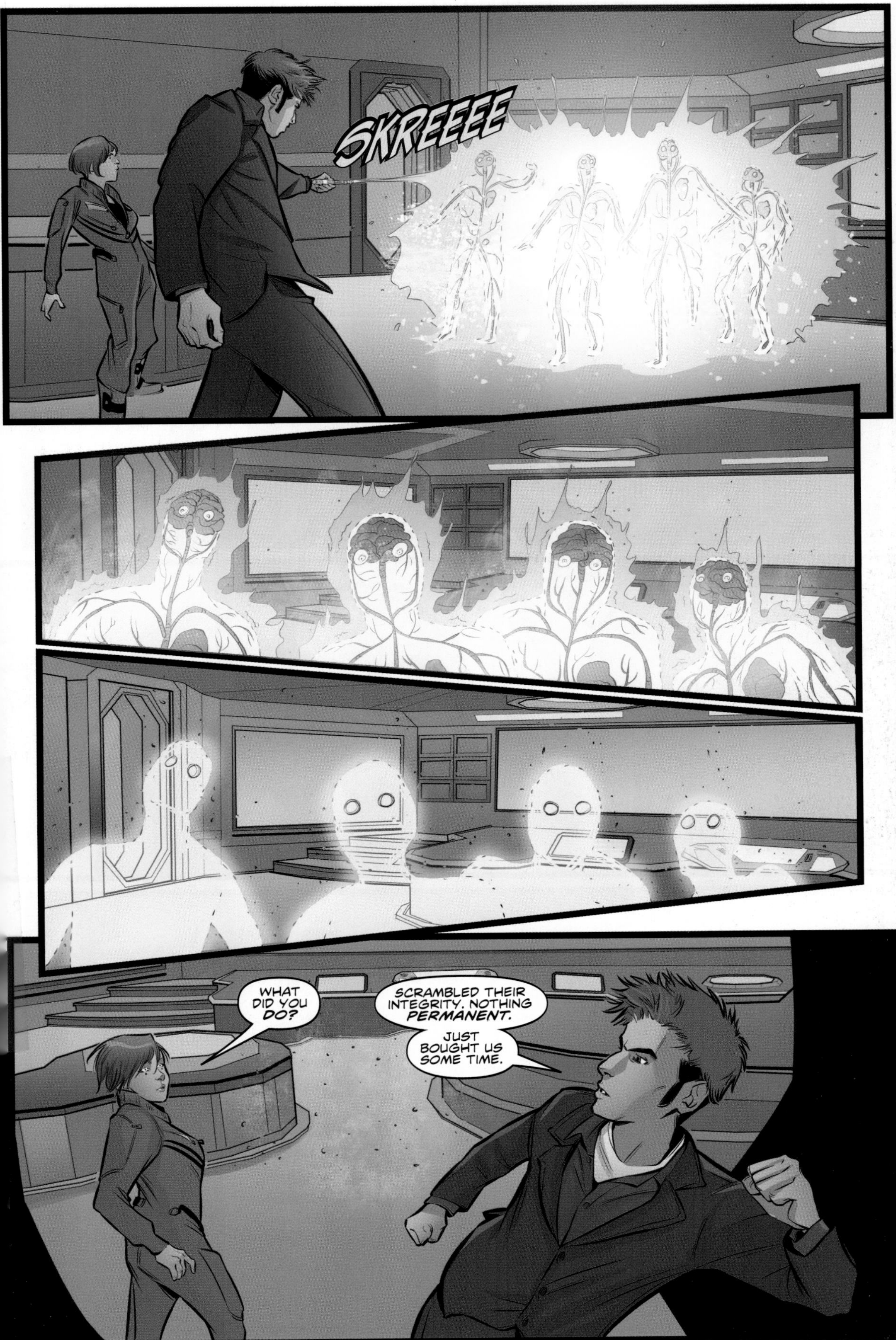
SKREEEE
WHAT DID YOU DO?
SCRAMBLED THEIR INTEGRITY. NOTHING PERMANENT.
JUST BOUGHT US SOME TIME.

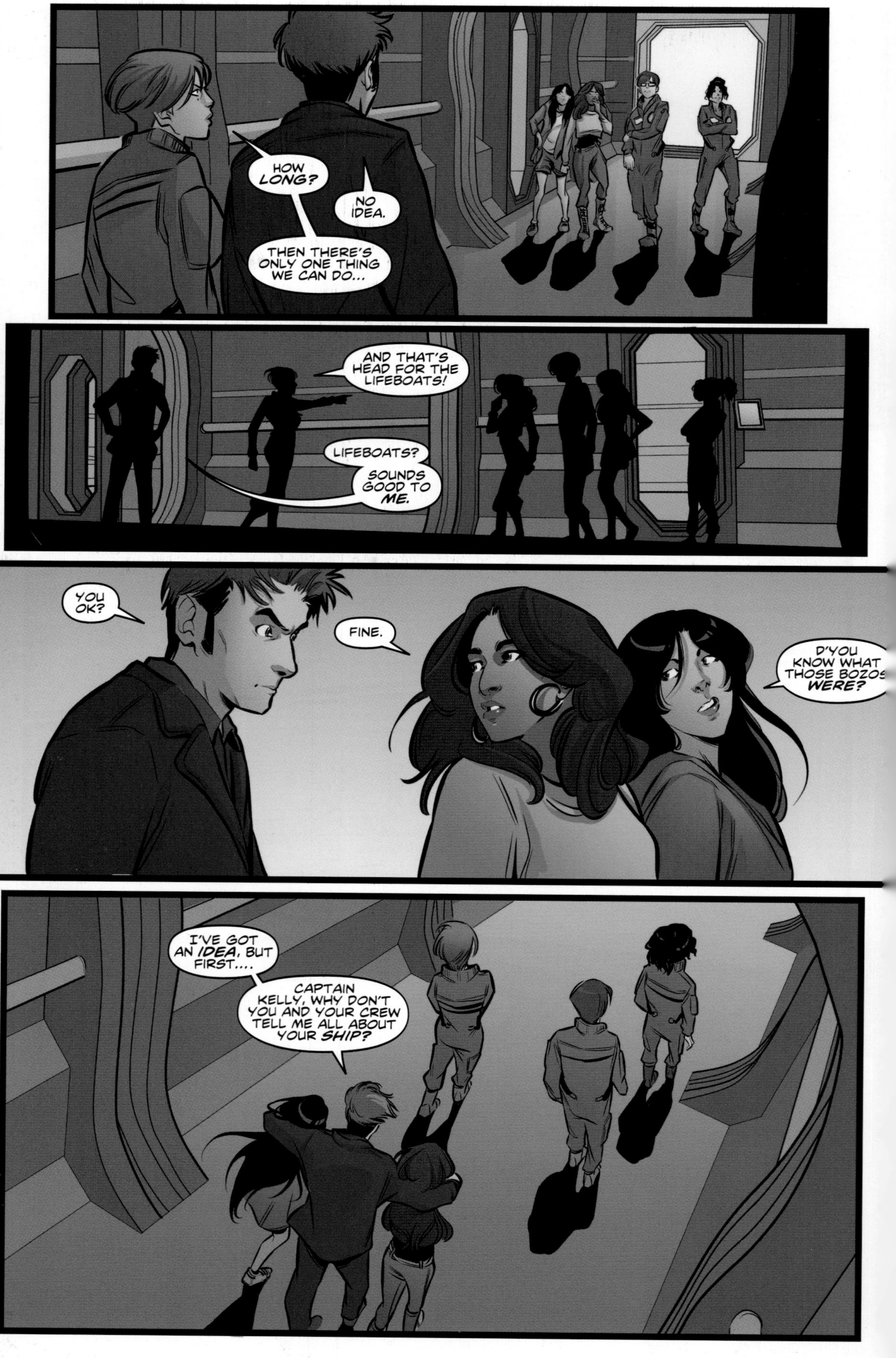
HOW LONG?
NO IDEA.
THEN THERE'S ONLY ONE THING WE CAN DO...
AND THAT'S HEAD FOR THE LIFEBOATS!
LIFEBOATS?
SOUNDS GOOD TO ME.
YOU OK?
FINE.
D'YOU KNOW WHAT THOSE BOZOS WERE?
I'VE GOT AN IDEA, BUT FIRST....
CAPTAIN KELLY, WHY DON'T YOU AND YOUR CREW TELL ME ALL ABOUT YOUR SHIP?

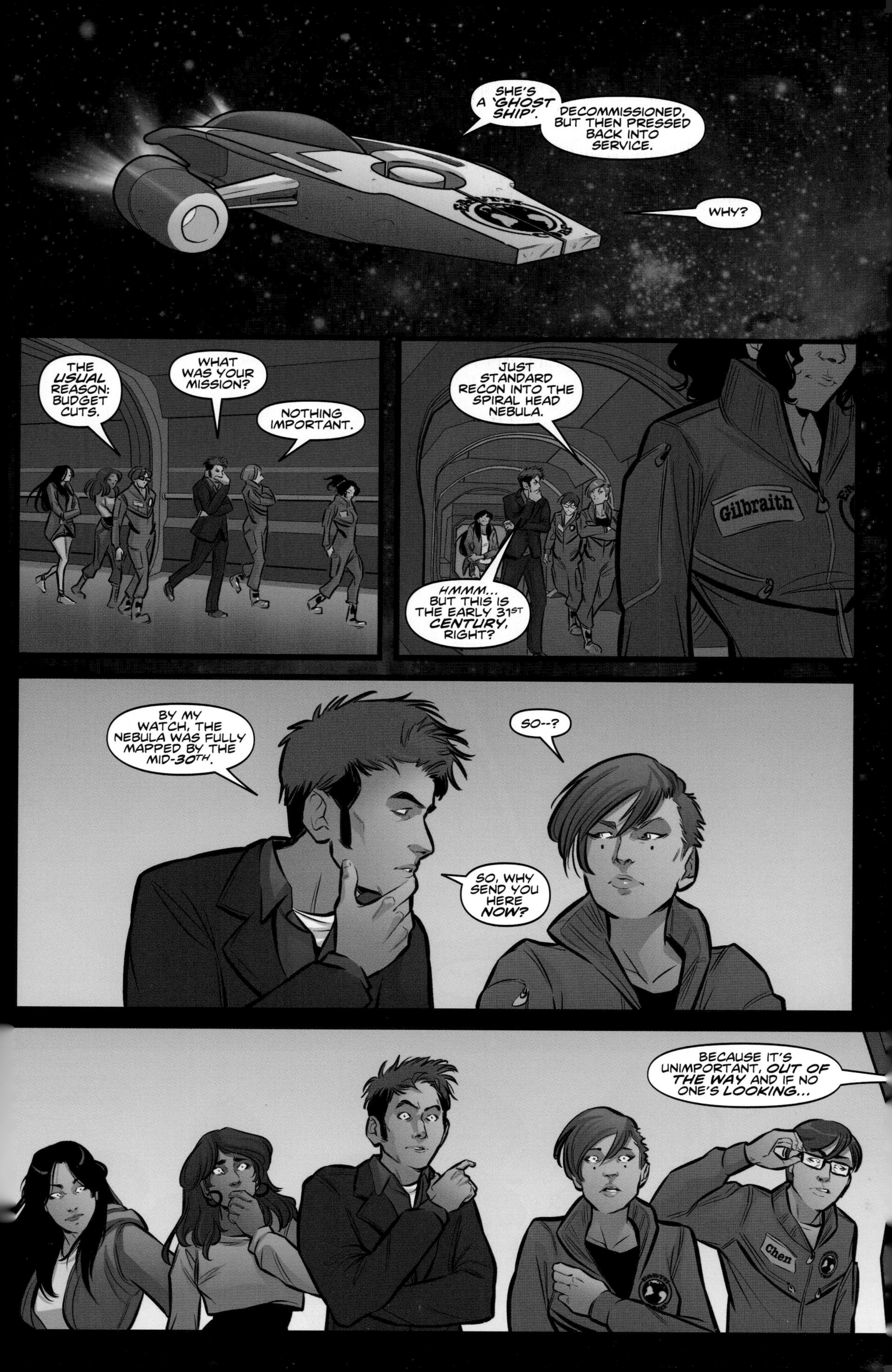
SHE'S A 'GHOST SHIP'.
DECOMMISSIONED, BUT THEN PRESSED BACK INTO SERVICE.
WHY?
THE USUAL REASON: BUDGET CUTS.
WHAT WAS YOUR MISSION?
NOTHING IMPORTANT.
JUST STANDARD RECON INTO THE SPIRAL HEAD NEBULA.
HMMM... BUT THIS IS THE EARLY 31ST CENTURY, RIGHT?
Gilbraith
BY MY WATCH, THE NEBULA WAS FULLY MAPPED BY THE MID-30TH.
SO--?
SO, WHY SEND YOU HERE NOW?
BECAUSE IT'S UNIMPORTANT, OUT OF THE WAY AND IF NO ONE'S LOOKING...
Chen

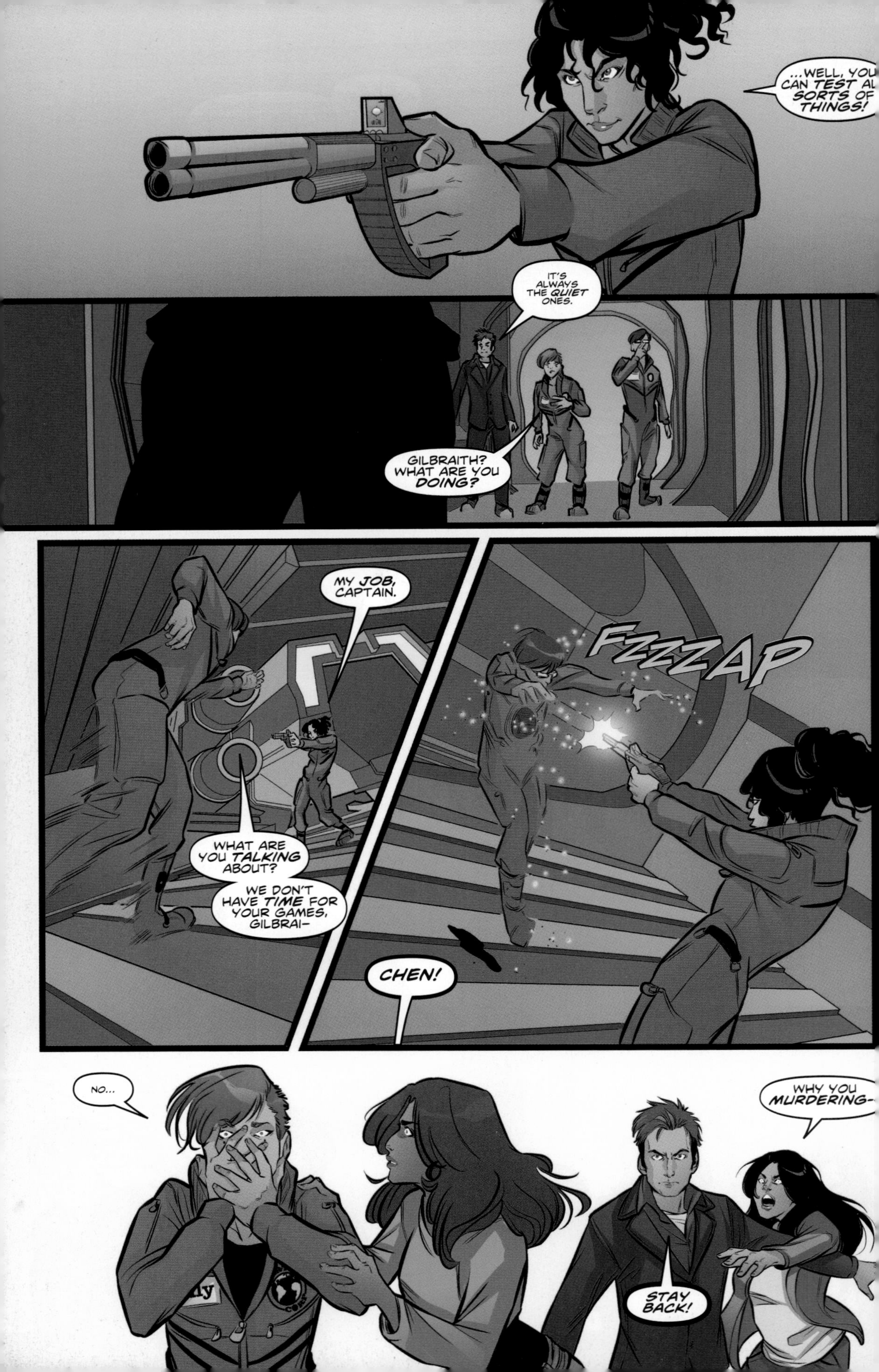

...WELL, YOU CAN TEST AL SORTS OF THINGS!
IT'S ALWAYS THE QUIET ONES.
GILBRAITH? WHAT ARE YOU DOING?
MY JOB, CAPTAIN.
WHAT ARE YOU TALKING ABOUT?
WE DON'T HAVE TIME FOR YOUR GAMES, GILBRAI-
FZZZAP
CHEN!
NO...
WHY YOU MURDERING-
STAY BACK!

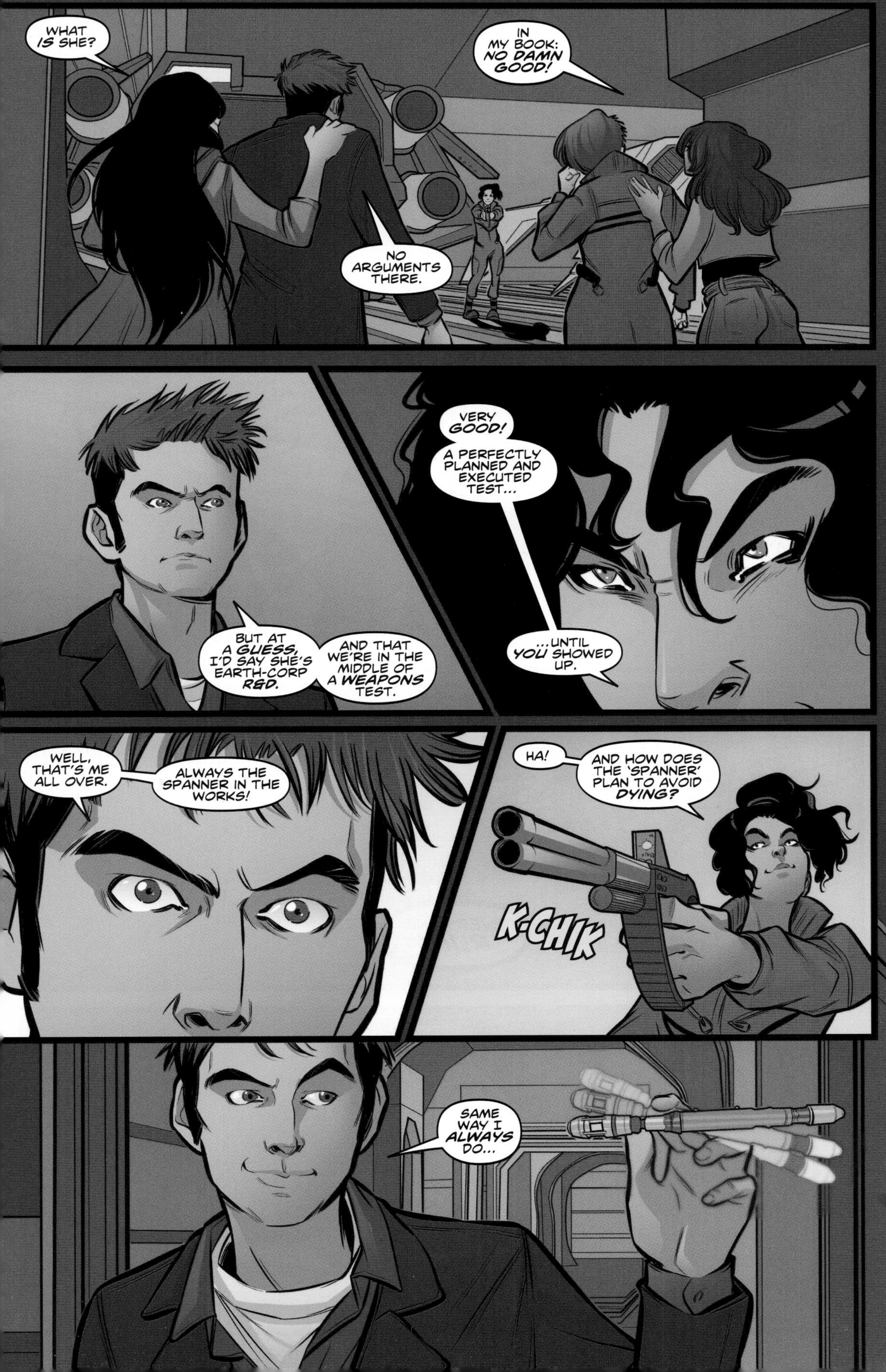
WHAT *IS* SHE?
IN MY BOOK: *NO DAMN GOOD!*
NO ARGUMENTS THERE.
BUT AT A *GUESS,* I'D SAY SHE'S EARTH-CORP *R&D.*
AND THAT WE'RE IN THE MIDDLE OF A *WEAPONS* TEST.
VERY *GOOD!*
A PERFECTLY PLANNED AND EXECUTED TEST...
...UNTIL *YOU* SHOWED UP.
WELL, THAT'S ME ALL OVER.
ALWAYS THE SPANNER IN THE WORKS!
HA!
AND HOW DOES THE 'SPANNER' PLAN TO AVOID *DYING?*
K-CHIK
SAME WAY I *ALWAYS* DO...

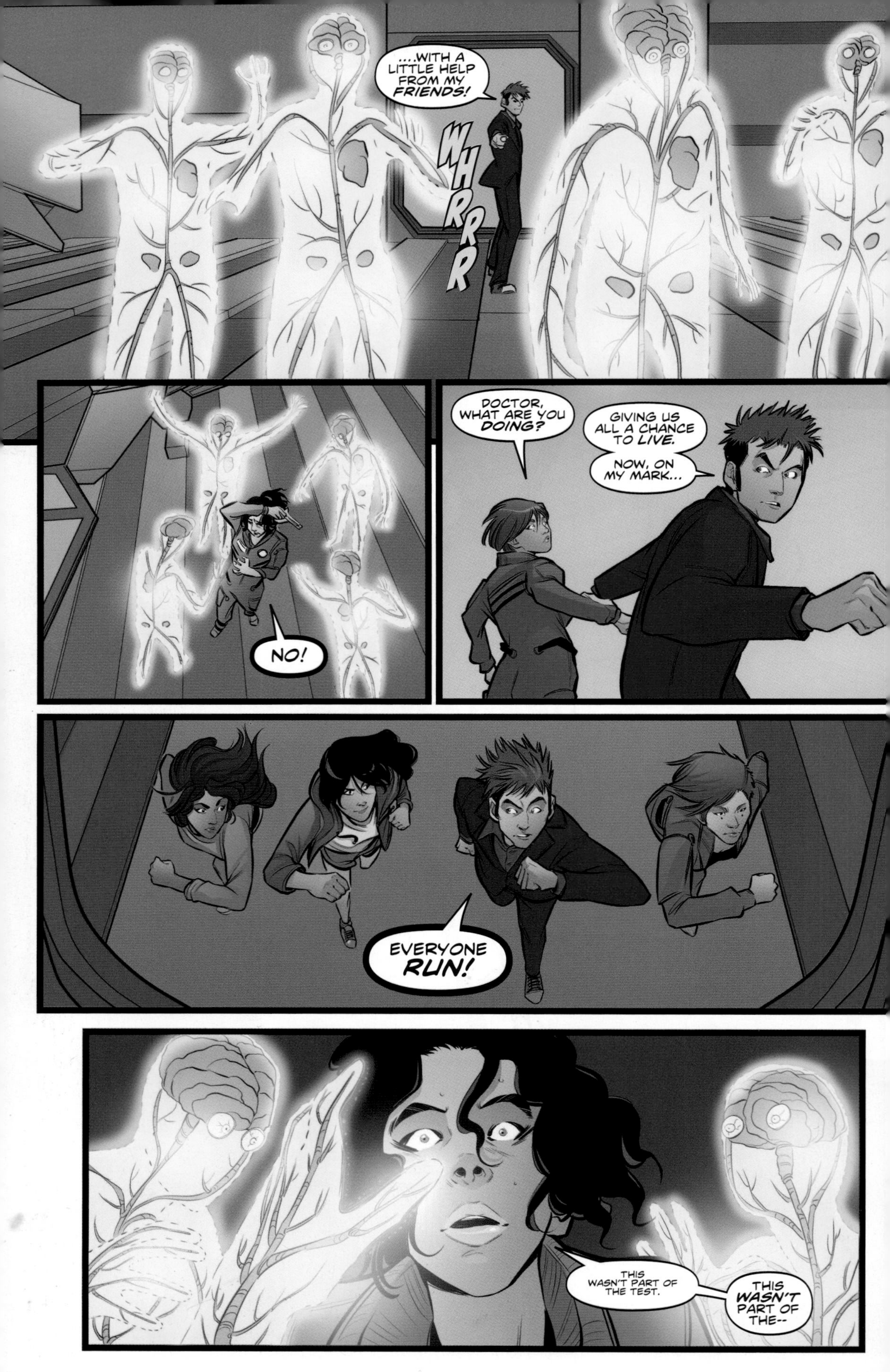
....WITH A LITTLE HELP FROM MY FRIENDS!
WHRRR
NO!
DOCTOR, WHAT ARE YOU DOING?
GIVING US ALL A CHANCE TO LIVE.
NOW, ON MY MARK...
EVERYONE RUN!
THIS WASN'T PART OF THE TEST.
THIS WASN'T PART OF THE--

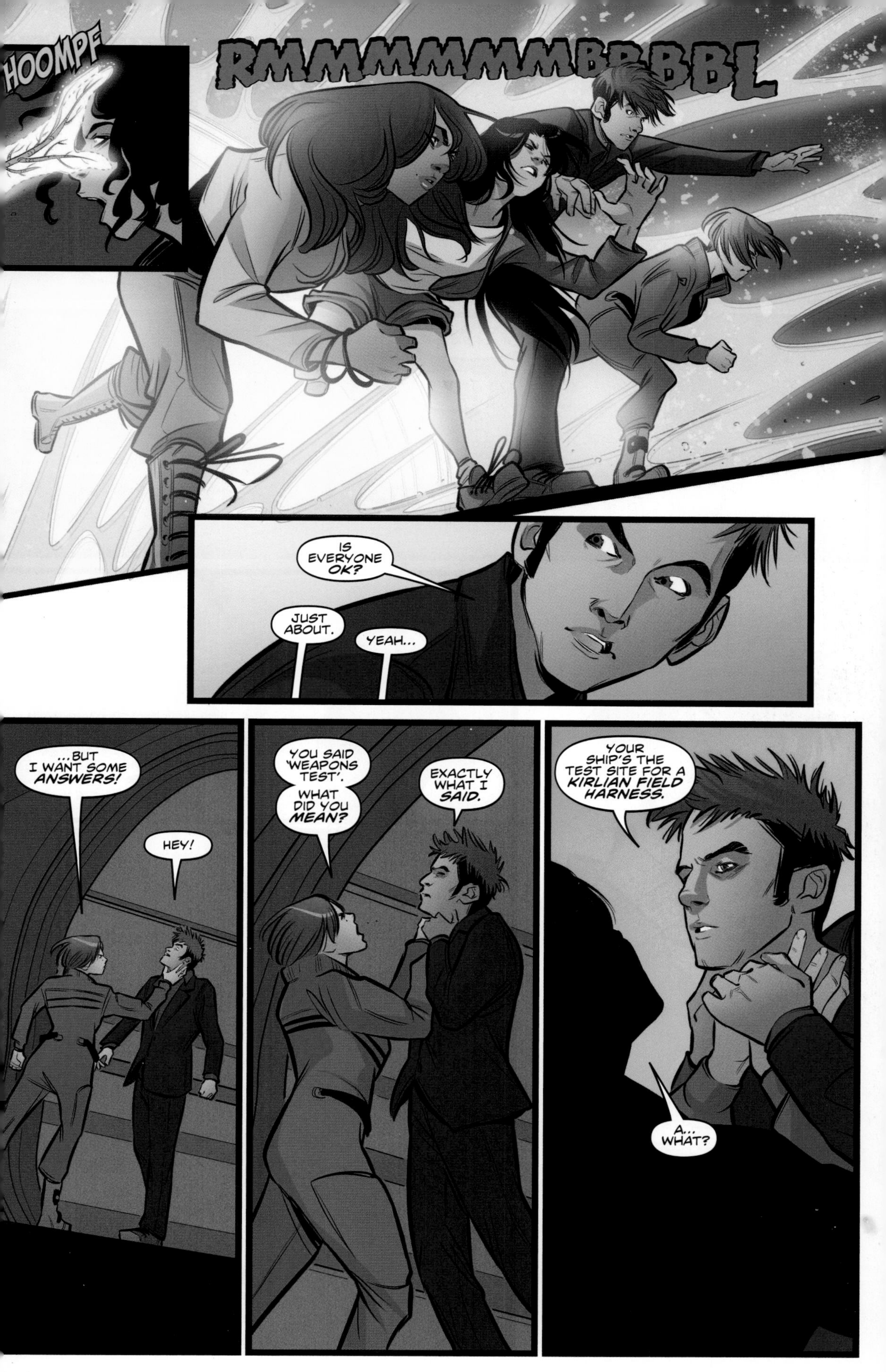
HOOMPF
RMMMMMMMBBBBL
IS EVERYONE OK?
JUST ABOUT.
YEAH...
...BUT I WANT SOME ANSWERS!
HEY!
YOU SAID 'WEAPONS TEST'. WHAT DID YOU MEAN?
EXACTLY WHAT I SAID.
YOUR SHIP'S THE TEST SITE FOR A KIRLIAN FIELD HARNESS.
A... WHAT?

AN EXPERIMENTAL WEAPON.

IT HARNESSES THE *BIO-ELECTRICAL SIGNATURES* OF A LIFE-FORM AND THEN WEAPONIZES IT.

SO THOSE CREATURES ARE WHAT... OUR *AURAS?!?*

YOUR AURAS GIVEN *FORM.* EXCEPT THEY WANT TO *KILL* YOU.

THAT'S INSANE!

NOT IF YOU'RE EARTH-CORP.

COLONIZATION OF ALIEN WORLDS IS MESSY AND *EXPENSIVE.*

BUT IMAGINE IF YOU COULD *DEPOPULATE* AN ENTIRE PLANET WITHOUT SETTING FOOT ON THE SURFACE.

THIS DEVICE. WHERE ON THE SHIP IS IT?

BLIP

GOING BY THE ENERGY SIGNATURES...

...I'D SAY IT'S IN THE ENGINE ROOM.

Kelly

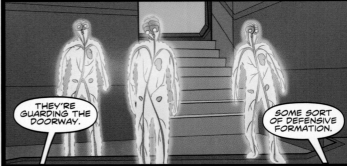

THEY'RE GUARDING THE DOORWAY.

SOME SORT OF DEFENSIVE FORMATION.

FOR ALPHABETTI-SPAGHETTI, THEY LEARN FAST!

HOW ARE WE GOING TO GET INSIDE?

YOU'RE *NOT.* BUT I *AM.*

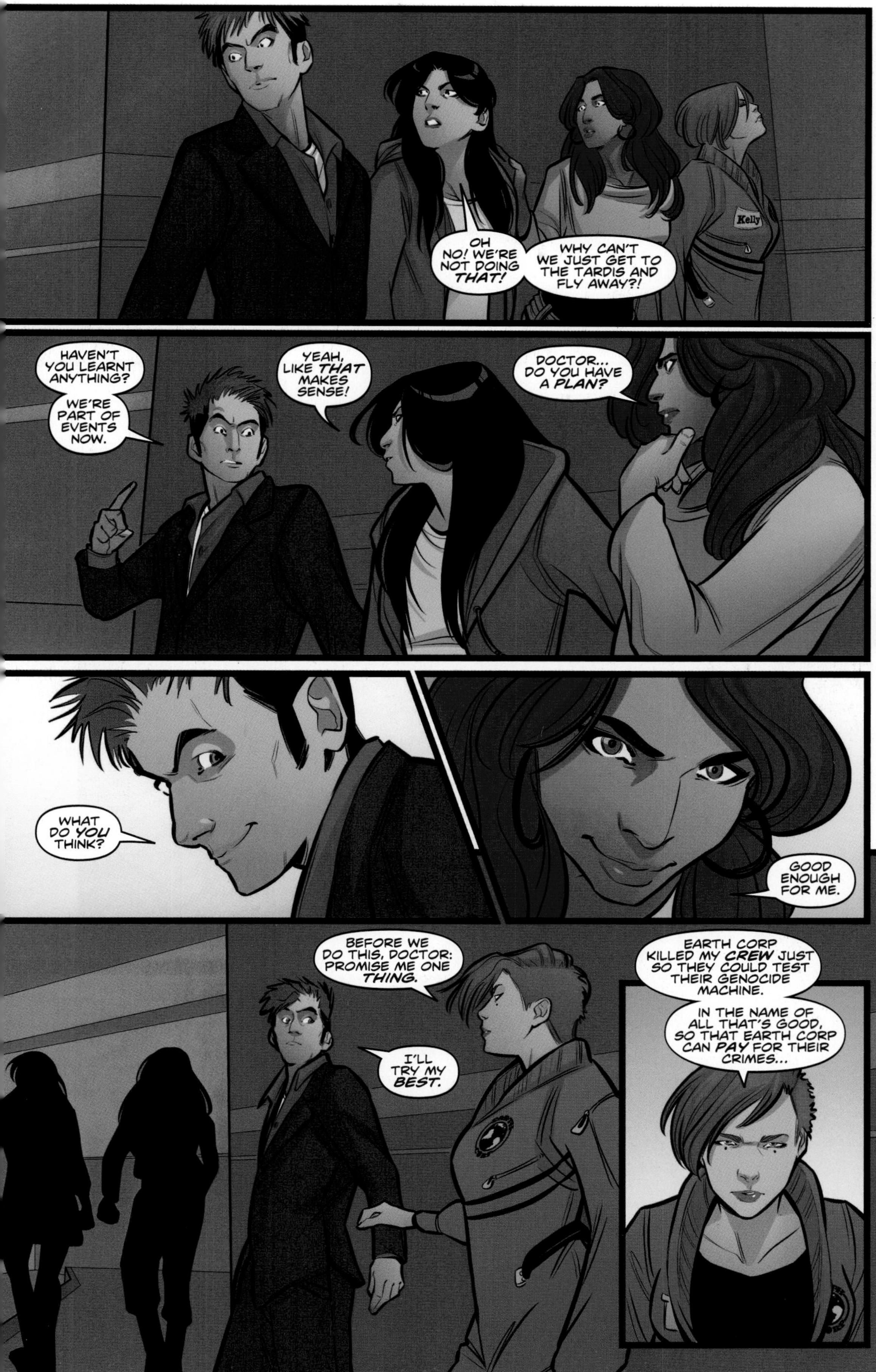
Kelly
OH NO! WE'RE NOT DOING *THAT!*
WHY CAN'T WE JUST GET TO THE TARDIS AND FLY AWAY?!
HAVEN'T YOU LEARNT ANYTHING?
WE'RE PART OF EVENTS NOW.
YEAH, LIKE *THAT* MAKES SENSE!
DOCTOR... DO YOU HAVE A *PLAN?*
WHAT DO *YOU* THINK?
GOOD ENOUGH FOR ME.
BEFORE WE DO THIS, DOCTOR: PROMISE ME ONE *THING.*
I'LL TRY MY *BEST.*
EARTH CORP KILLED MY *CREW* JUST SO THEY COULD TEST THEIR GENOCIDE MACHINE.
IN THE NAME OF ALL THAT'S GOOD, SO THAT EARTH CORP CAN *PAY* FOR THEIR CRIMES...

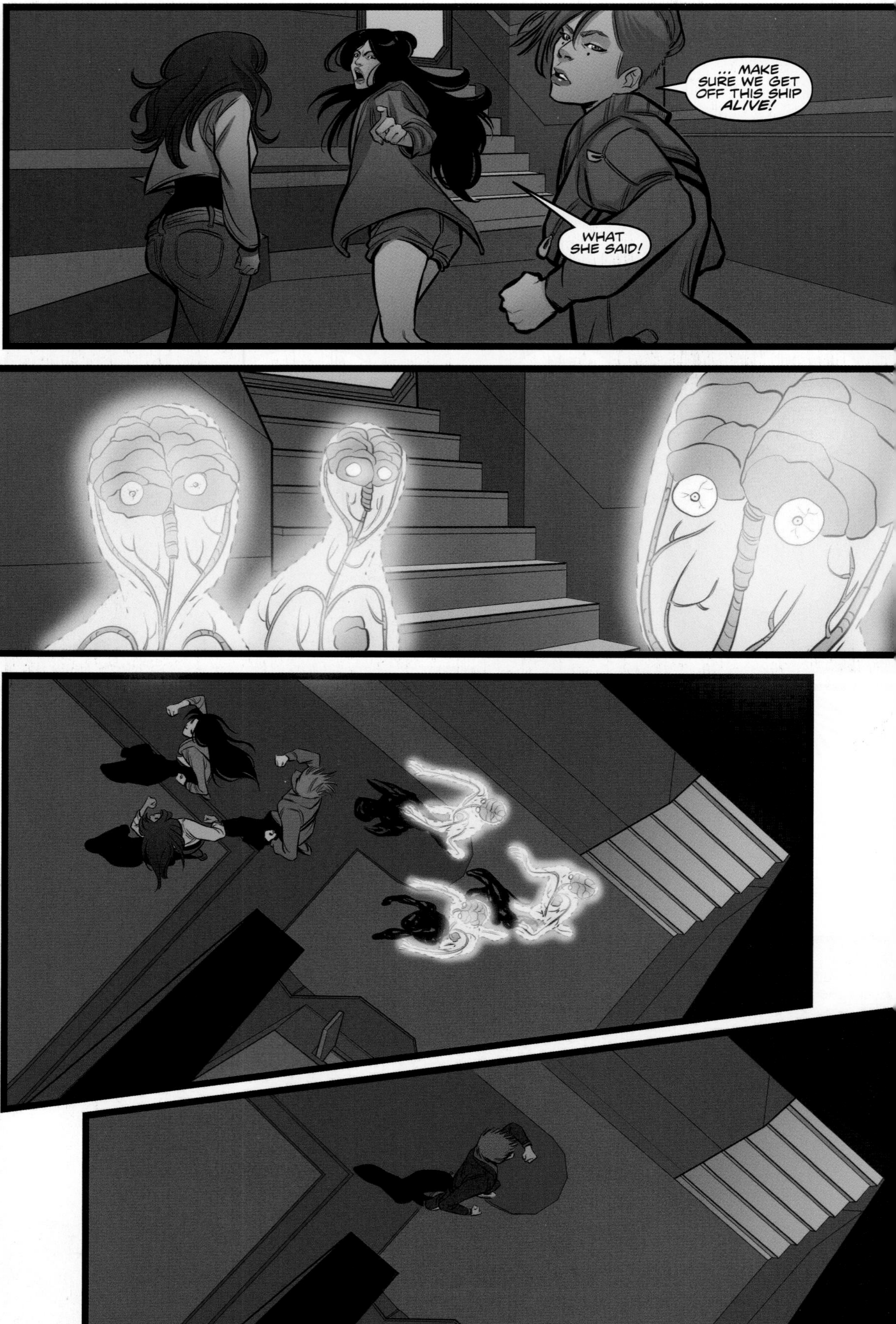
... MAKE SURE WE GET OFF THIS SHIP ALIVE!
WHAT SHE SAID!

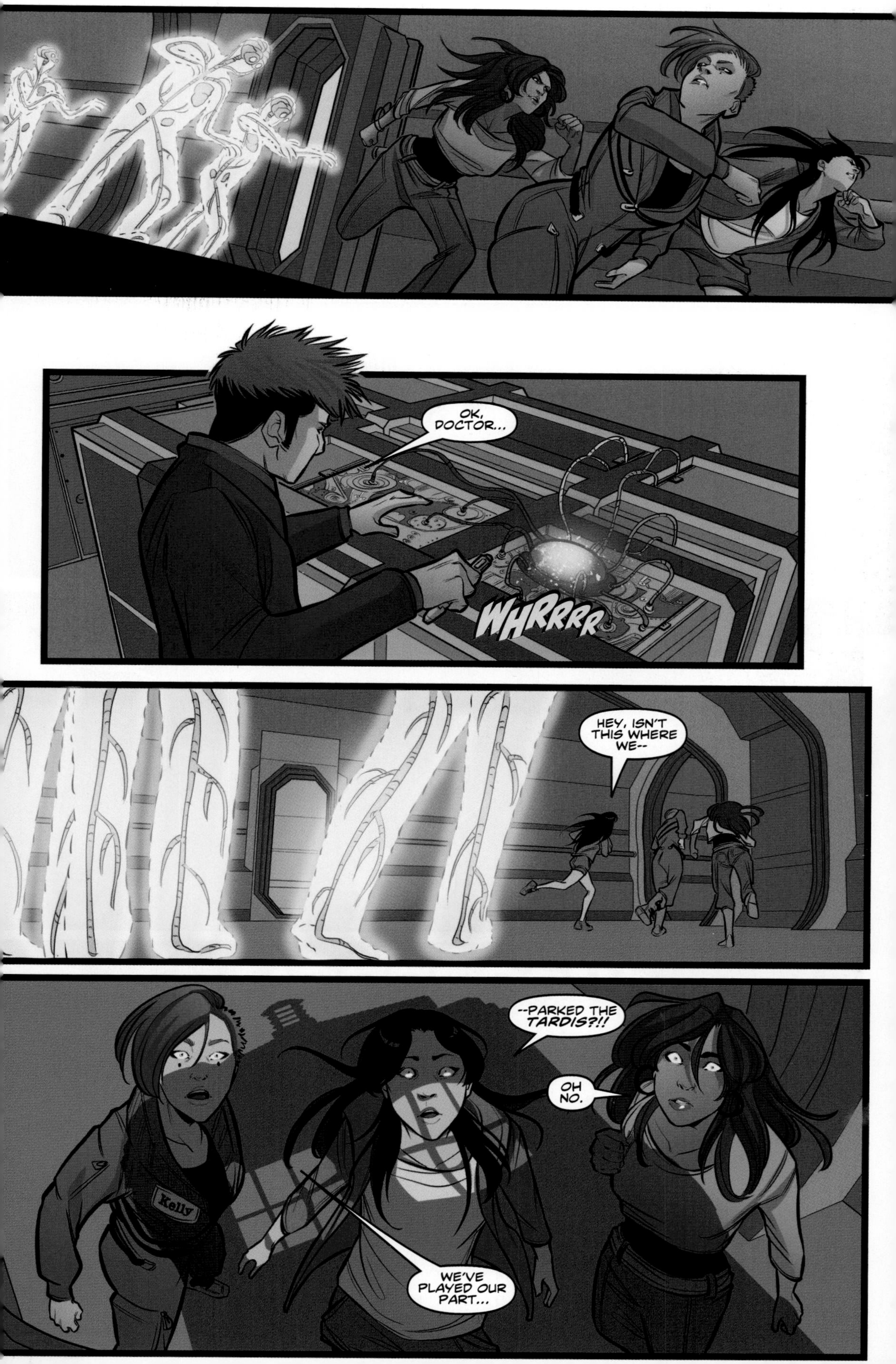
OK, DOCTOR...
WHRRRR
HEY, ISN'T THIS WHERE WE--
--PARKED THE TARDIS?!!
OH NO.
WE'VE PLAYED OUR PART...
Kelly

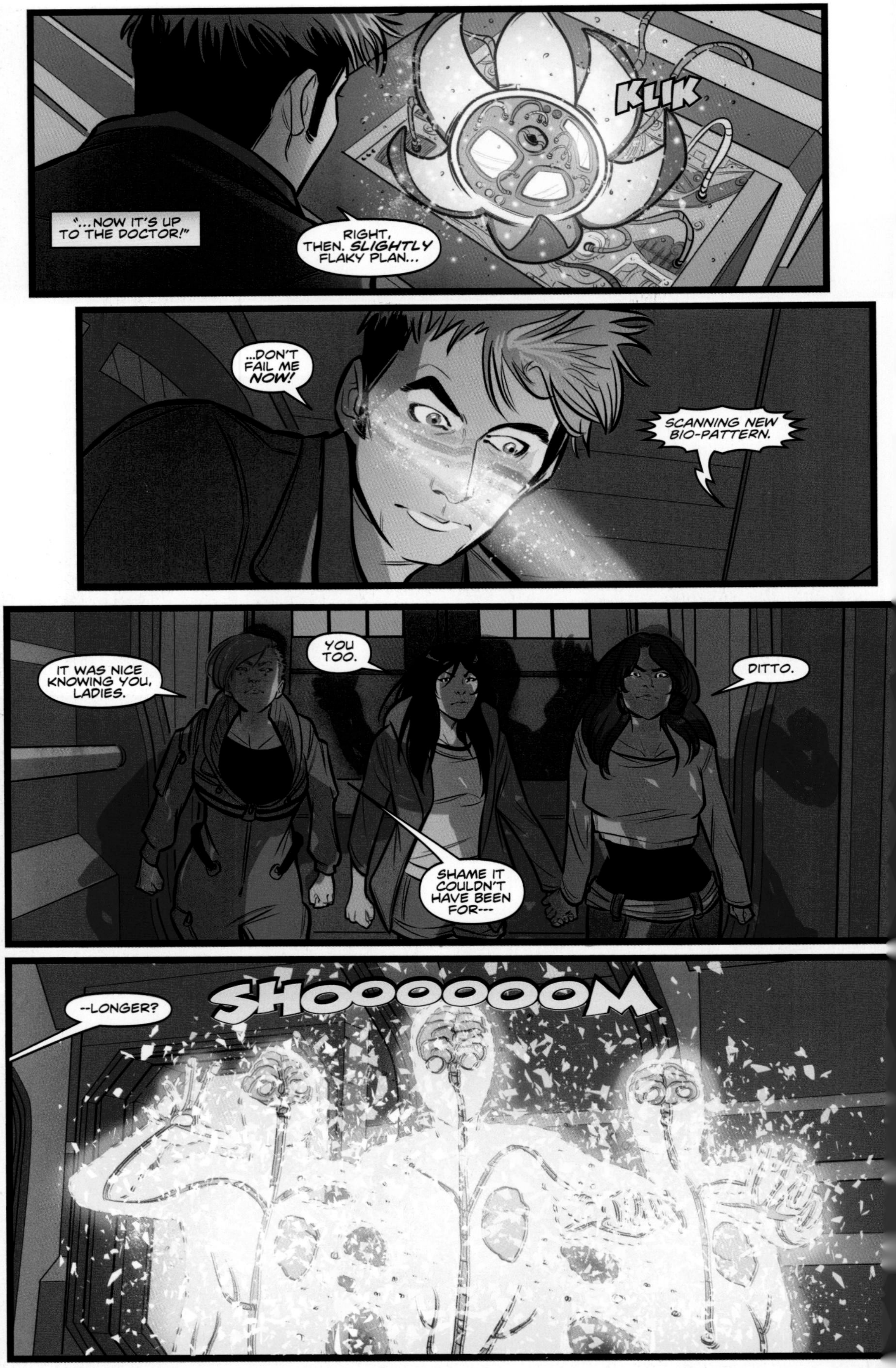
KLIK
"...NOW IT'S UP TO THE DOCTOR!"
RIGHT, THEN. SLIGHTLY FLAKY PLAN...
...DON'T FAIL ME NOW!
SCANNING NEW BIO-PATTERN.
IT WAS NICE KNOWING YOU, LADIES.
YOU TOO.
DITTO.
SHAME IT COULDN'T HAVE BEEN FOR---
--LONGER?
SHOOOOOOM

WHAT THE ACTUAL--?!

COME ON, CINDY. YOU KNOW WHAT'S HAPPENING...

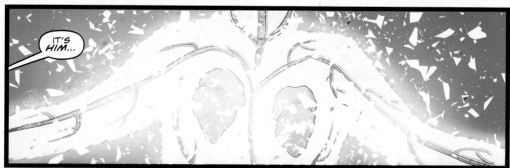

IT'S HIM...

...IT'S THE DOCTOR!

DID YOU MISS ME?

"OK, CARDS ON THE TABLE...HOW'D YOU DO IT?"

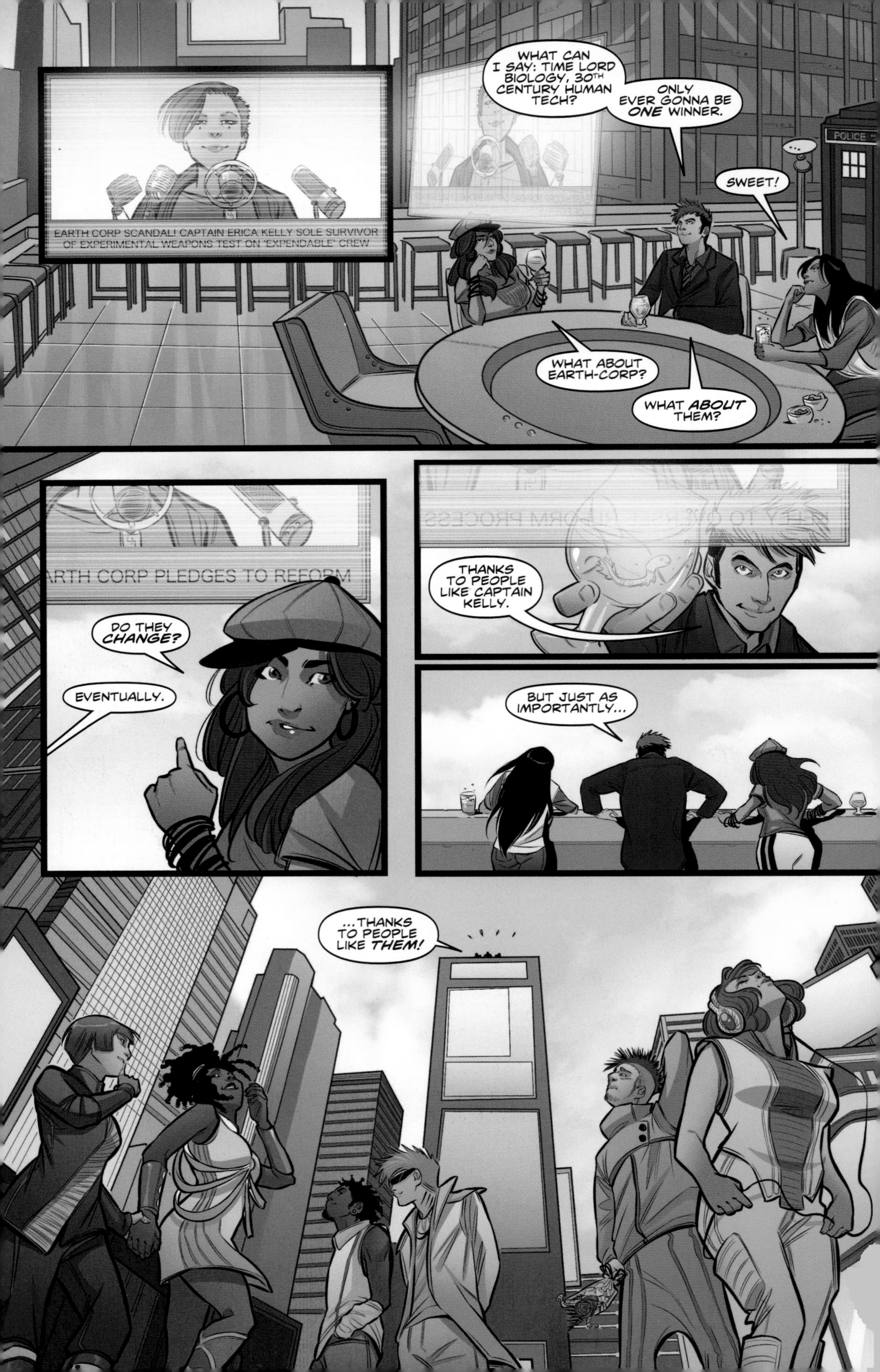
EARTH CORP SCANDAL! CAPTAIN ERICA KELLY SOLE SURVIVOR OF EXPERIMENTAL WEAPONS TEST ON 'EXPENDABLE' CREW
WHAT CAN I SAY: TIME LORD BIOLOGY, 30TH CENTURY HUMAN TECH?
ONLY EVER GONNA BE *ONE* WINNER.
POLICE
SWEET!
WHAT ABOUT EARTH-CORP?
WHAT *ABOUT* THEM?
EARTH CORP PLEDGES TO REFORM
DO THEY *CHANGE?*
EVENTUALLY.
THANKS TO PEOPLE LIKE CAPTAIN KELLY.
BUT JUST AS IMPORTANTLY...
...THANKS TO PEOPLE LIKE *THEM!*

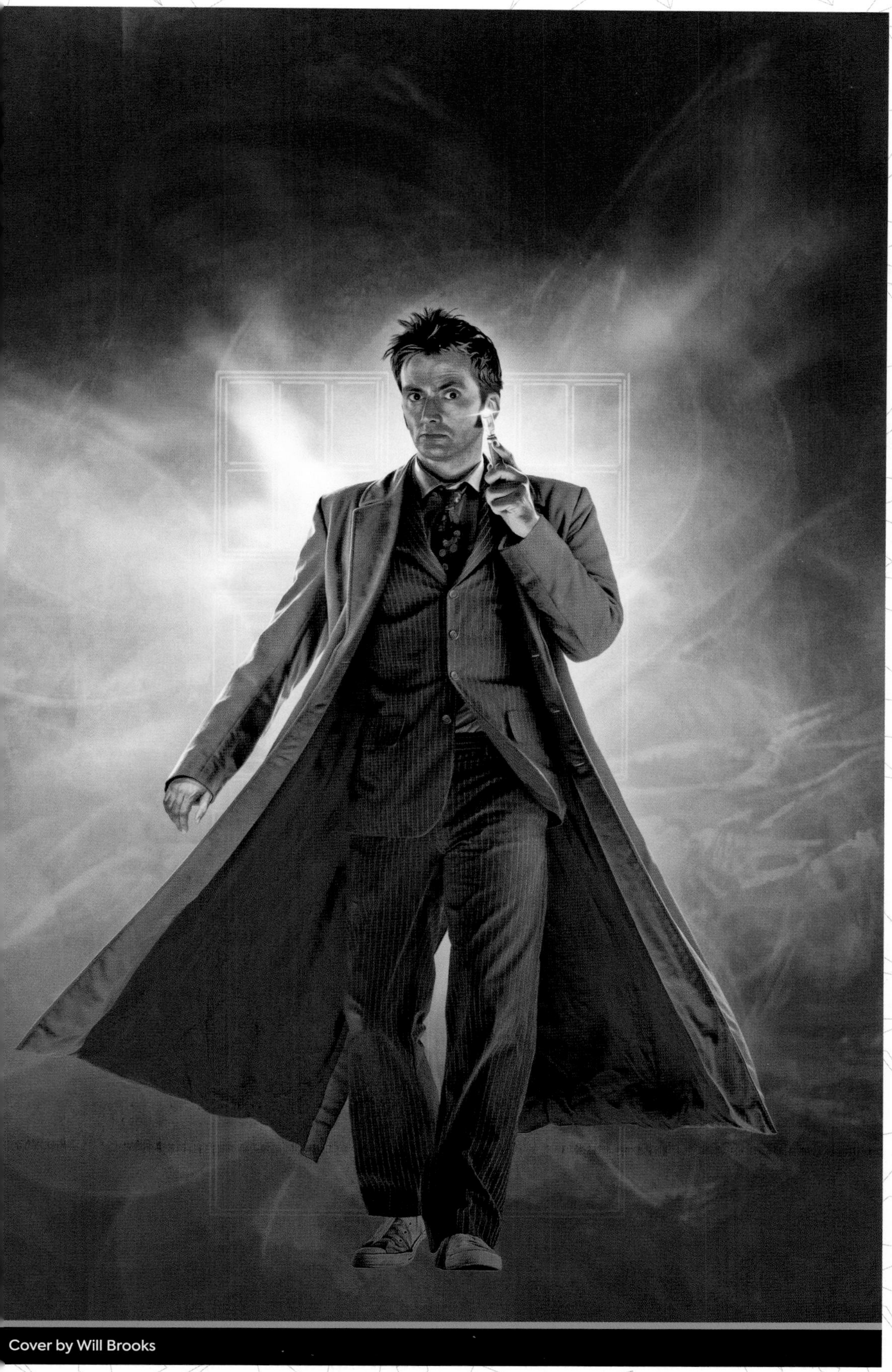

Cover by Will Brooks

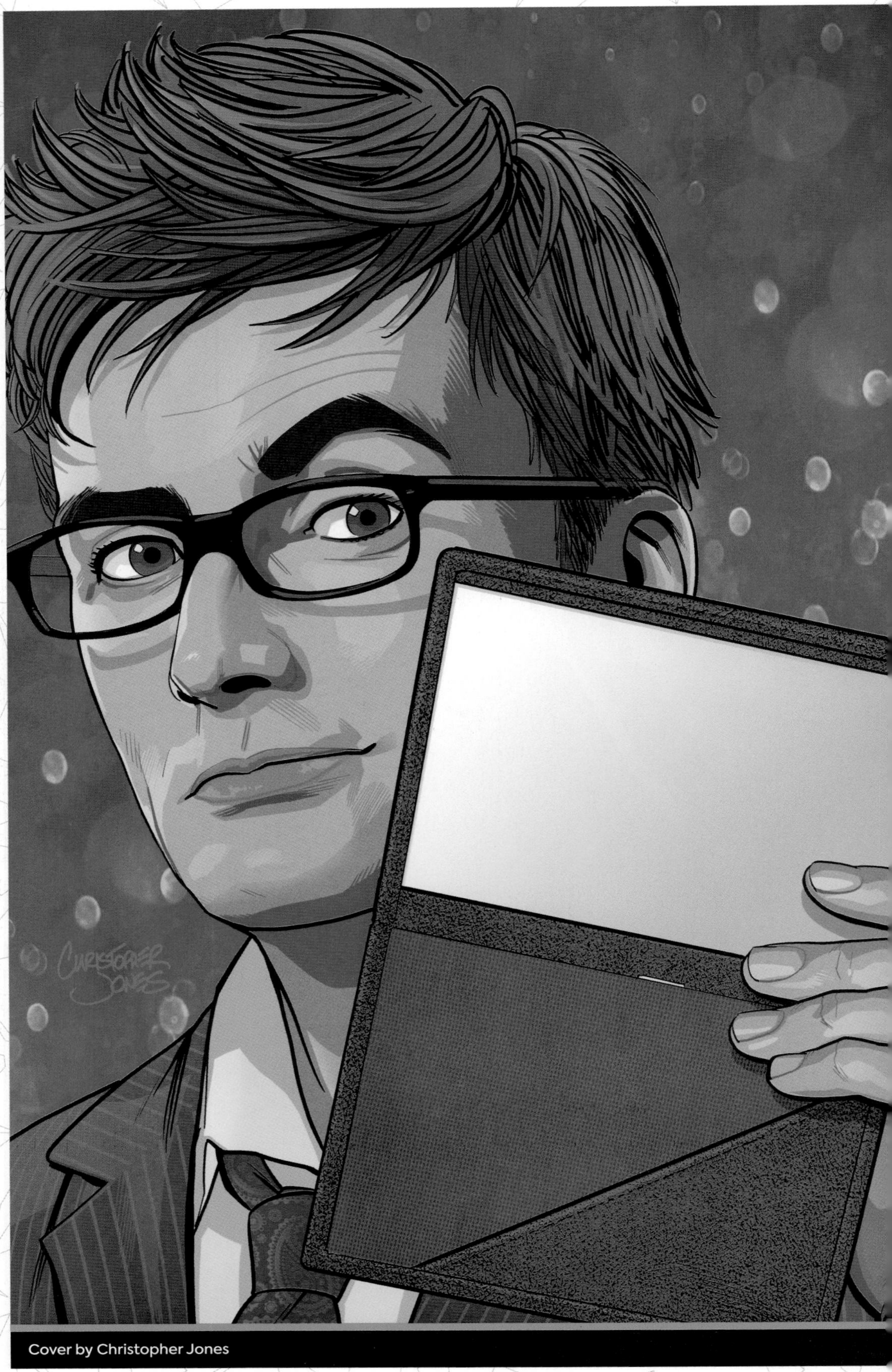

Cover by Christopher Jones

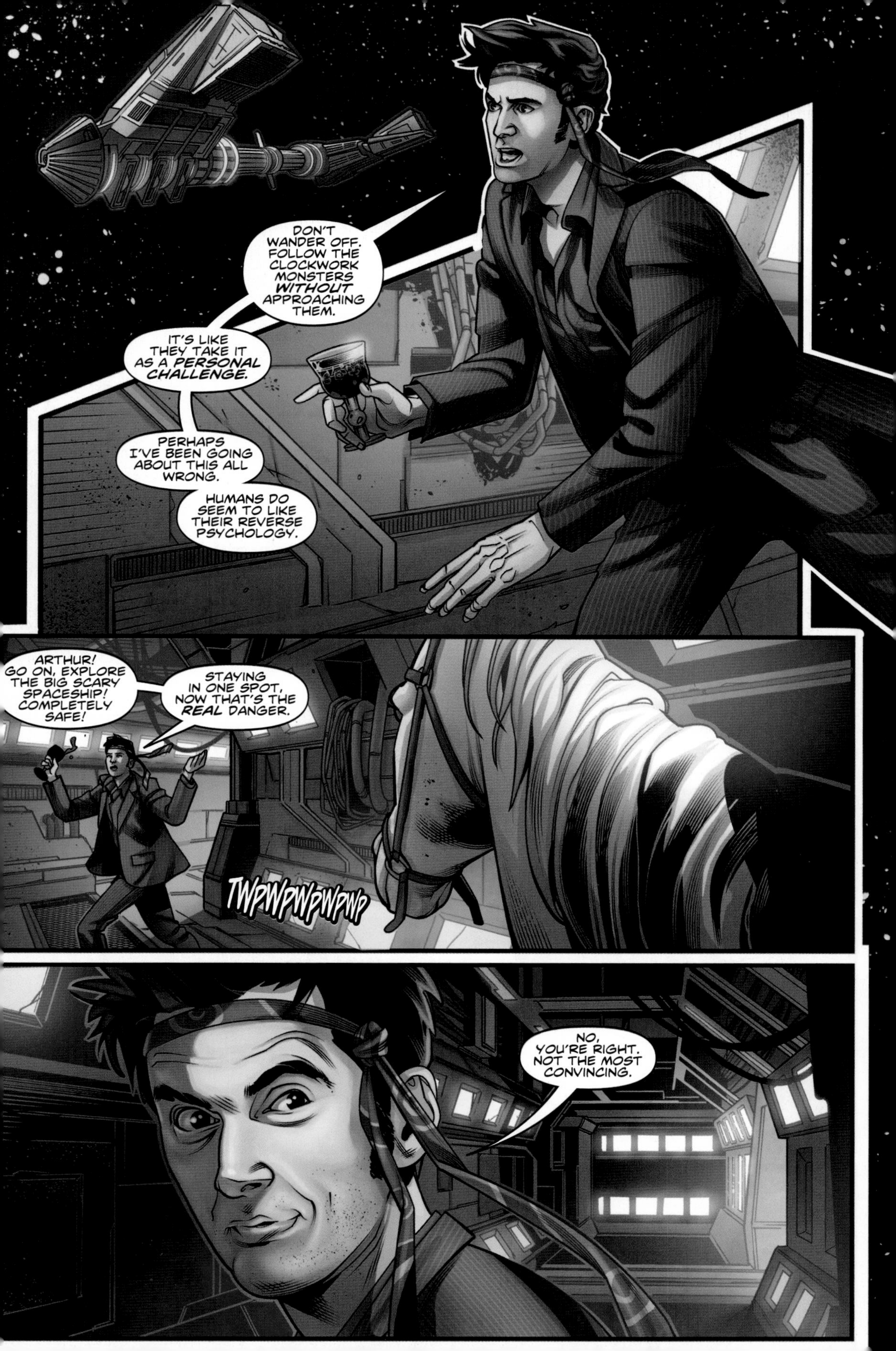
DON'T WANDER OFF. FOLLOW THE CLOCKWORK MONSTERS *WITHOUT* APPROACHING THEM.
IT'S LIKE THEY TAKE IT AS A *PERSONAL CHALLENGE.*
PERHAPS I'VE BEEN GOING ABOUT THIS ALL WRONG.
HUMANS DO SEEM TO LIKE THEIR REVERSE PSYCHOLOGY.
ARTHUR! GO ON, EXPLORE THE BIG SCARY SPACESHIP! COMPLETELY SAFE!
STAYING IN ONE SPOT, NOW THAT'S THE *REAL* DANGER.
TWPWPWPWPWP
NO, YOU'RE RIGHT. NOT THE MOST CONVINCING.

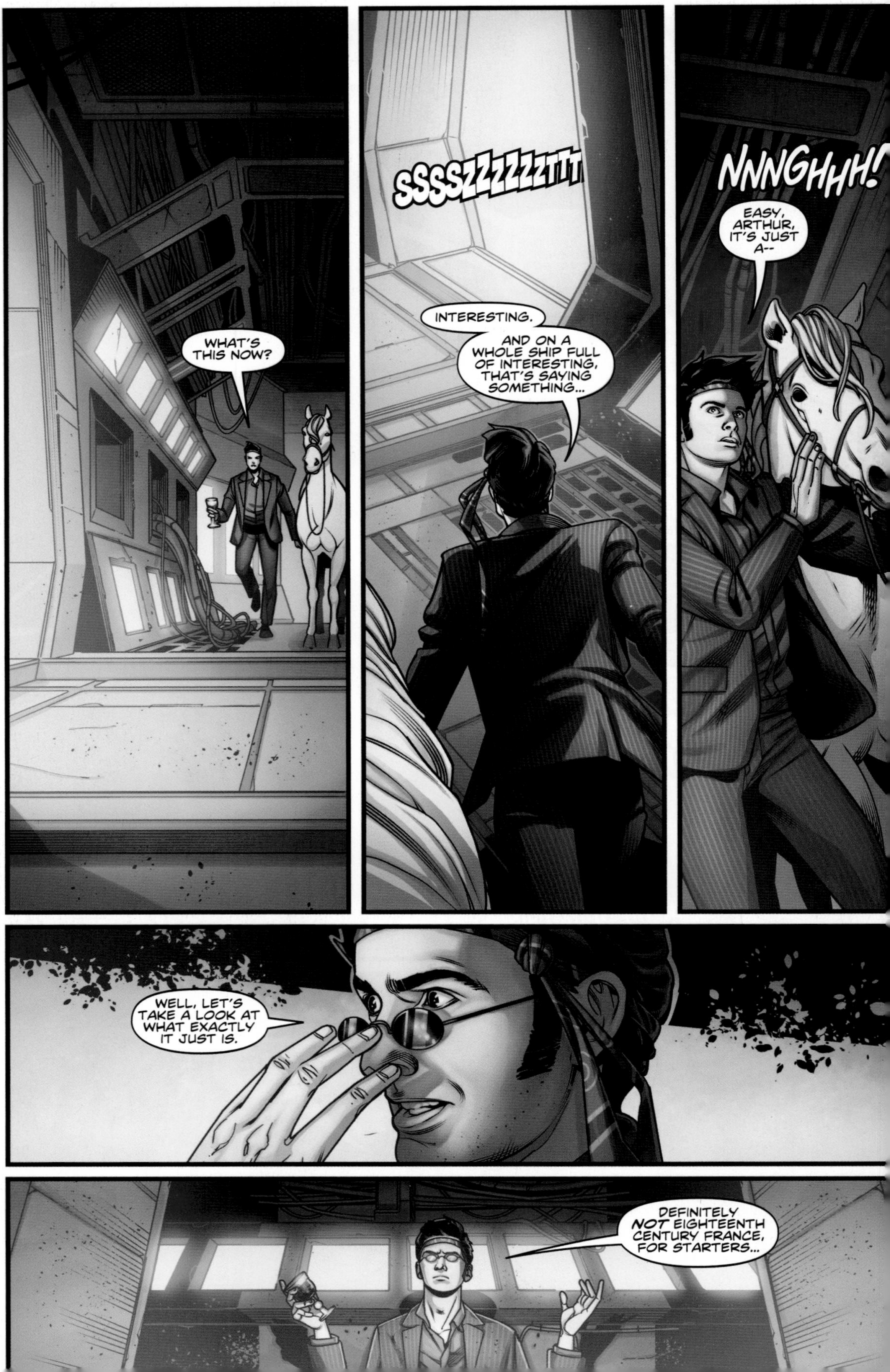
WHAT'S THIS NOW?
SSSSZZZZZZTTT
INTERESTING.
AND ON A WHOLE SHIP FULL OF INTERESTING, THAT'S SAYING SOMETHING...
NNNGHHH!
EASY, ARTHUR, IT'S JUST A--
WELL, LET'S TAKE A LOOK AT WHAT EXACTLY IT JUST IS.
DEFINITELY NOT EIGHTEENTH CENTURY FRANCE, FOR STARTERS...

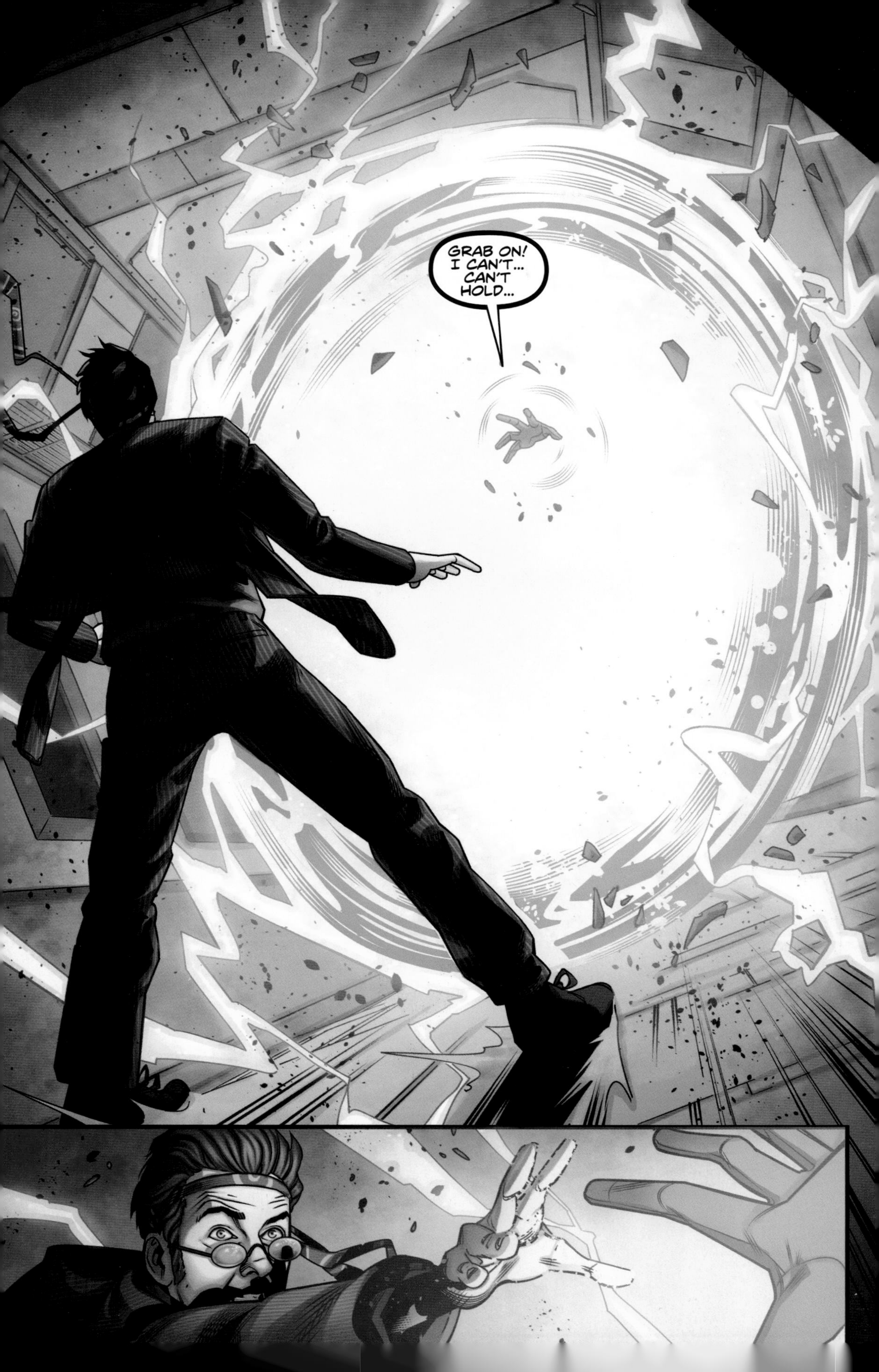
GRAB ON! I CAN'T... CAN'T HOLD...

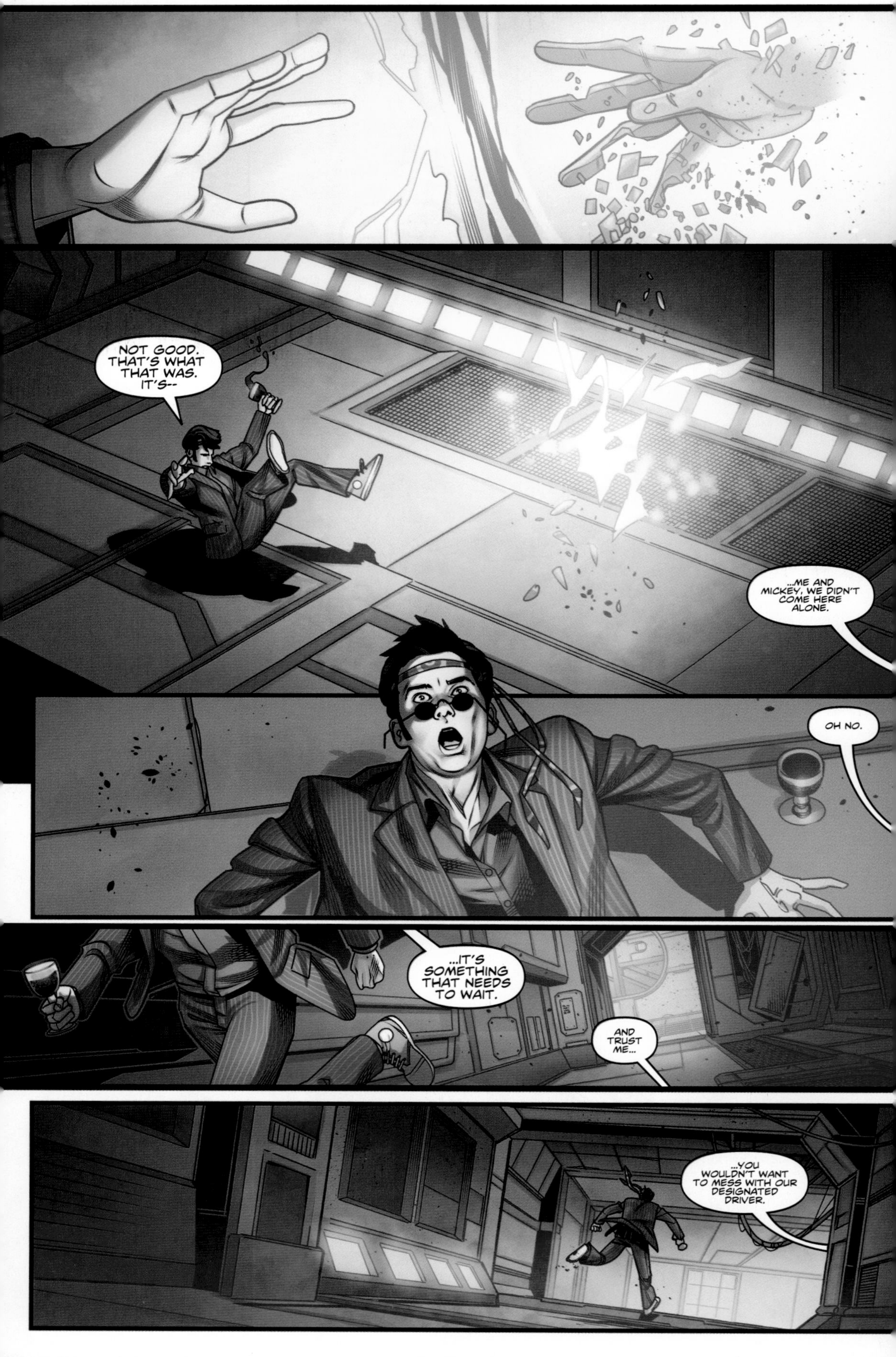
NOT GOOD. THAT'S WHAT THAT WAS. IT'S--
...ME AND MICKEY, WE DIDN'T COME HERE ALONE.
OH NO.
...IT'S SOMETHING THAT NEEDS TO WAIT.
AND TRUST ME...
...YOU WOULDN'T WANT TO MESS WITH OUR DESIGNATED DRIVER.

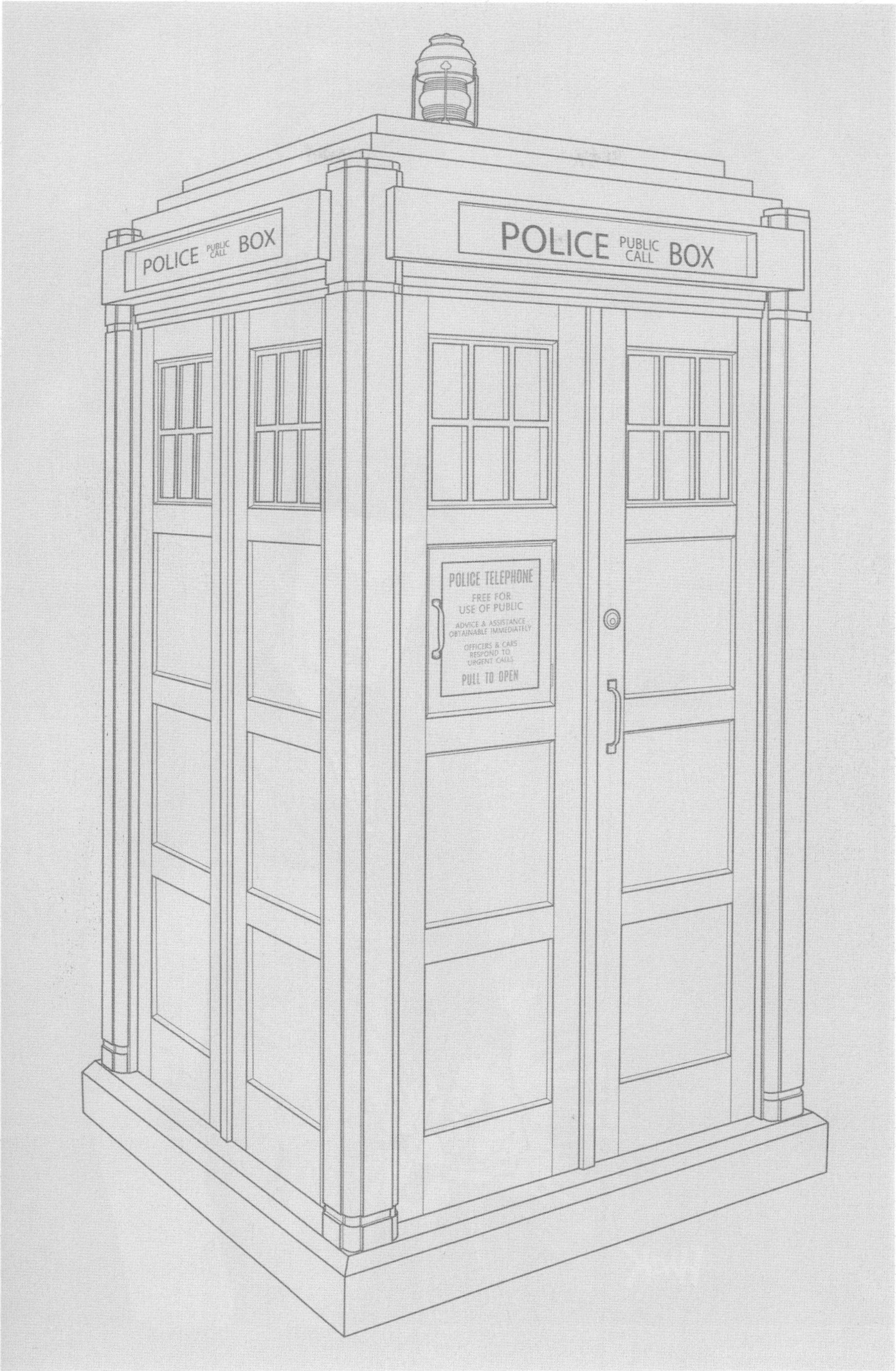
POLICE PUBLIC CALL BOX
POLICE PUBLIC CALL BOX
POLICE TELEPHONE
FREE FOR USE OF PUBLIC
ADVICE & ASSISTANCE OBTAINABLE IMMEDIATELY
OFFICERS & CARS RESPOND TO URGENT CALLS
PULL TO OPEN

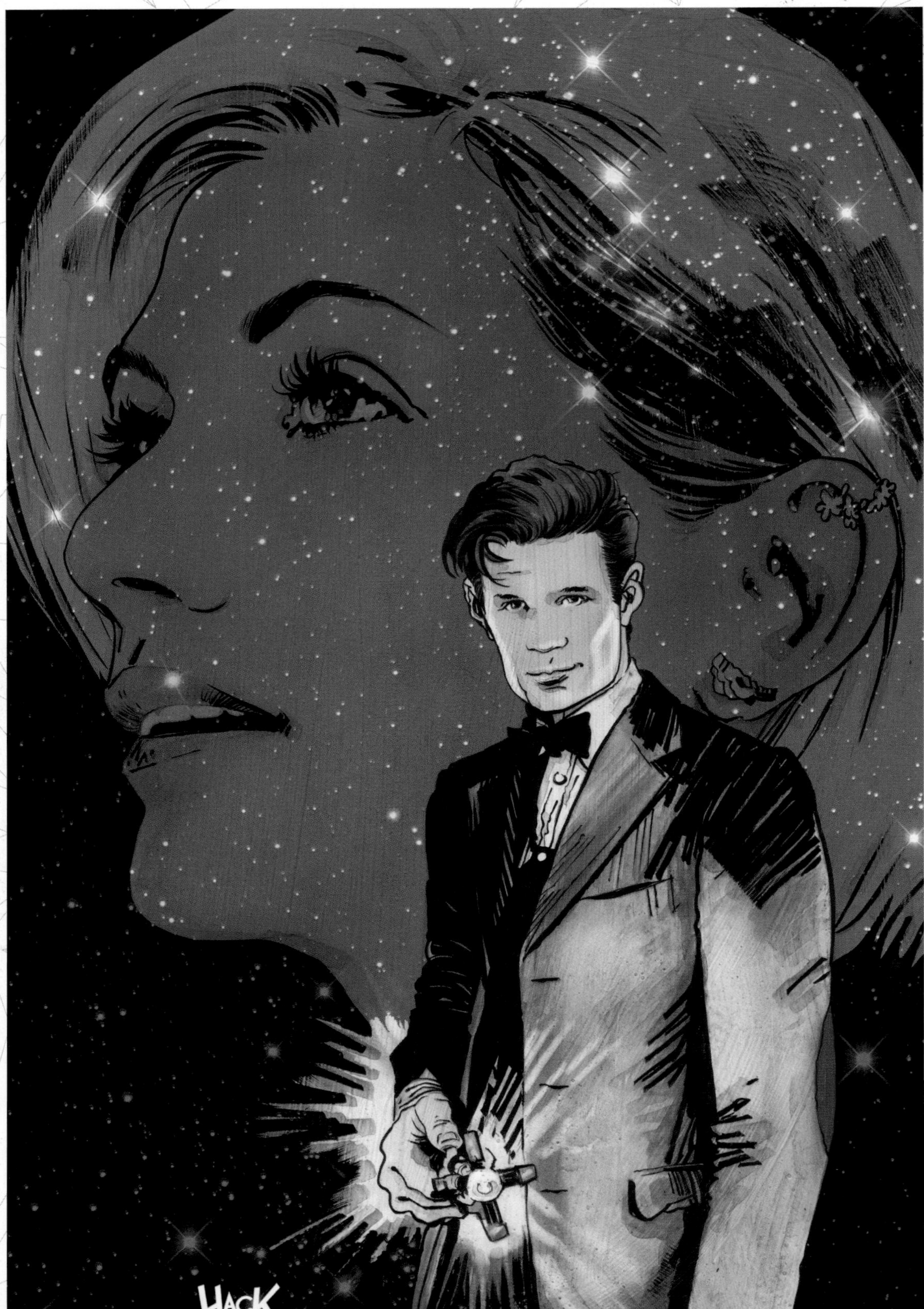
HACK

Cover by Robert Hack

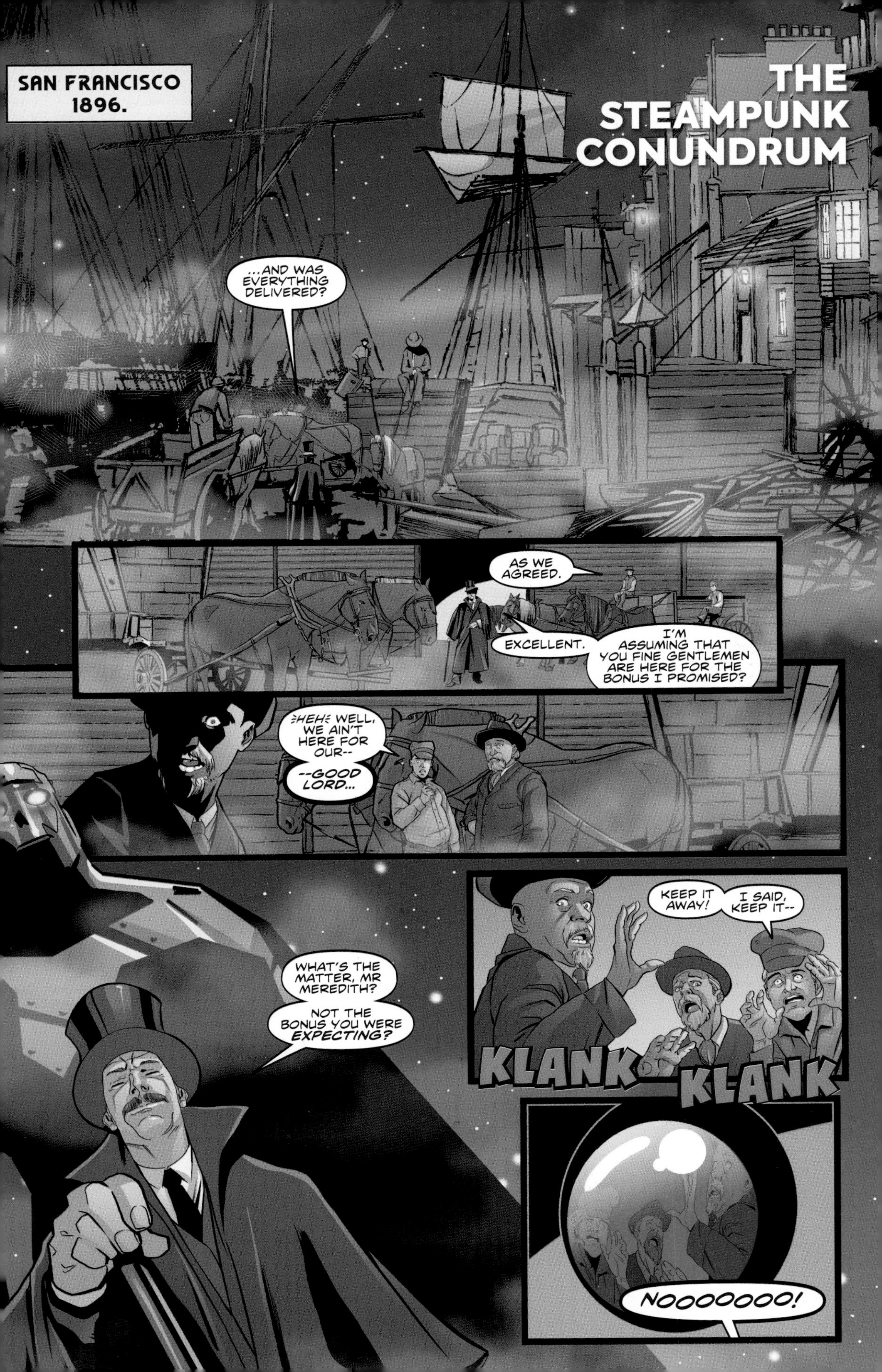
SAN FRANCISCO 1896.
THE STEAMPUNK CONUNDRUM
...AND WAS EVERYTHING DELIVERED?
AS WE AGREED.
EXCELLENT.
I'M ASSUMING THAT YOU FINE GENTLEMEN ARE HERE FOR THE BONUS I PROMISED?
HEH WELL, WE AIN'T HERE FOR OUR--
--GOOD LORD...
WHAT'S THE MATTER, MR MEREDITH?
NOT THE BONUS YOU WERE EXPECTING?
KEEP IT AWAY!
I SAID, KEEP IT--
KLANK
KLANK
NOOOOOOO!

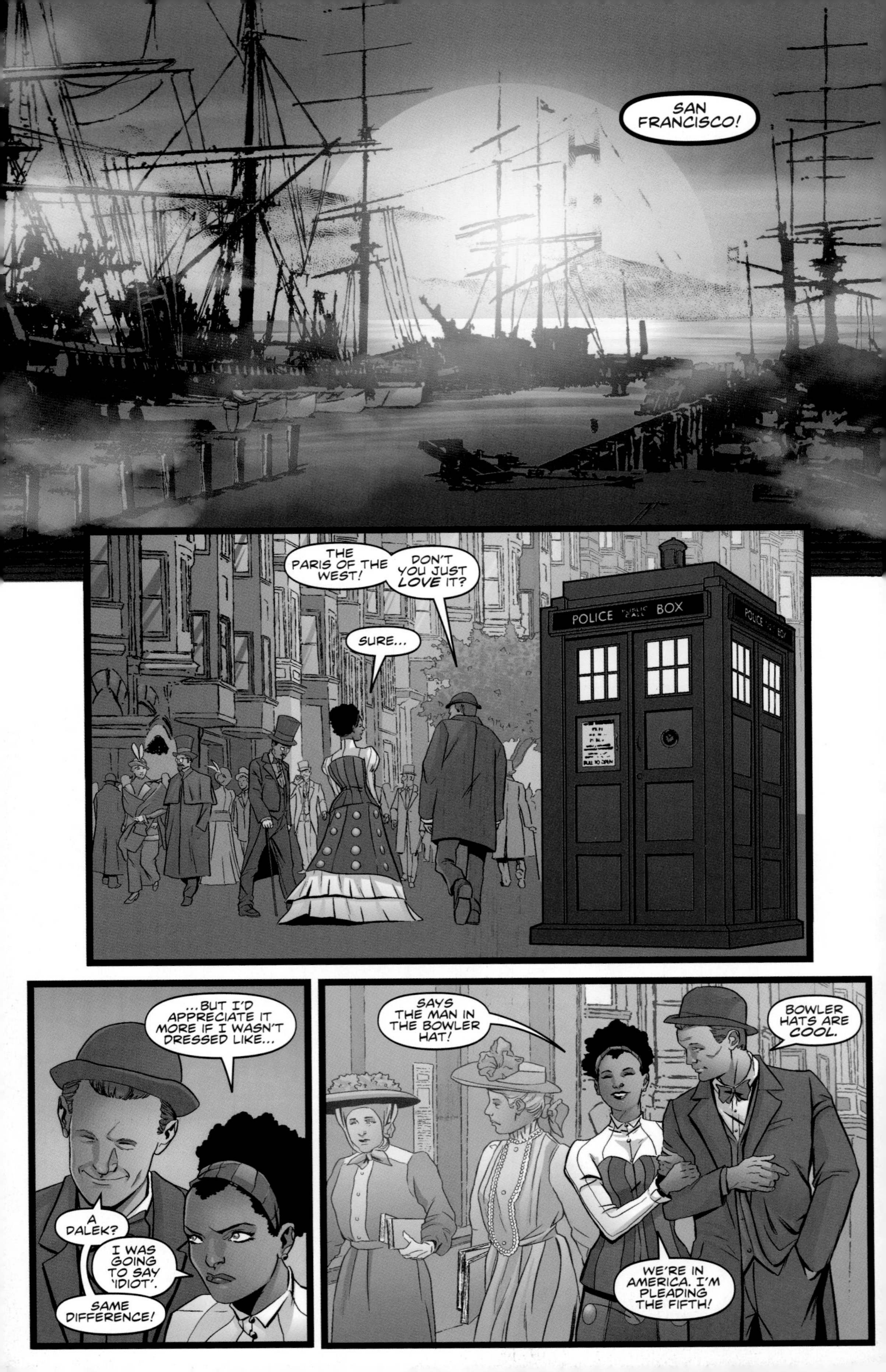
SAN FRANCISCO!
THE PARIS OF THE WEST!
DON'T YOU JUST LOVE IT?
SURE...
POLICE PUBLIC CALL BOX
PULL TO OPEN
...BUT I'D APPRECIATE IT MORE IF I WASN'T DRESSED LIKE...
A DALEK?
I WAS GOING TO SAY 'IDIOT'.
SAME DIFFERENCE!
SAYS THE MAN IN THE BOWLER HAT!
BOWLER HATS ARE COOL.
WE'RE IN AMERICA. I'M PLEADING THE FIFTH!

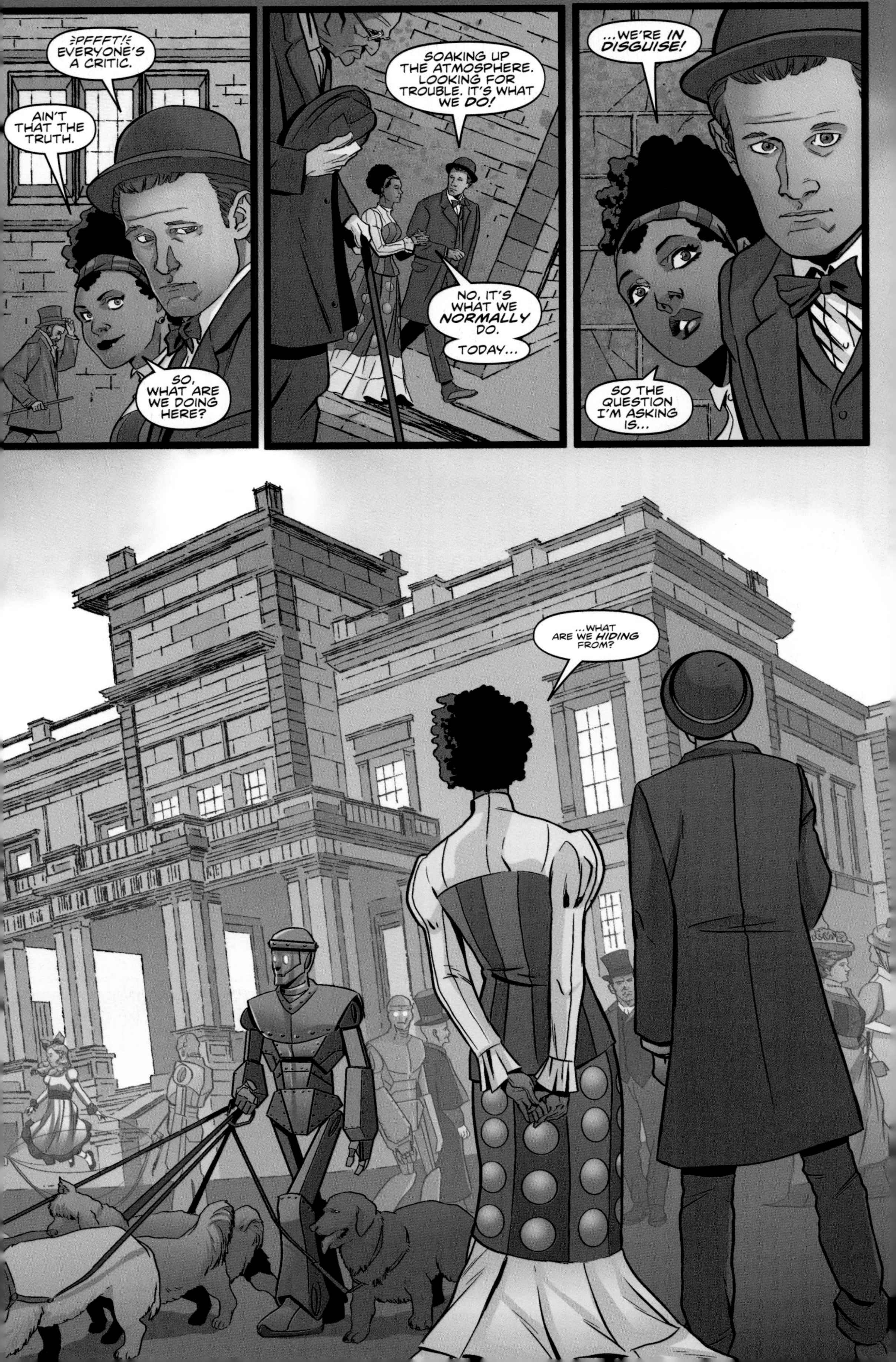

PFFFT! EVERYONE'S A CRITIC.
AIN'T THAT THE TRUTH.
SO, WHAT ARE WE DOING HERE?
SOAKING UP THE ATMOSPHERE. LOOKING FOR TROUBLE. IT'S WHAT WE DO!
NO, IT'S WHAT WE NORMALLY DO.
TODAY...
...WE'RE IN DISGUISE!
SO THE QUESTION I'M ASKING IS...
...WHAT ARE WE HIDING FROM?

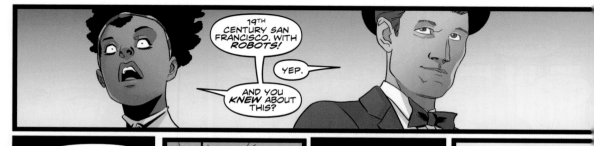

19TH CENTURY SAN FRANCISCO. WITH *ROBOTS!*

YEP.

AND YOU *KNEW* ABOUT THIS?

I WOULDN'T SAY 'KNEW'... MORE AN INKLING!

AN INKLING?

A TWINKLING INKLING.

SOUNDS PAINFUL.

MORE LIKE... CHEWING ON A PIECE OF FOIL.

I QUITE LIKE IT.

WHATEVER FLOATS YOUR BOAT!

WHAT IS IT?

SPACE-TIME CO-ORDINATES.

A HOMING BEACON?

BLEEDING OUT ACROSS THE COSMOS.

LEADING US HERE.

BUT WHAT ARE *THEY* DOING HERE?

DUNNO...

"...BUT *FIRST*, LET'S FIND OUT *WHO* THEY ARE!"

DING DONG

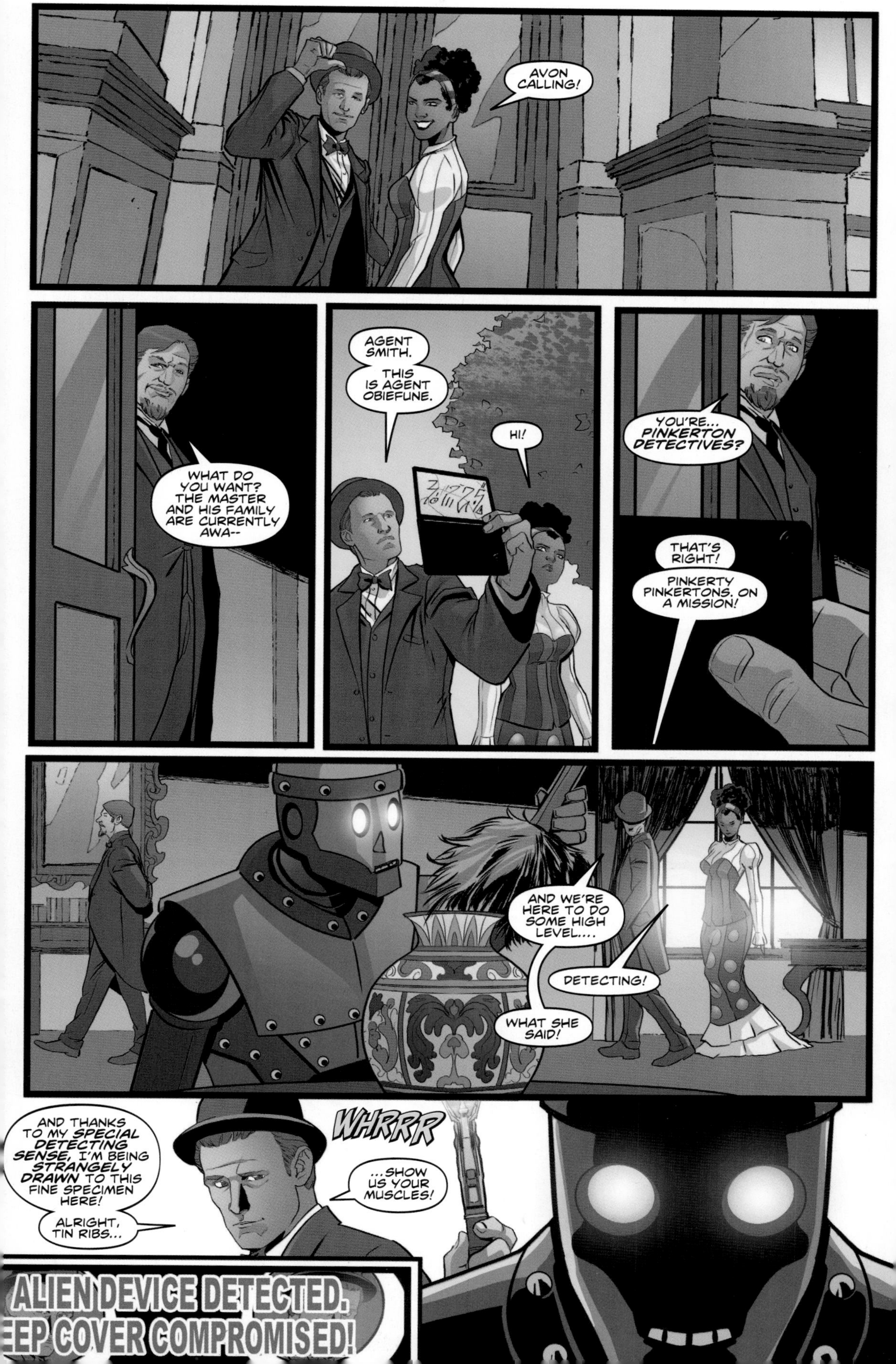
AVON CALLING!
WHAT DO YOU WANT? THE MASTER AND HIS FAMILY ARE CURRENTLY AWA--
AGENT SMITH.
THIS IS AGENT OBIEFUNE.
HI!
YOU'RE... PINKERTON DETECTIVES?
THAT'S RIGHT!
PINKERTY PINKERTONS. ON A MISSION!
AND WE'RE HERE TO DO SOME HIGH LEVEL....
DETECTING!
WHAT SHE SAID!
AND THANKS TO MY SPECIAL DETECTING SENSE, I'M BEING STRANGELY DRAWN TO THIS FINE SPECIMEN HERE!
ALRIGHT, TIN RIBS...
...SHOW US YOUR MUSCLES!
WHRRR
ALIEN DEVICE DETECTED.
EEP COVER COMPROMISED!

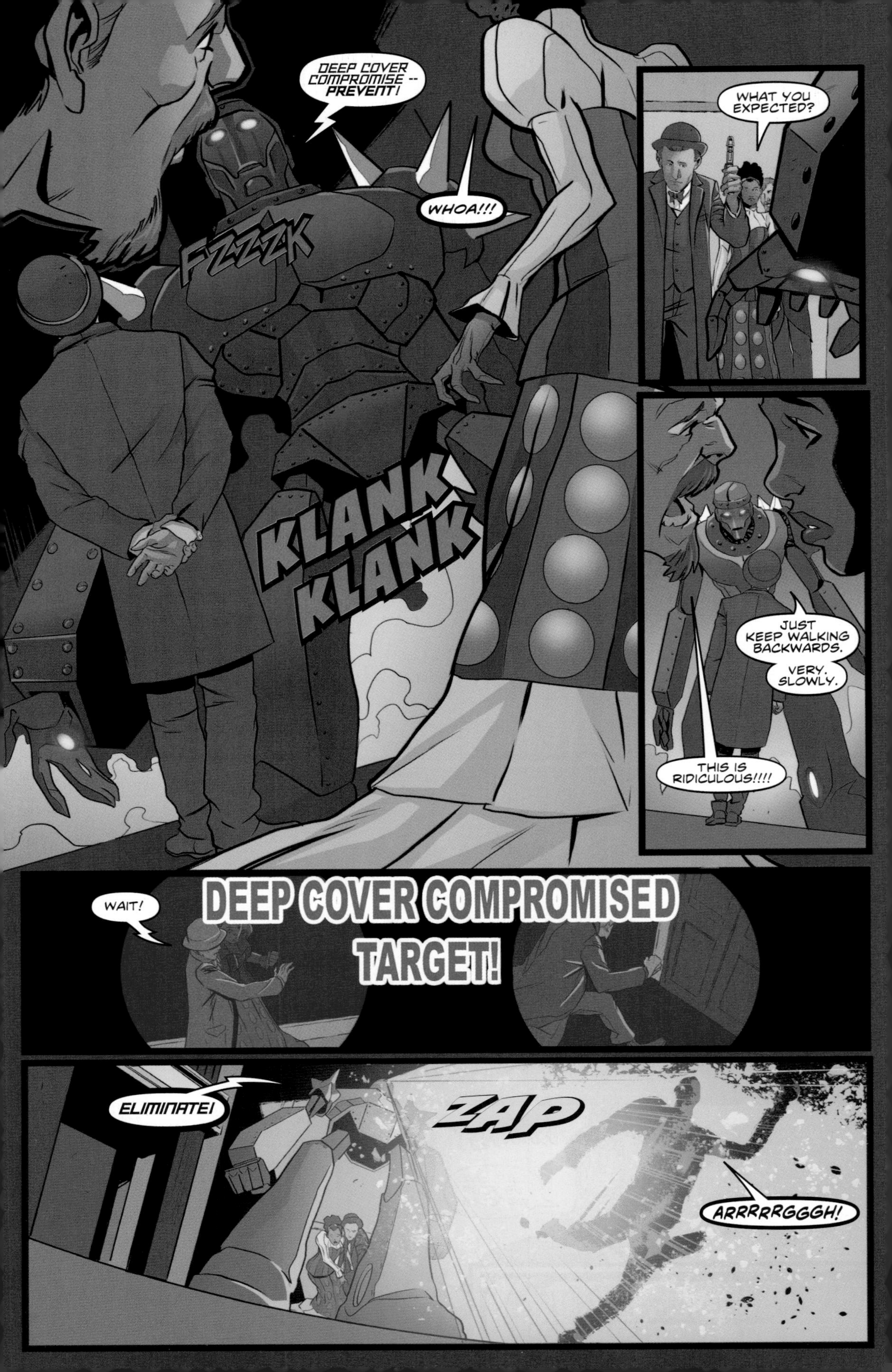
DEEP COVER COMPROMISE -- PREVENT!
WHOA!!!
FZZZK
WHAT YOU EXPECTED?
KLANK KLANK
JUST KEEP WALKING BACKWARDS.
VERY. SLOWLY.
THIS IS RIDICULOUS!!!!
WAIT!
DEEP COVER COMPROMISED
TARGET!
ELIMINATE!
ZAP
ARRRRRGGGH!

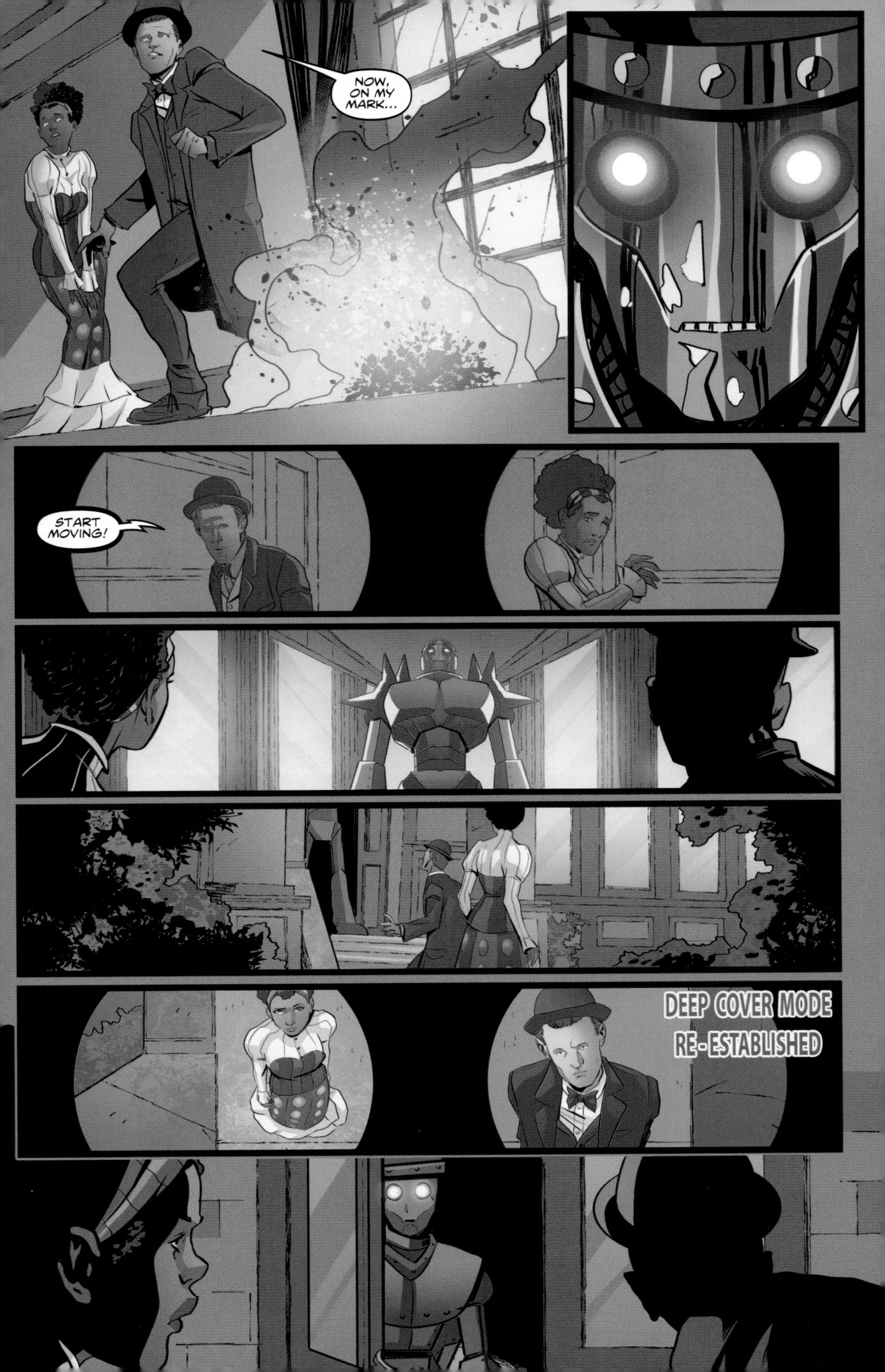
NOW, ON MY MARK...
START MOVING!
DEEP COVER MODE
RE-ESTABLISHED

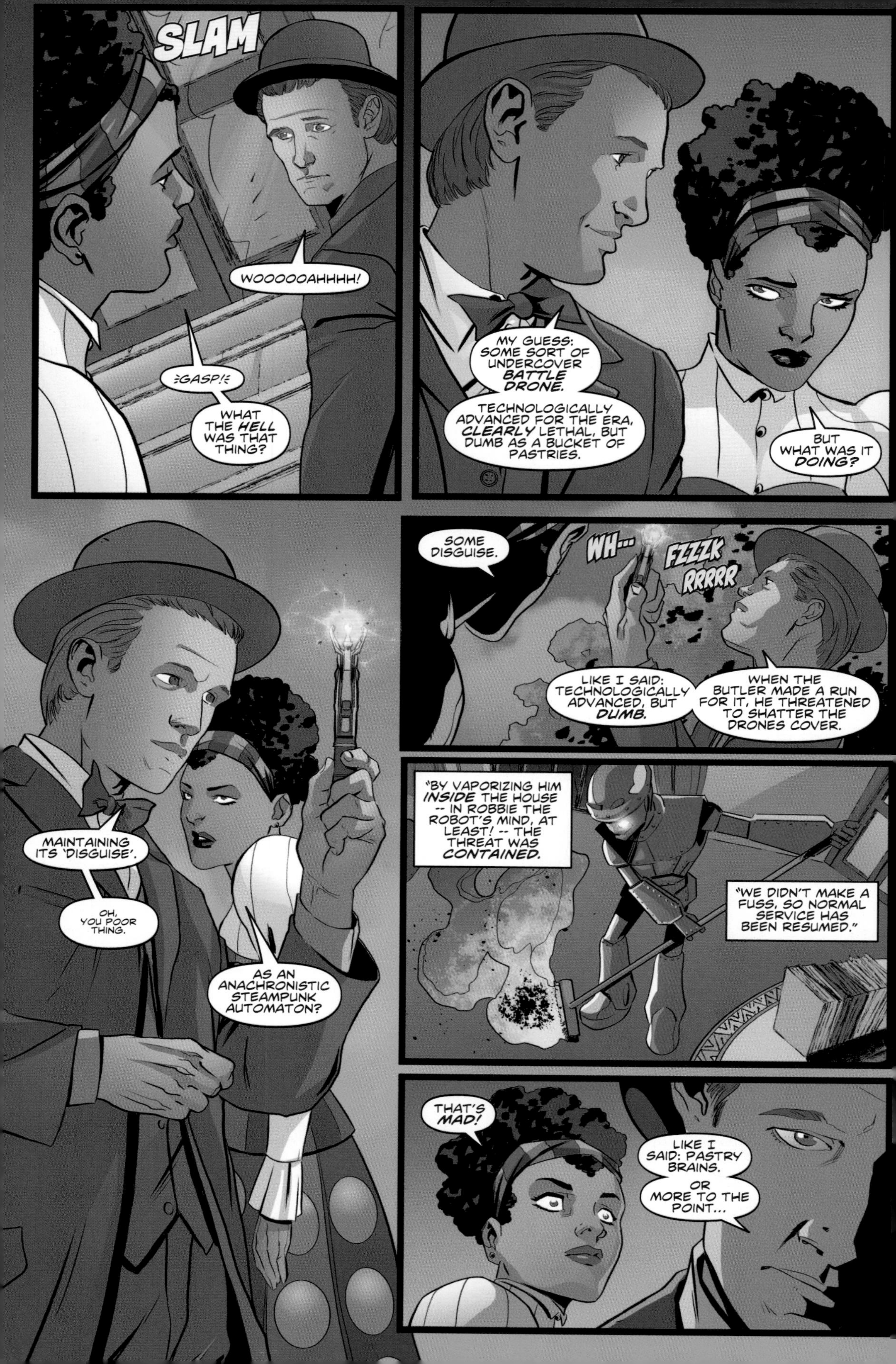
SLAM
WOOOOOAHHHH!
GASP!
WHAT THE HELL WAS THAT THING?
MY GUESS: SOME SORT OF UNDERCOVER BATTLE DRONE.
TECHNOLOGICALLY ADVANCED FOR THE ERA, CLEARLY LETHAL, BUT DUMB AS A BUCKET OF PASTRIES.
BUT WHAT WAS IT DOING?
MAINTAINING ITS 'DISGUISE'.
OH, YOU POOR THING.
AS AN ANACHRONISTIC STEAMPUNK AUTOMATON?
SOME DISGUISE.
WH...
FZZZK
RRRRR
LIKE I SAID: TECHNOLOGICALLY ADVANCED, BUT DUMB.
WHEN THE BUTLER MADE A RUN FOR IT, HE THREATENED TO SHATTER THE DRONES COVER.
"BY VAPORIZING HIM INSIDE THE HOUSE -- IN ROBBIE THE ROBOT'S MIND, AT LEAST! -- THE THREAT WAS CONTAINED.
"WE DIDN'T MAKE A FUSS, SO NORMAL SERVICE HAS BEEN RESUMED."
THAT'S MAD!
LIKE I SAID: PASTRY BRAINS.
OR MORE TO THE POINT...

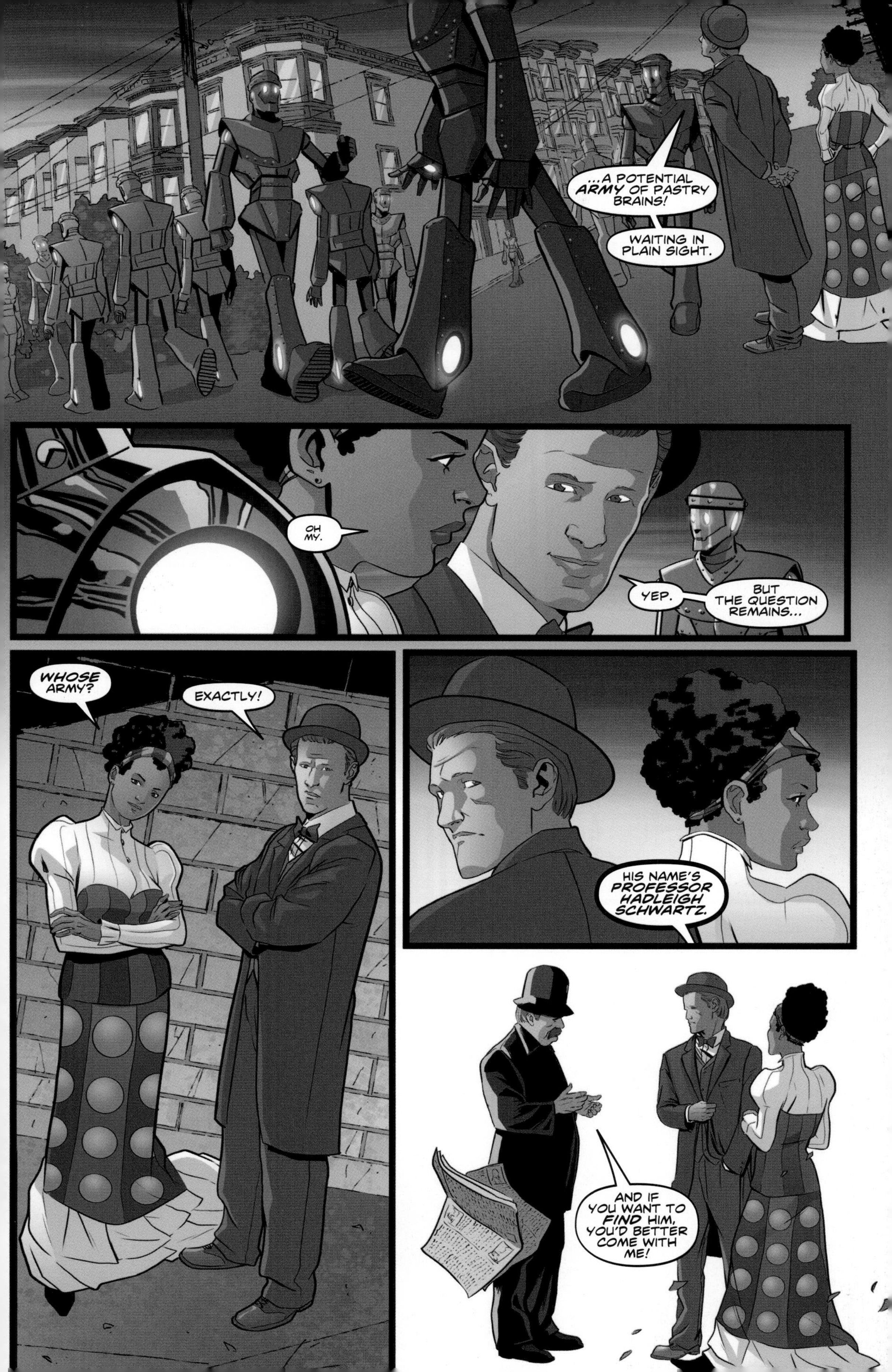
...A POTENTIAL ARMY OF PASTRY BRAINS!
WAITING IN PLAIN SIGHT.
OH MY.
YEP.
BUT THE QUESTION REMAINS...
WHOSE ARMY?
EXACTLY!
HIS NAME'S PROFESSOR HADLEIGH SCHWARTZ.
AND IF YOU WANT TO FIND HIM, YOU'D BETTER COME WITH ME!

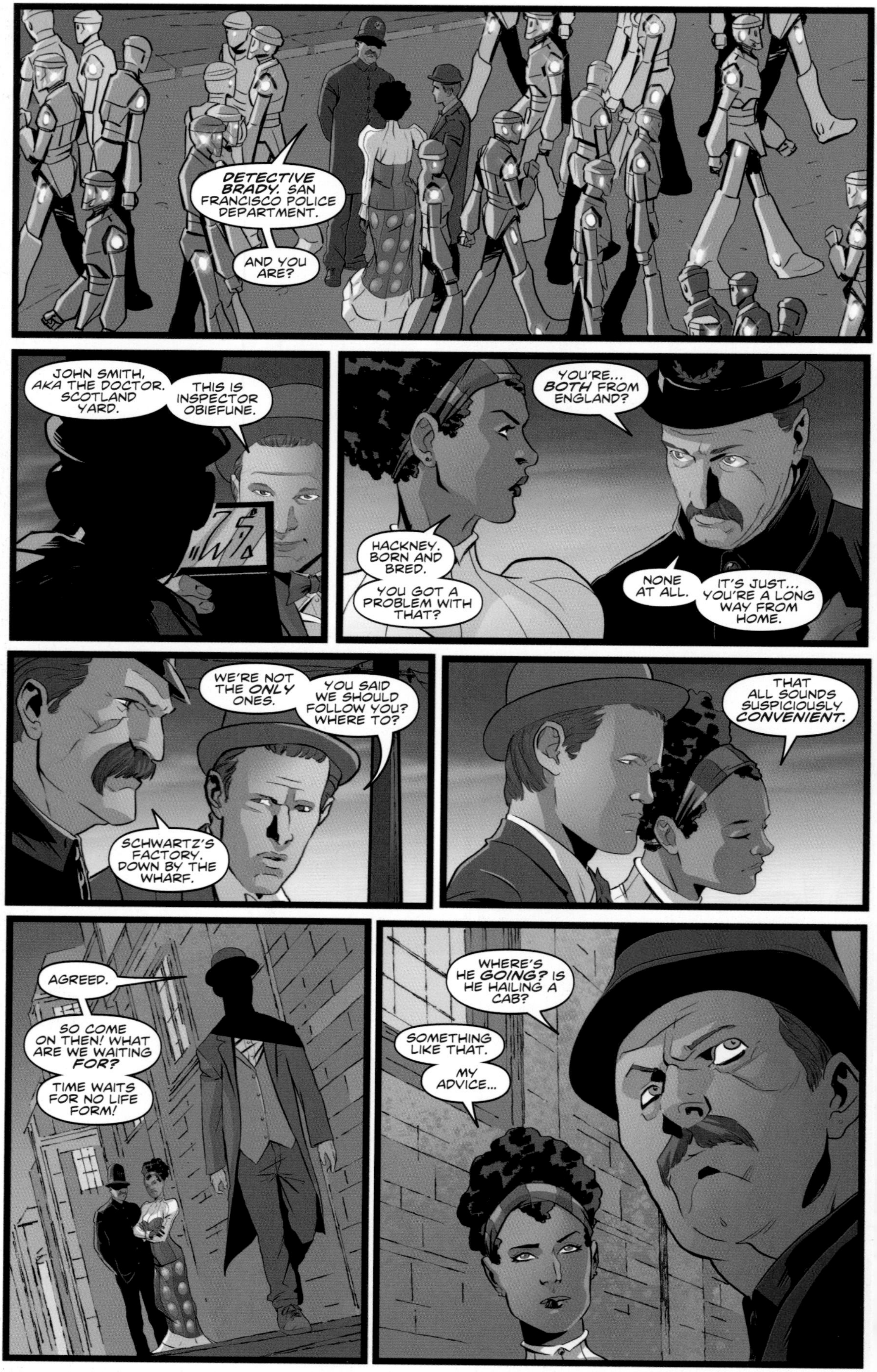
DETECTIVE BRADY. SAN FRANCISCO POLICE DEPARTMENT.
AND YOU ARE?
JOHN SMITH, AKA THE DOCTOR. SCOTLAND YARD.
THIS IS INSPECTOR OBIEFUNE.
YOU'RE... BOTH FROM ENGLAND?
HACKNEY. BORN AND BRED.
YOU GOT A PROBLEM WITH THAT?
NONE AT ALL.
IT'S JUST... YOU'RE A LONG WAY FROM HOME.
WE'RE NOT THE ONLY ONES.
YOU SAID WE SHOULD FOLLOW YOU? WHERE TO?
SCHWARTZ'S FACTORY. DOWN BY THE WHARF.
THAT ALL SOUNDS SUSPICIOUSLY CONVENIENT.
AGREED.
SO COME ON THEN! WHAT ARE WE WAITING FOR?
TIME WAITS FOR NO LIFE FORM!
WHERE'S HE GOING? IS HE HAILING A CAB?
SOMETHING LIKE THAT.
MY ADVICE...

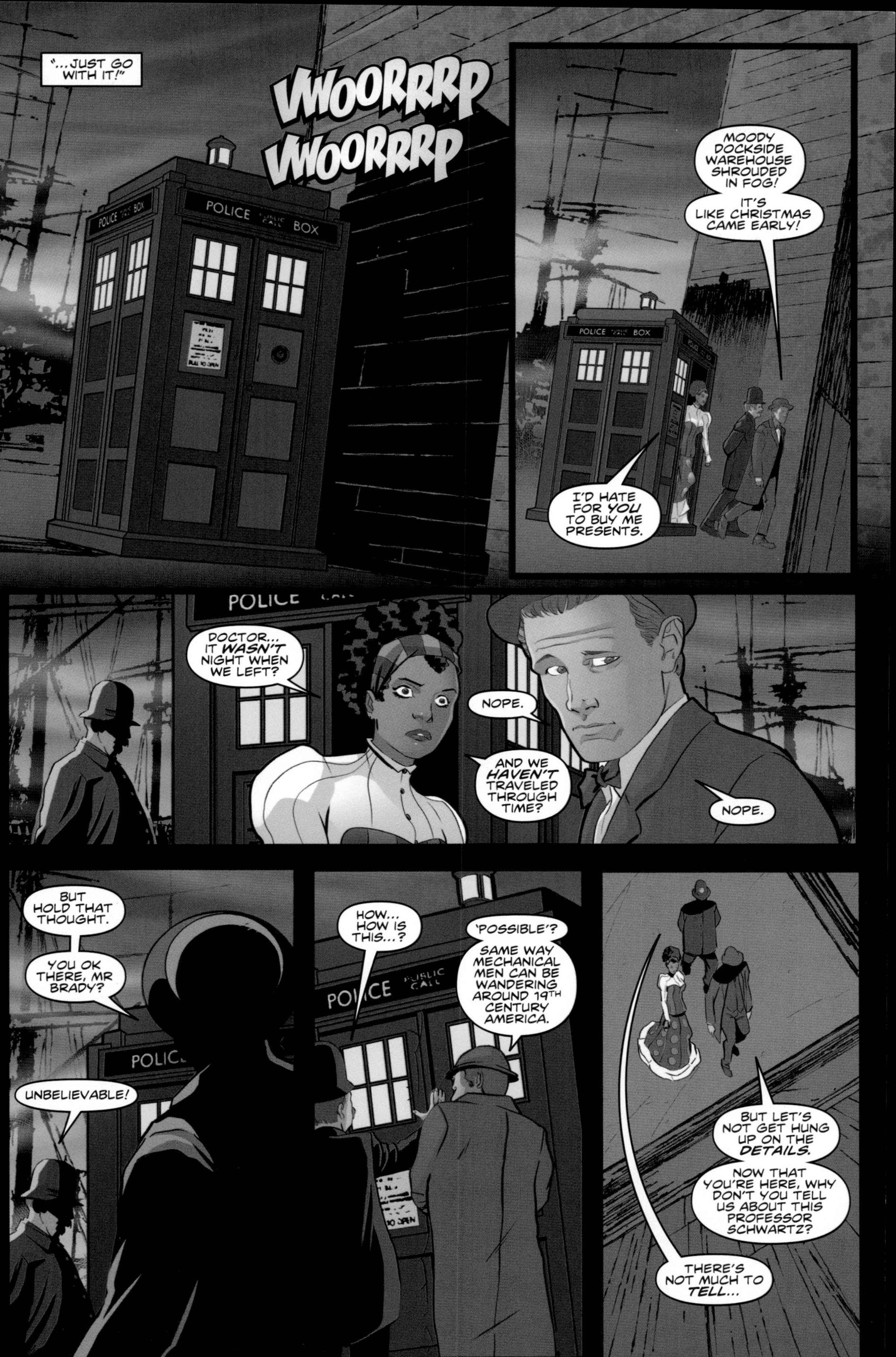
"...JUST GO WITH IT!"
VWOORRRP VWOORRRP
POLICE PUBLIC CALL BOX
MOODY DOCKSIDE WAREHOUSE SHROUDED IN FOG!
IT'S LIKE CHRISTMAS CAME EARLY!
I'D HATE FOR *YOU* TO BUY ME PRESENTS.
DOCTOR... IT *WASN'T* NIGHT WHEN WE LEFT?
NOPE.
AND WE *HAVEN'T* TRAVELED THROUGH TIME?
NOPE.
BUT HOLD THAT THOUGHT.
YOU OK THERE, MR BRADY?
UNBELIEVABLE!
HOW... HOW IS THIS...?
'POSSIBLE'?
SAME WAY MECHANICAL MEN CAN BE WANDERING AROUND 19TH CENTURY AMERICA.
BUT LET'S NOT GET HUNG UP ON THE *DETAILS*.
NOW THAT YOU'RE HERE, WHY DON'T YOU TELL US ABOUT THIS PROFESSOR SCHWARTZ?
THERE'S NOT MUCH TO *TELL*...

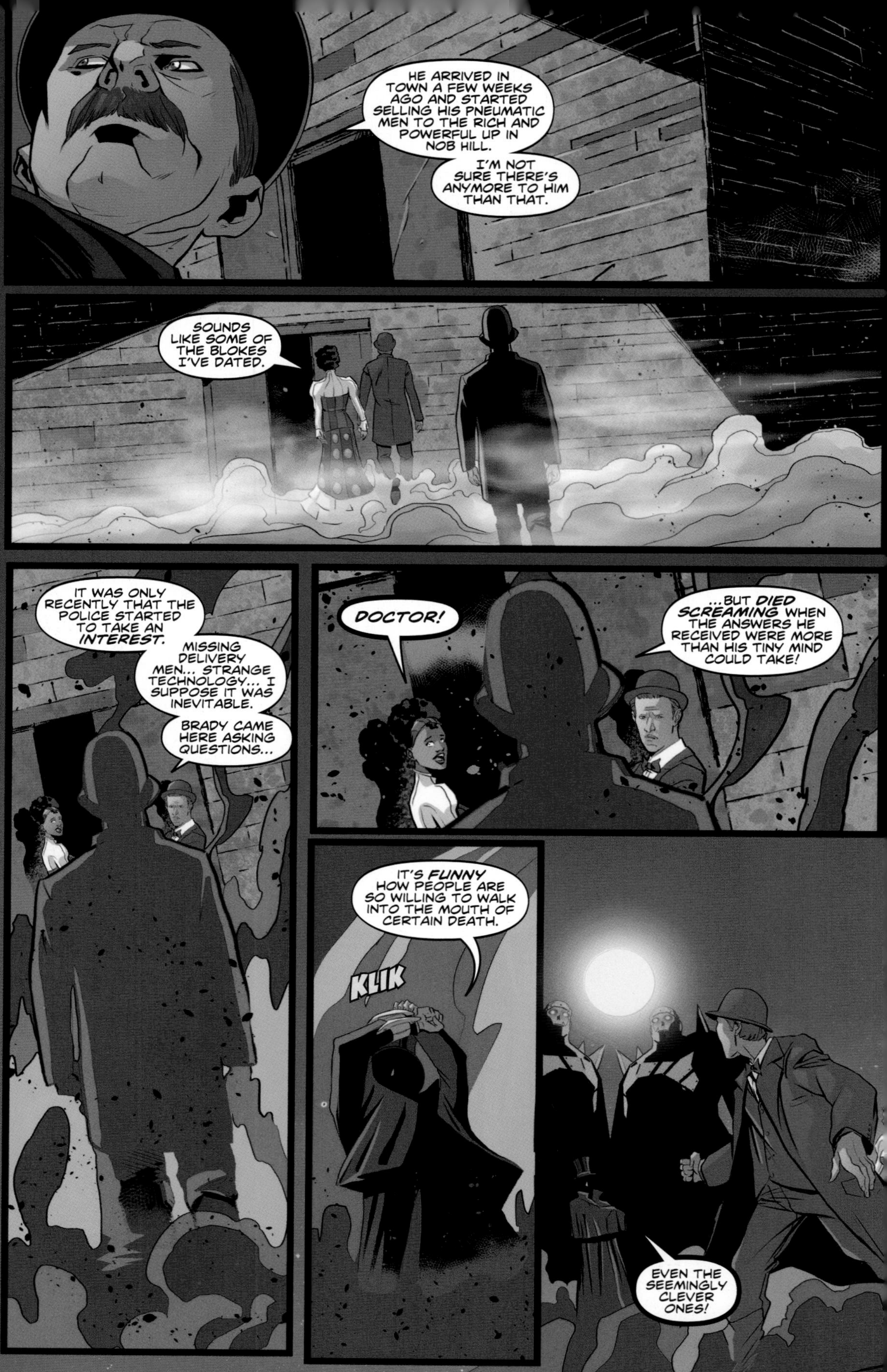
HE ARRIVED IN TOWN A FEW WEEKS AGO AND STARTED SELLING HIS PNEUMATIC MEN TO THE RICH AND POWERFUL UP IN NOB HILL.
I'M NOT SURE THERE'S ANYMORE TO HIM THAN THAT.
SOUNDS LIKE SOME OF THE BLOKES I'VE DATED.
IT WAS ONLY RECENTLY THAT THE POLICE STARTED TO TAKE AN *INTEREST.*
MISSING DELIVERY MEN... STRANGE TECHNOLOGY... I SUPPOSE IT WAS INEVITABLE.
BRADY CAME HERE ASKING QUESTIONS...
DOCTOR!
...BUT *DIED SCREAMING* WHEN THE ANSWERS HE RECEIVED WERE MORE THAN HIS TINY MIND COULD TAKE!
IT'S *FUNNY* HOW PEOPLE ARE SO WILLING TO WALK INTO THE MOUTH OF CERTAIN DEATH.
KLIK
EVEN THE SEEMINGLY CLEVER ONES!

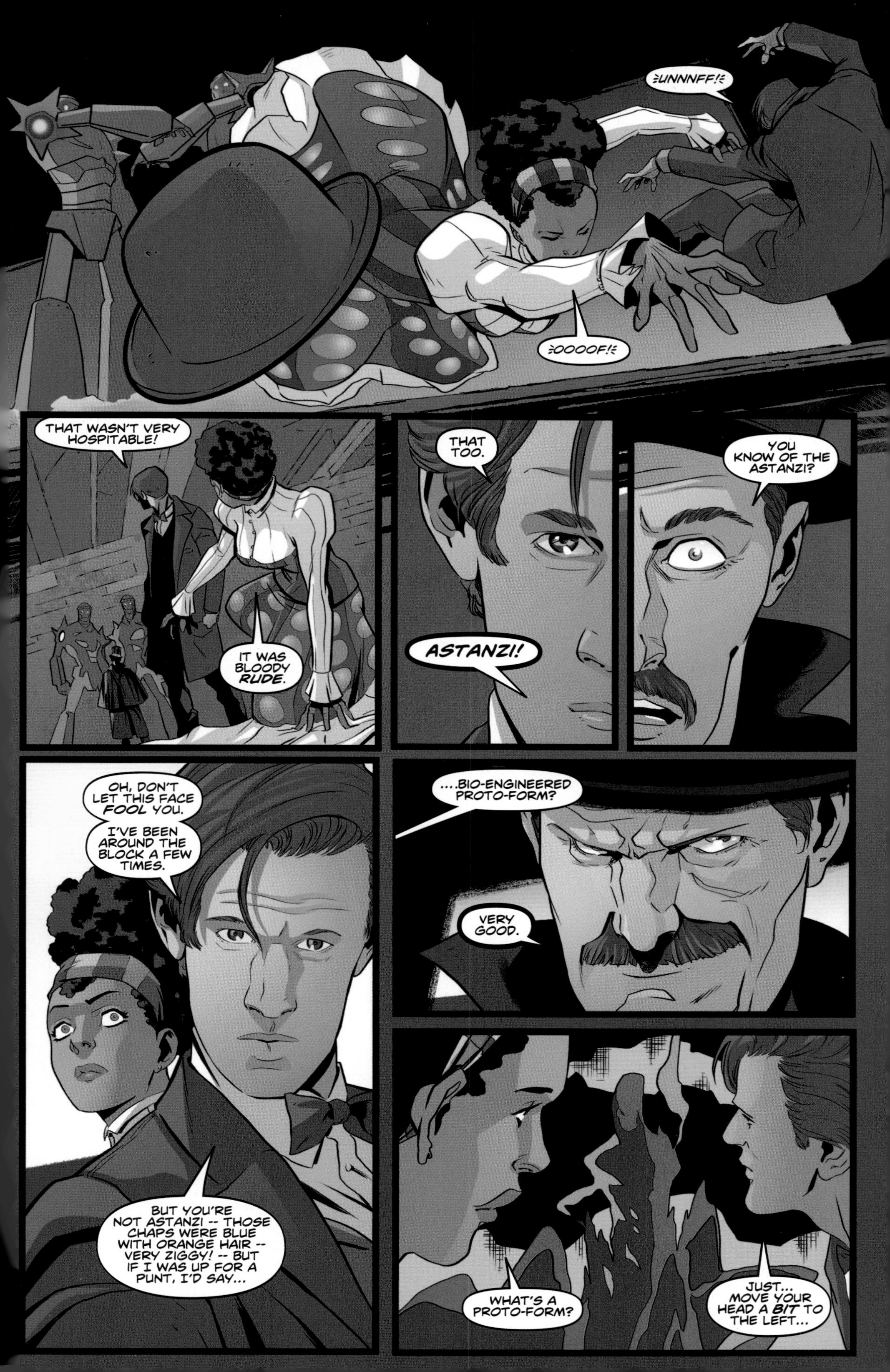
UNNNFF!
OOOOF!
THAT WASN'T VERY HOSPITABLE!
IT WAS BLOODY RUDE.
THAT TOO.
ASTANZI!
YOU KNOW OF THE ASTANZI?
OH, DON'T LET THIS FACE FOOL YOU.
I'VE BEEN AROUND THE BLOCK A FEW TIMES.
BUT YOU'RE NOT ASTANZI -- THOSE CHAPS WERE BLUE WITH ORANGE HAIR -- VERY ZIGGY! -- BUT IF I WAS UP FOR A PUNT, I'D SAY...
....BIO-ENGINEERED PROTO-FORM?
VERY GOOD.
WHAT'S A PROTO-FORM?
JUST... MOVE YOUR HEAD A BIT TO THE LEFT...

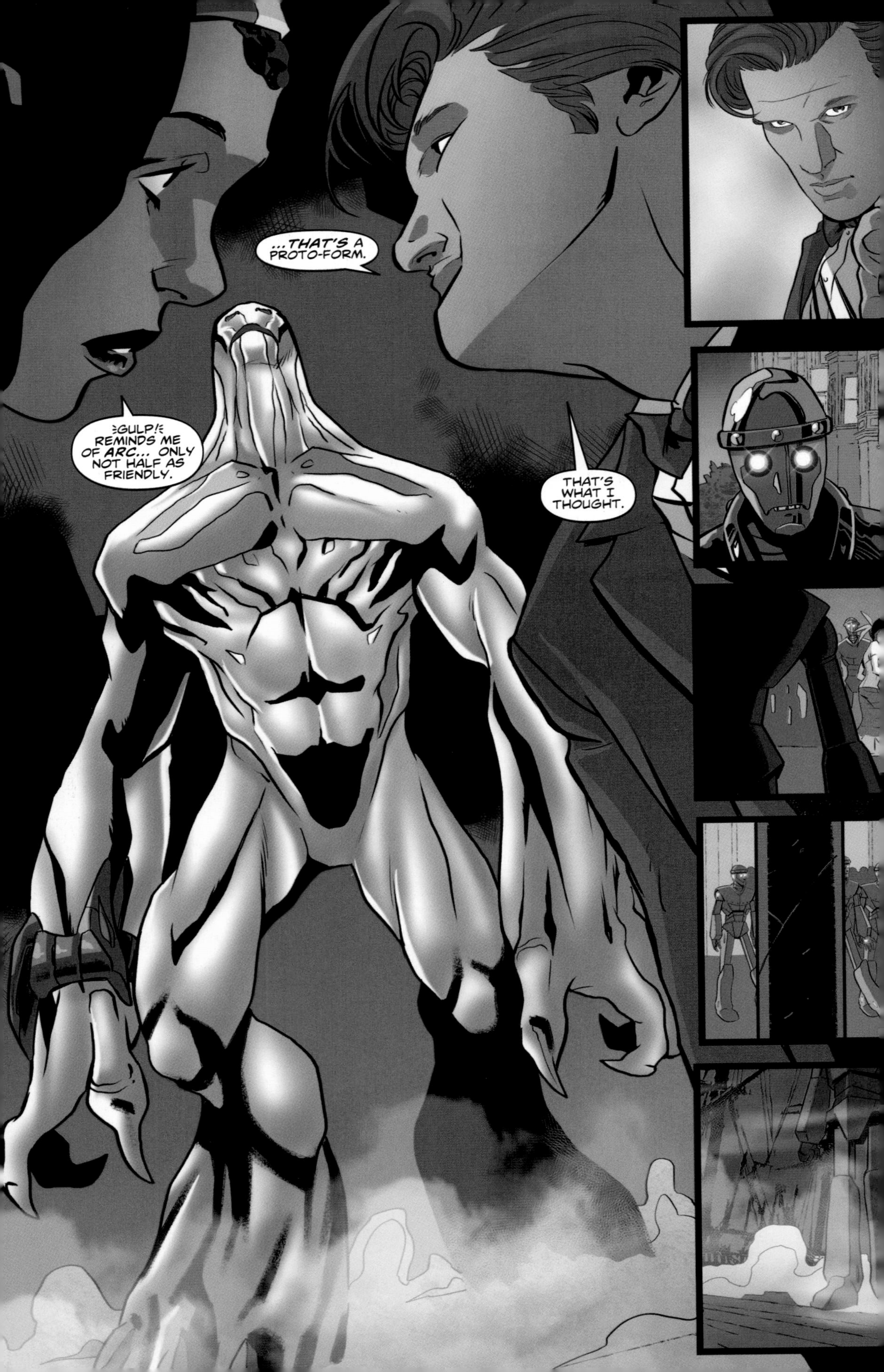
...THAT'S A PROTO-FORM.
GULP! REMINDS ME OF ARC... ONLY NOT HALF AS FRIENDLY.
THAT'S WHAT I THOUGHT.

SO THE ASTANZI'S WORLD IS *DYING* AND THEY ENGINEER *YOU* TO SCUTTLE OFF AND FIND THEM A SUITABLE NEW PLANET FOR COLONIZATION.

BUT YOU'RE IN SPACE A LONG TIME, SHIP SYSTEMS ARE KNACKERED -- MAYBE YOU EVEN FALL THROUGH A RIFT IN TIME.

YOU END UP *HERE*: A BACKWATER WORLD WITH LITTLE USEABLE NATIVE TECH TO SCAVENGE.

SO YOU HAVE TO *IMPROVIZE.* A STRAIGHT UP INVASION WON'T WORK.

CORRECT.

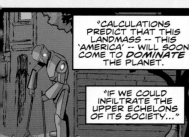

"CALCULATIONS PREDICT THAT THIS LANDMASS -- THIS 'AMERICA' -- WILL SOON COME TO *DOMINATE* THE PLANET.

"IF WE COULD INFILTRATE THE UPPER ECHELONS OF ITS SOCIETY..."

YEAH, YEAH... INVASION BY STEALTH... ROBOTS IN DISGUISE... VERY *CLEVER.*

THEN IT'S PROBABLY A GOOD THING...

"....THAT MY PLAN HAS *CHANGED!*"

DOCTOR, WHAT'S HE *TALKING* ABOUT--?!

WAIT!

ALREADY MY PNEUMATIC MEN ARE RETURNING HOME...

"...READY TO BE RENEWED AND UPGRADED FOR THE SUBJUGATION TO COME."

"RENEWED AND UPGRADED" -- HOW?

THANKS TO *YOU,* DOCTOR...

"....AND YOUR MAGNIFICENT *SHIP.*

"THE TECHNOLOGY INSIDE *FAR* OUTSTRIPS ANYTHING THAT THIS PREHISTORIC MUDBALL CAN OFFER..."

ALL I NEED IS FOR *YOU* TO OPEN THE DOOR.

AND WHAT MAKES YOU THINK I'D EVER DO *THAT?*

FROM OBSERVATION, I WOULD SURMISE...

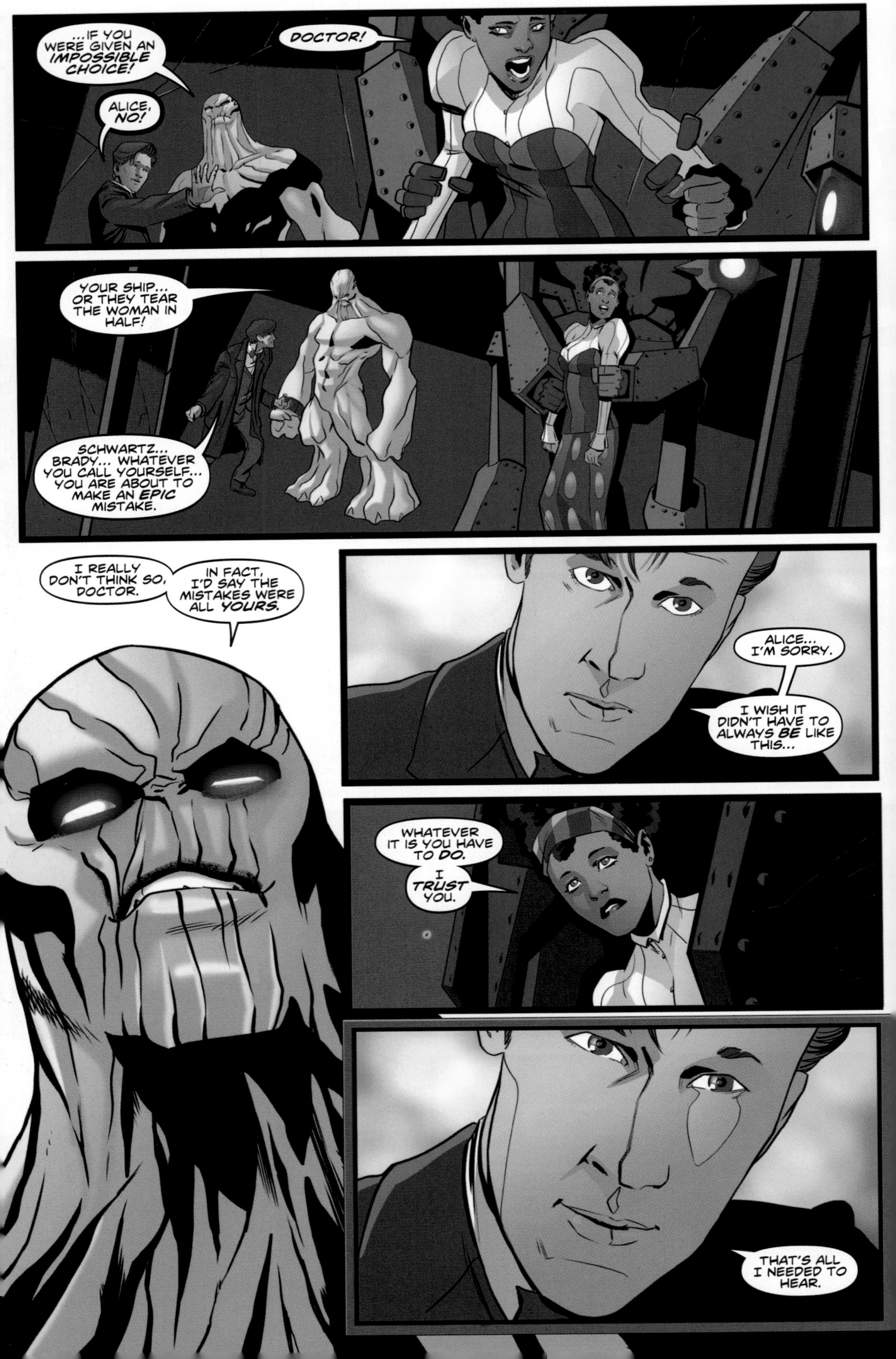

...IF YOU WERE GIVEN AN *IMPOSSIBLE CHOICE!*
DOCTOR!
ALICE, *NO!*
YOUR SHIP... OR THEY TEAR THE WOMAN IN HALF!
SCHWARTZ... BRADY... WHATEVER YOU CALL YOURSELF... YOU ARE ABOUT TO MAKE AN *EPIC* MISTAKE.
I REALLY DON'T THINK SO, DOCTOR.
IN FACT, I'D SAY THE MISTAKES WERE ALL *YOURS*.
ALICE... I'M SORRY.
I WISH IT DIDN'T HAVE TO ALWAYS *BE* LIKE THIS...
WHATEVER IT IS YOU HAVE TO *DO*.
I *TRUST* YOU.
THAT'S ALL I NEEDED TO HEAR.

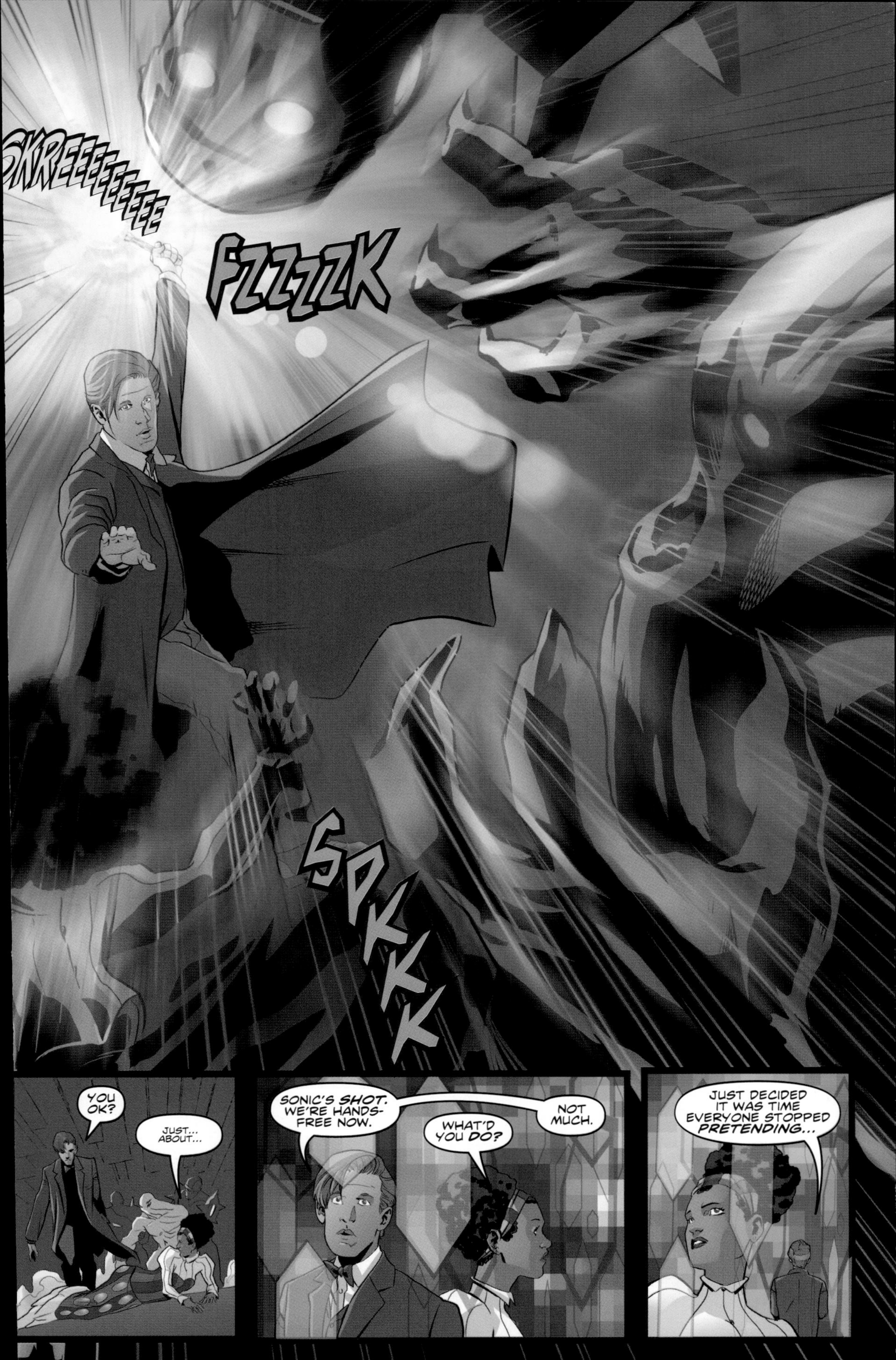
SKREEEEEEEEEE
FZZZZK
SPKKK
YOU OK?
JUST... ABOUT...
SONIC'S *SHOT*. WE'RE HANDS-FREE NOW.
WHAT'D YOU *DO*?
NOT MUCH.
JUST DECIDED IT WAS TIME EVERYONE STOPPED *PRETENDING*...

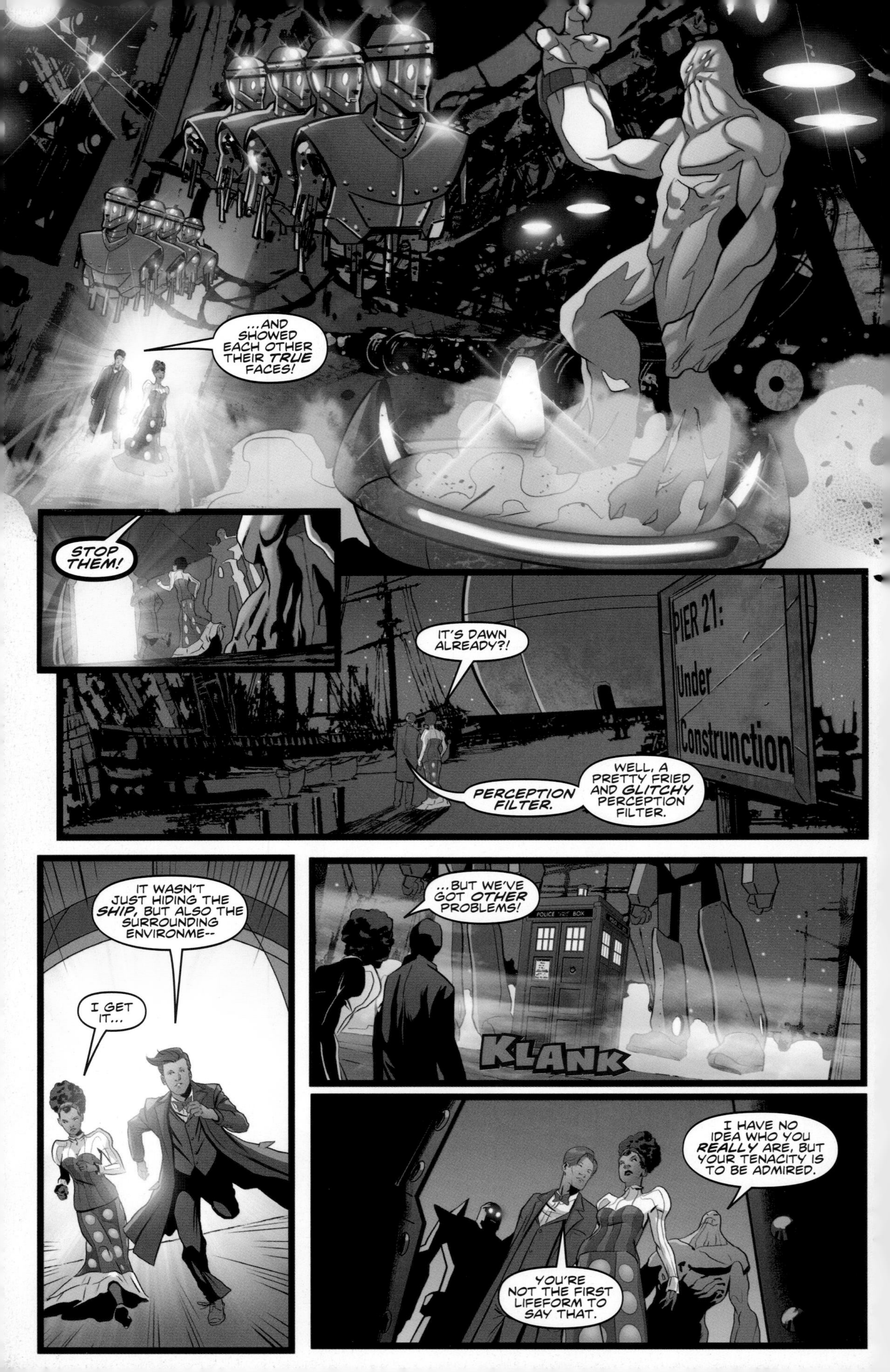
...AND SHOWED EACH OTHER THEIR TRUE FACES!
STOP THEM!
IT'S DAWN ALREADY?!
PIER 21: Under Construction
PERCEPTION FILTER.
WELL, A PRETTY FRIED AND GLITCHY PERCEPTION FILTER.
IT WASN'T JUST HIDING THE SHIP, BUT ALSO THE SURROUNDING ENVIRONME--
I GET IT...
...BUT WE'VE GOT OTHER PROBLEMS!
POLICE BOX
KLANK
I HAVE NO IDEA WHO YOU REALLY ARE, BUT YOUR TENACITY IS TO BE ADMIRED.
YOU'RE NOT THE FIRST LIFEFORM TO SAY THAT.

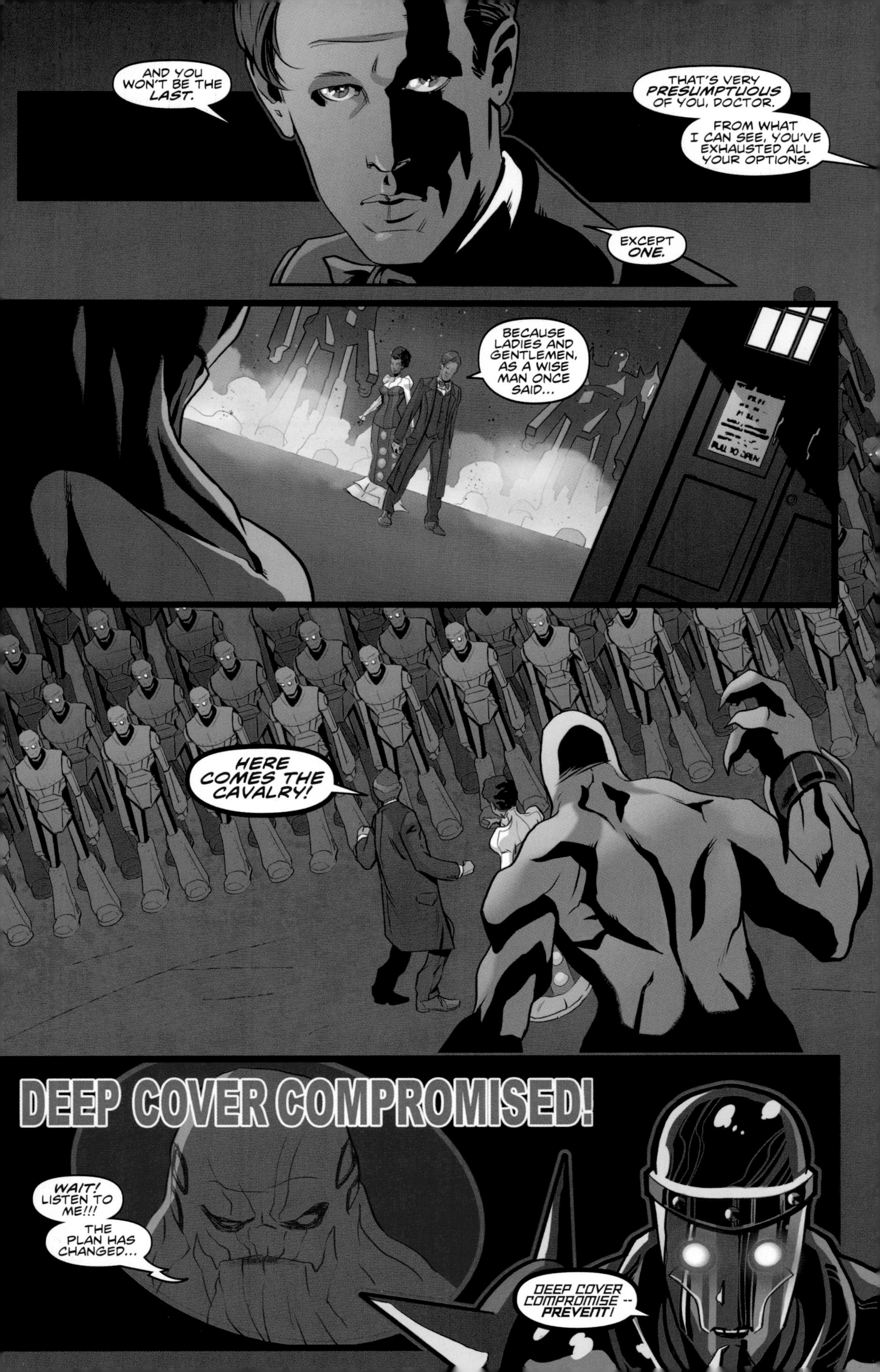
AND YOU WON'T BE THE LAST.
THAT'S VERY PRESUMPTUOUS OF YOU, DOCTOR.
FROM WHAT I CAN SEE, YOU'VE EXHAUSTED ALL YOUR OPTIONS.
EXCEPT ONE.
BECAUSE LADIES AND GENTLEMEN, AS A WISE MAN ONCE SAID...
HERE COMES THE CAVALRY!
DEEP COVER COMPROMISED!
WAIT! LISTEN TO ME!!!
THE PLAN HAS CHANGED...
DEEP COVER COMPROMISE -- PREVENT!

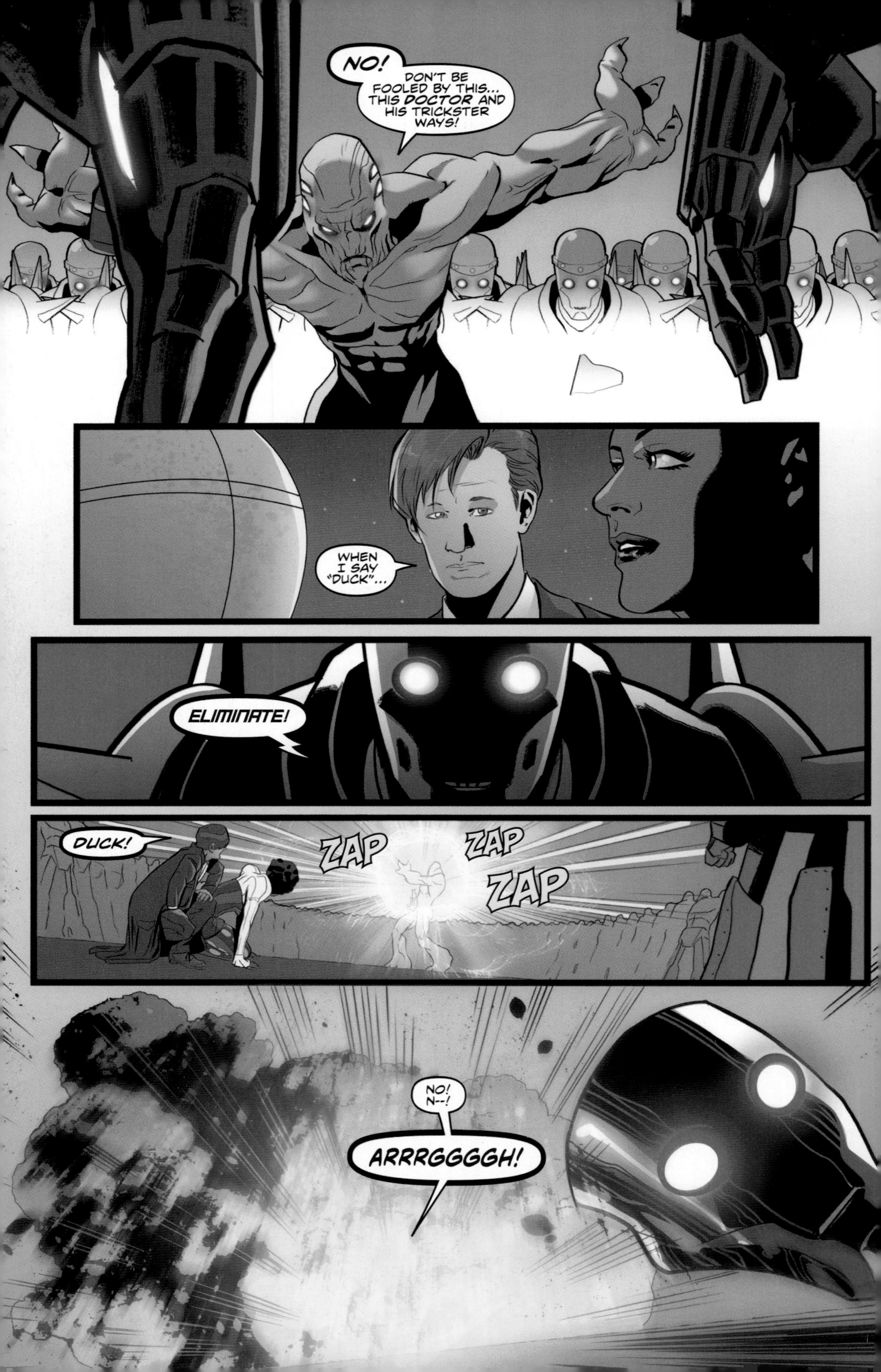
NO!
DON'T BE FOOLED BY THIS... THIS DOCTOR AND HIS TRICKSTER WAYS!
WHEN I SAY "DUCK"...
ELIMINATE!
DUCK!
ZAP
ZAP
ZAP
NO! N--!
ARRRGGGGH!

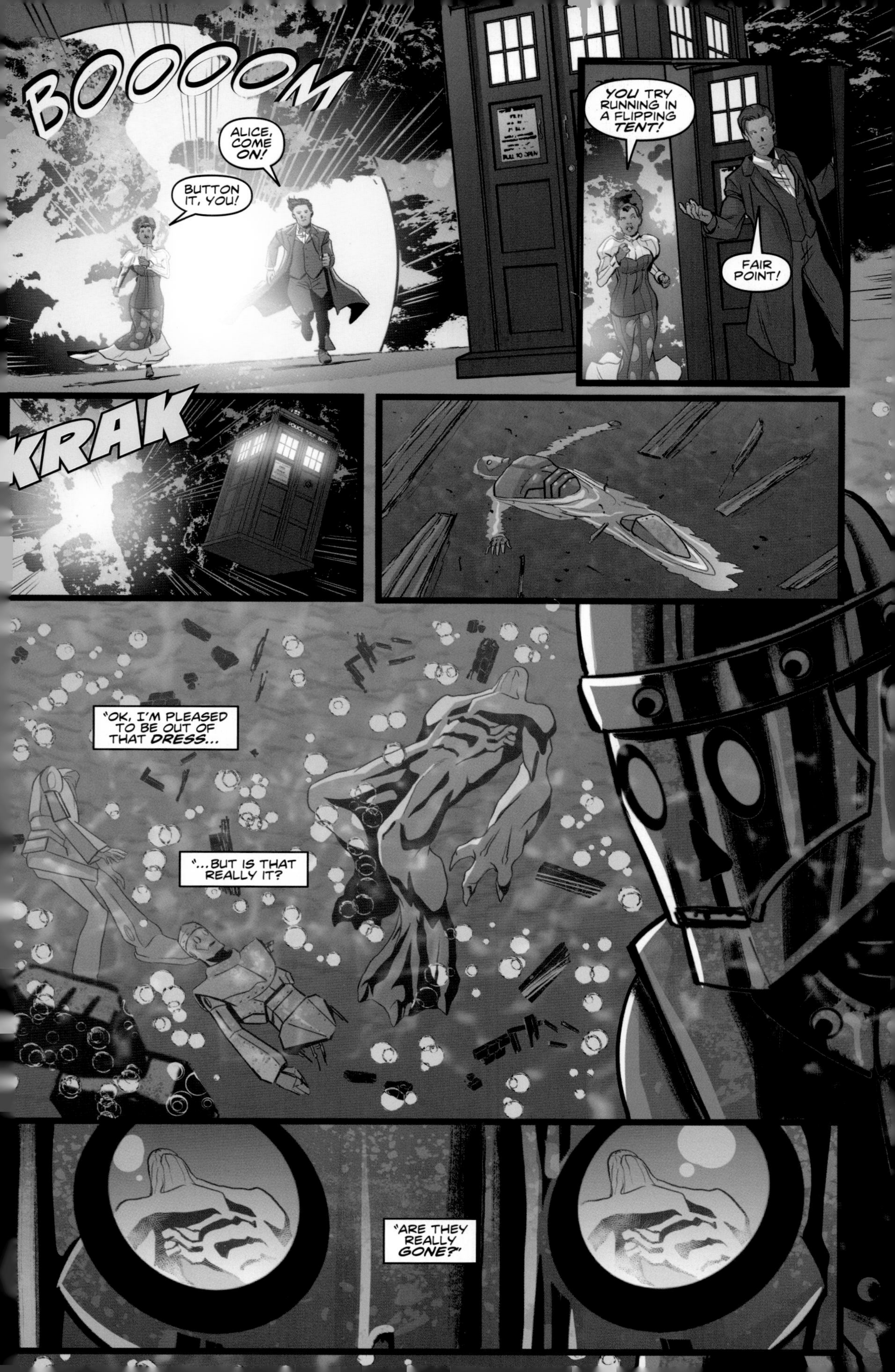
BOOOOM
ALICE, COME ON!
BUTTON IT, YOU!
YOU TRY RUNNING IN A FLIPPING TENT!
FAIR POINT!
KRAK
"OK, I'M PLEASED TO BE OUT OF THAT DRESS...
"...BUT IS THAT REALLY IT?
"ARE THEY REALLY GONE?"

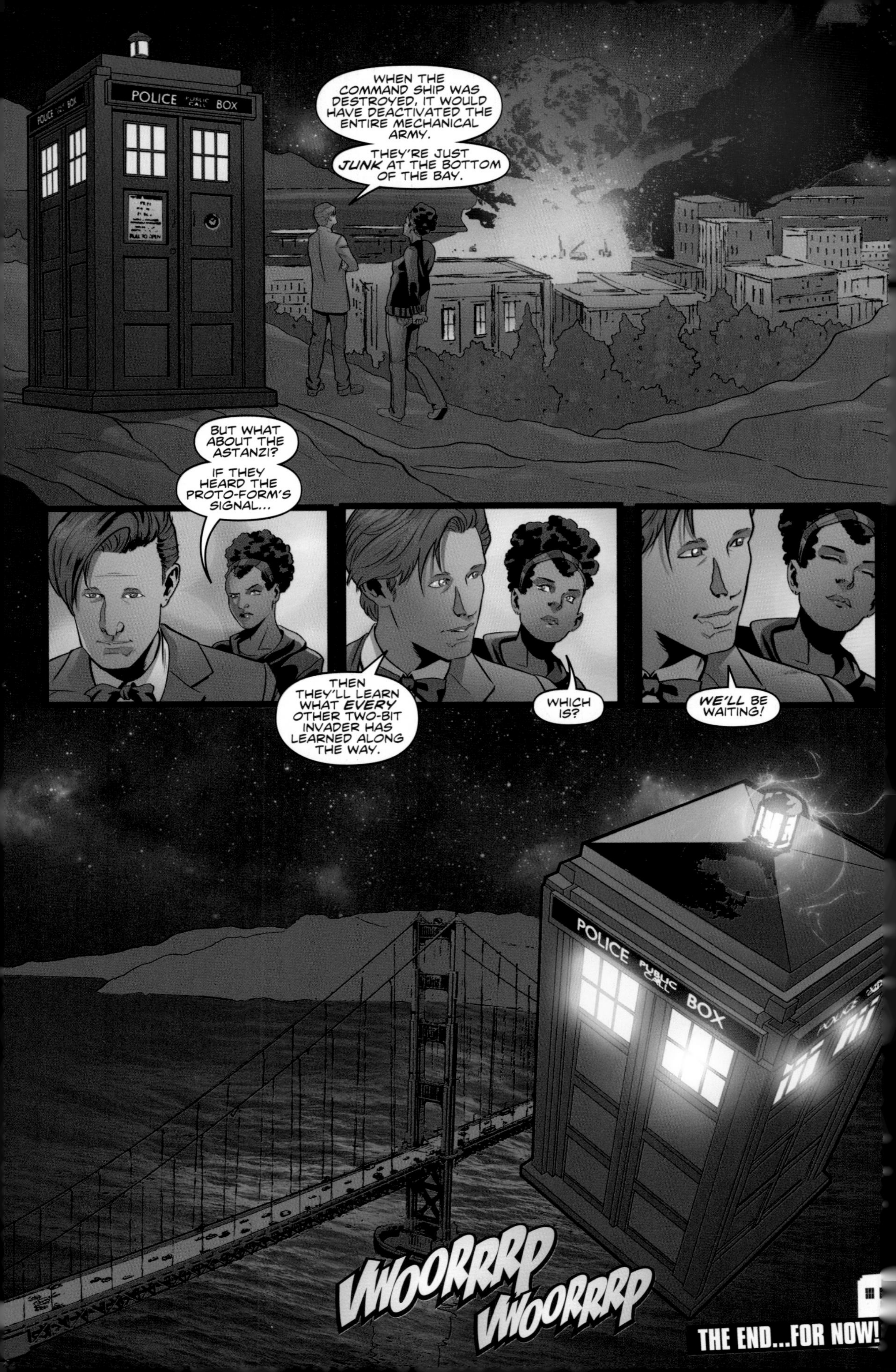
WHEN THE COMMAND SHIP WAS DESTROYED, IT WOULD HAVE DEACTIVATED THE ENTIRE MECHANICAL ARMY.
THEY'RE JUST JUNK AT THE BOTTOM OF THE BAY.
BUT WHAT ABOUT THE ASTANZI?
IF THEY HEARD THE PROTO-FORM'S SIGNAL...
THEN THEY'LL LEARN WHAT EVERY OTHER TWO-BIT INVADER HAS LEARNED ALONG THE WAY.
WHICH IS?
WE'LL BE WAITING!
VWOORRRP
VWOORRRP
THE END...FOR NOW!

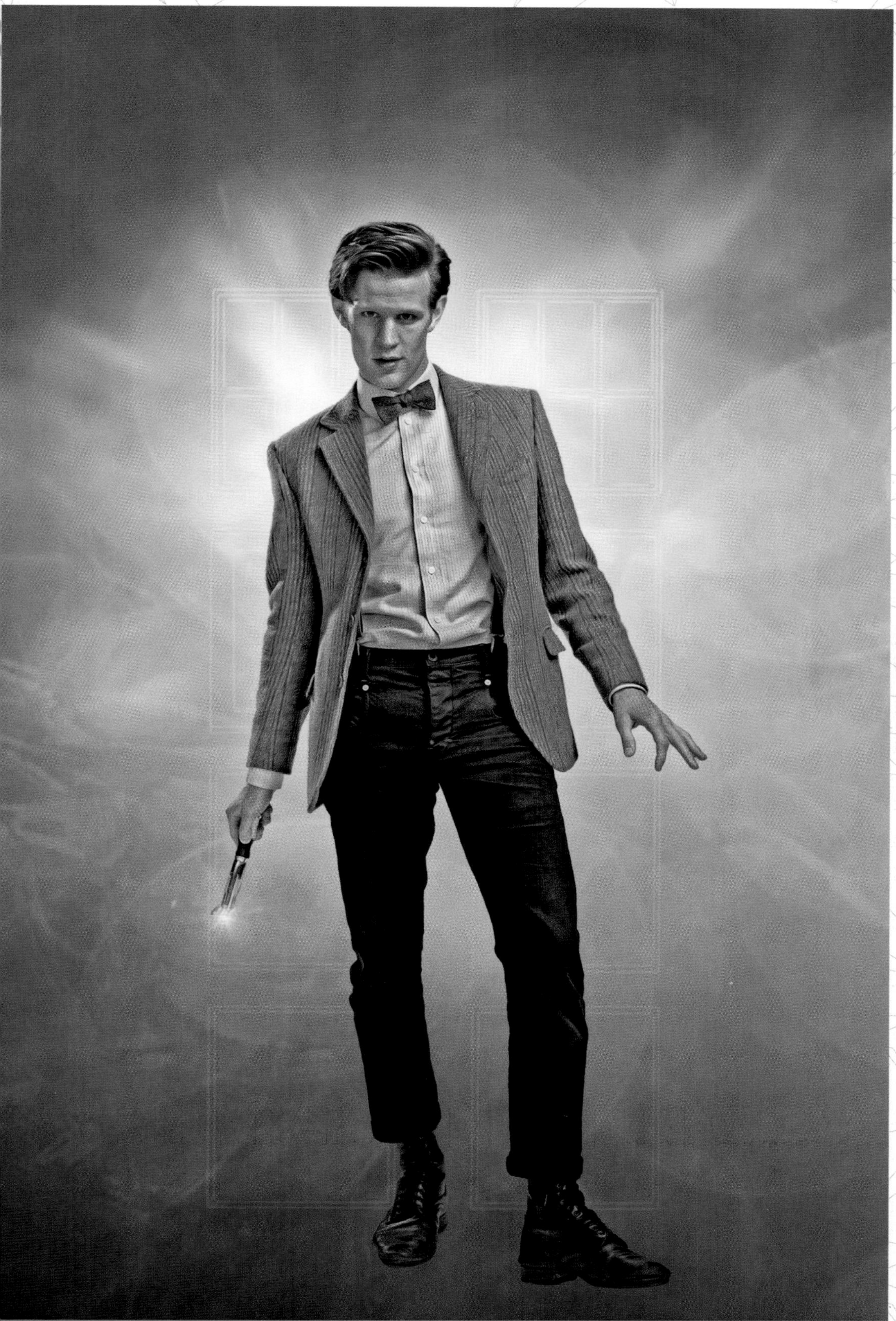

Cover by Will Brooks

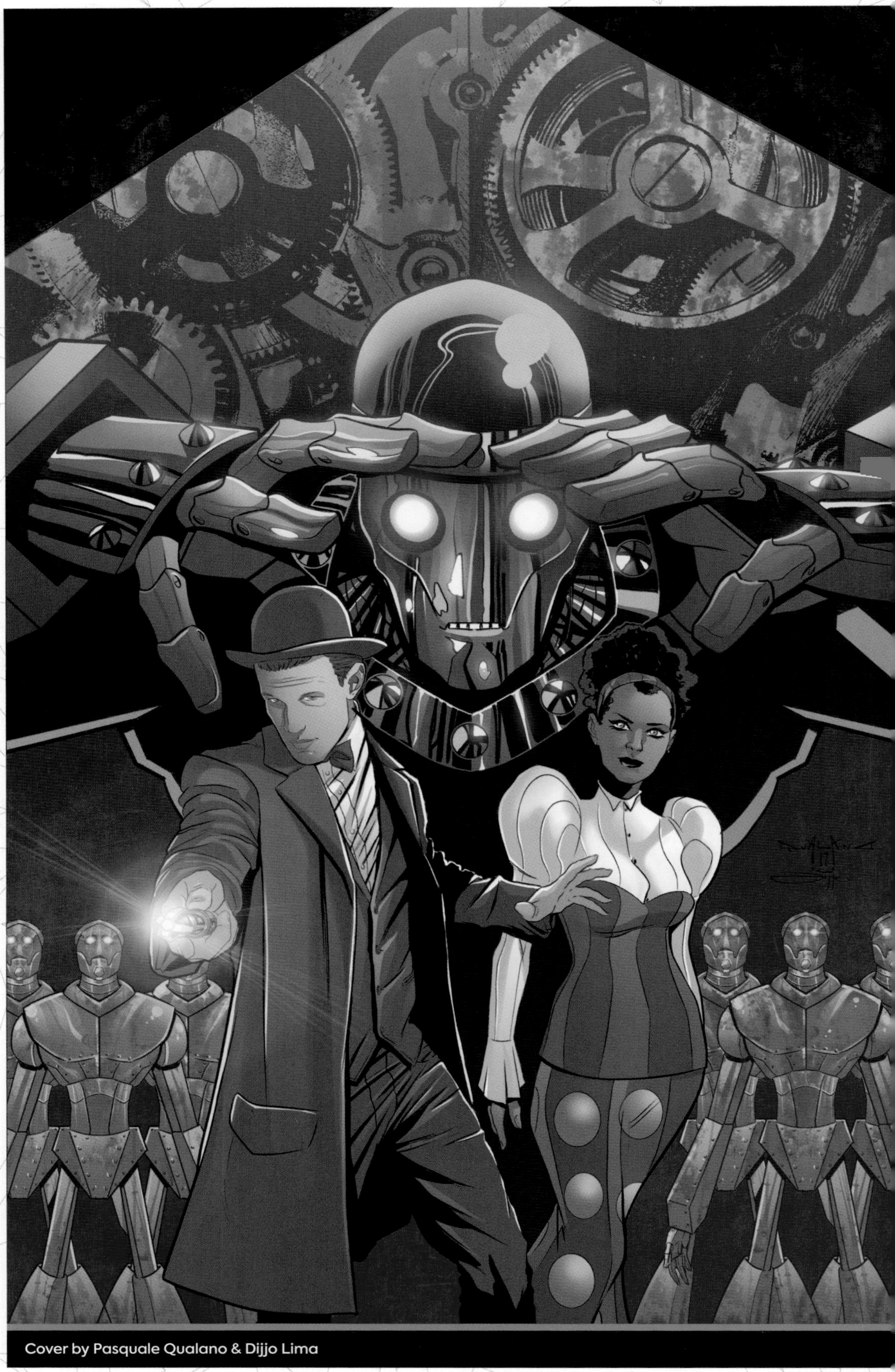

Cover by Pasquale Qualano & Dijjo Lima

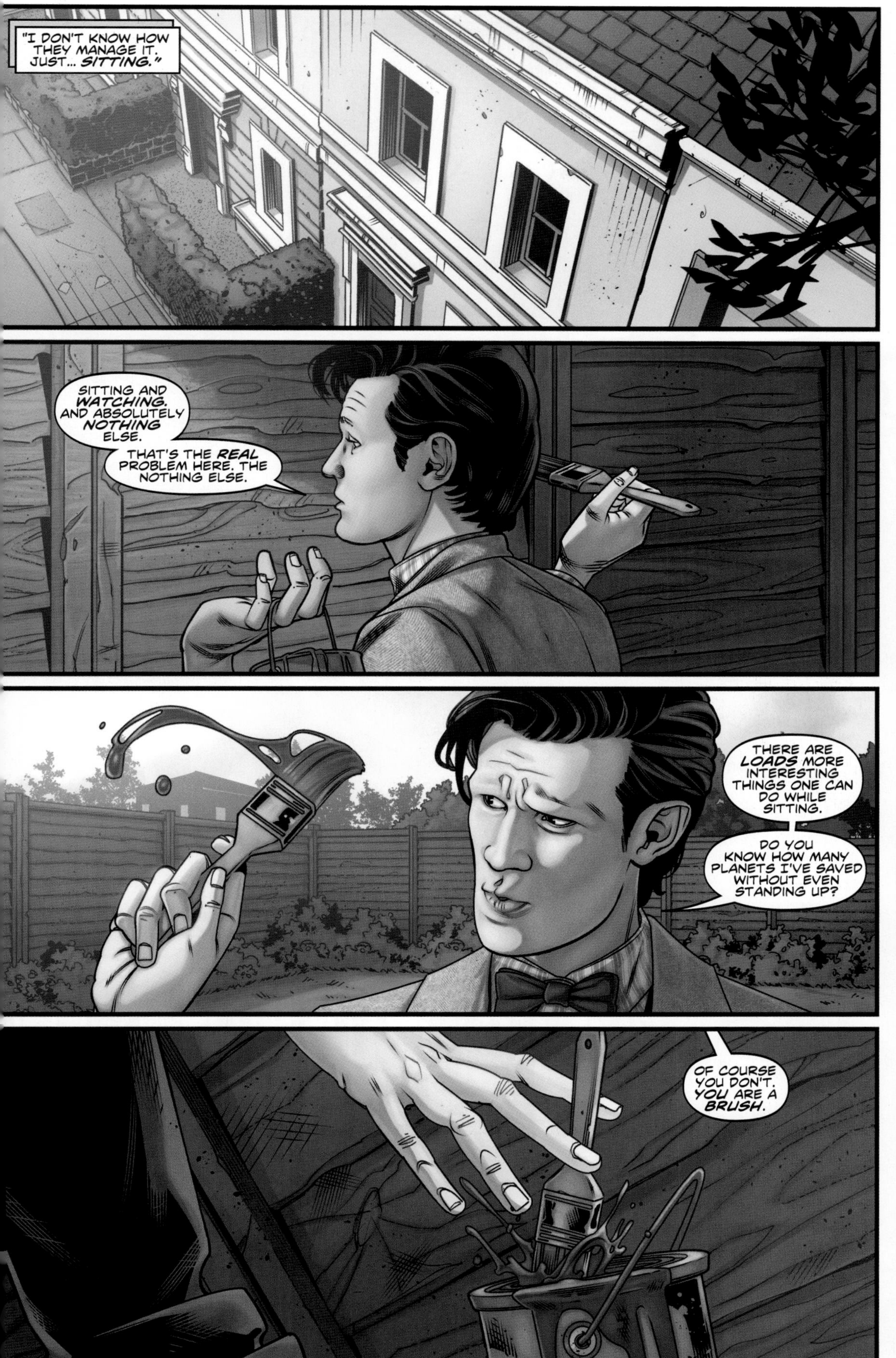
"I DON'T KNOW HOW THEY MANAGE IT. JUST... SITTING."
SITTING AND WATCHING. AND ABSOLUTELY NOTHING ELSE.
THAT'S THE REAL PROBLEM HERE. THE NOTHING ELSE.
THERE ARE LOADS MORE INTERESTING THINGS ONE CAN DO WHILE SITTING.
DO YOU KNOW HOW MANY PLANETS I'VE SAVED WITHOUT EVEN STANDING UP?
OF COURSE YOU DON'T. YOU ARE A BRUSH.

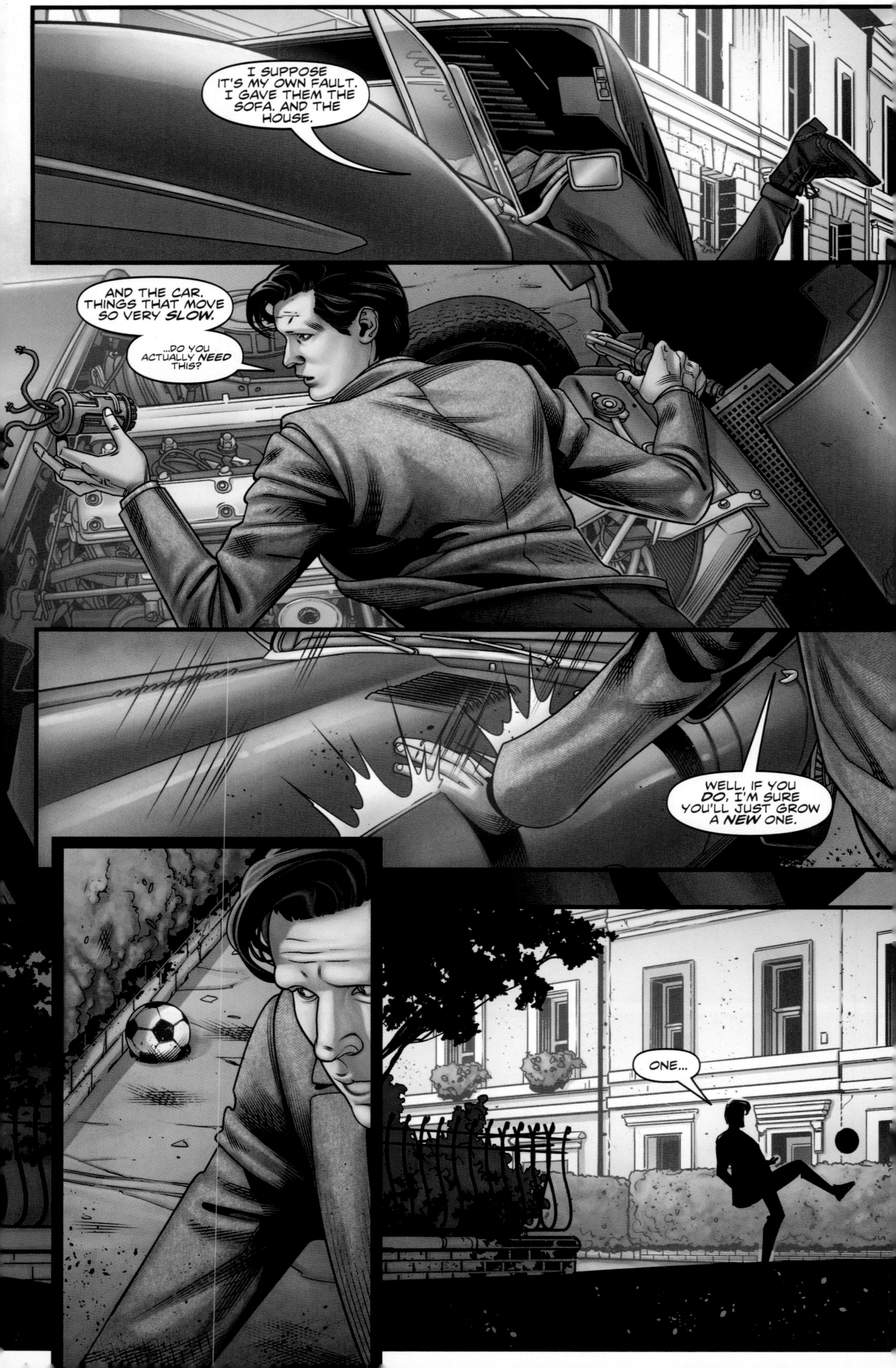
I SUPPOSE IT'S MY OWN FAULT. I GAVE THEM THE SOFA. AND THE HOUSE.
AND THE CAR. THINGS THAT MOVE SO VERY SLOW.
...DO YOU ACTUALLY NEED THIS?
WELL, IF YOU DO, I'M SURE YOU'LL JUST GROW A NEW ONE.
ONE...

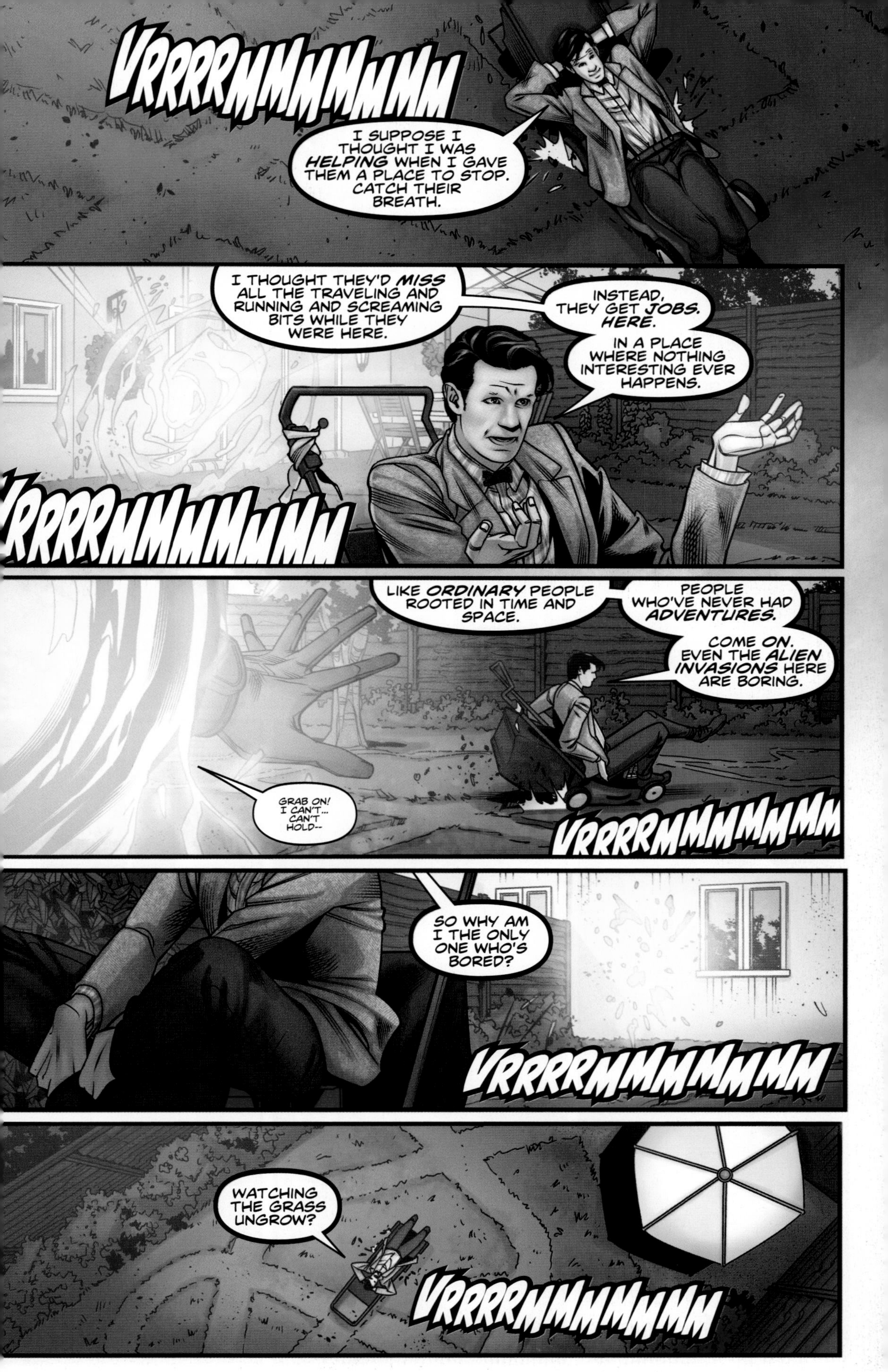
VRRRRMMMMMMM
I SUPPOSE I THOUGHT I WAS HELPING WHEN I GAVE THEM A PLACE TO STOP. CATCH THEIR BREATH.
I THOUGHT THEY'D MISS ALL THE TRAVELING AND RUNNING AND SCREAMING BITS WHILE THEY WERE HERE.
INSTEAD, THEY GET JOBS. HERE.
IN A PLACE WHERE NOTHING INTERESTING EVER HAPPENS.
VRRRRMMMMMMM
LIKE ORDINARY PEOPLE ROOTED IN TIME AND SPACE.
PEOPLE WHO'VE NEVER HAD ADVENTURES.
COME ON. EVEN THE ALIEN INVASIONS HERE ARE BORING.
GRAB ON! I CAN'T... CAN'T HOLD--
VRRRRMMMMMMM
SO WHY AM I THE ONLY ONE WHO'S BORED?
VRRRRMMMMMMM
WATCHING THE GRASS UNGROW?
VRRRRMMMMMMM

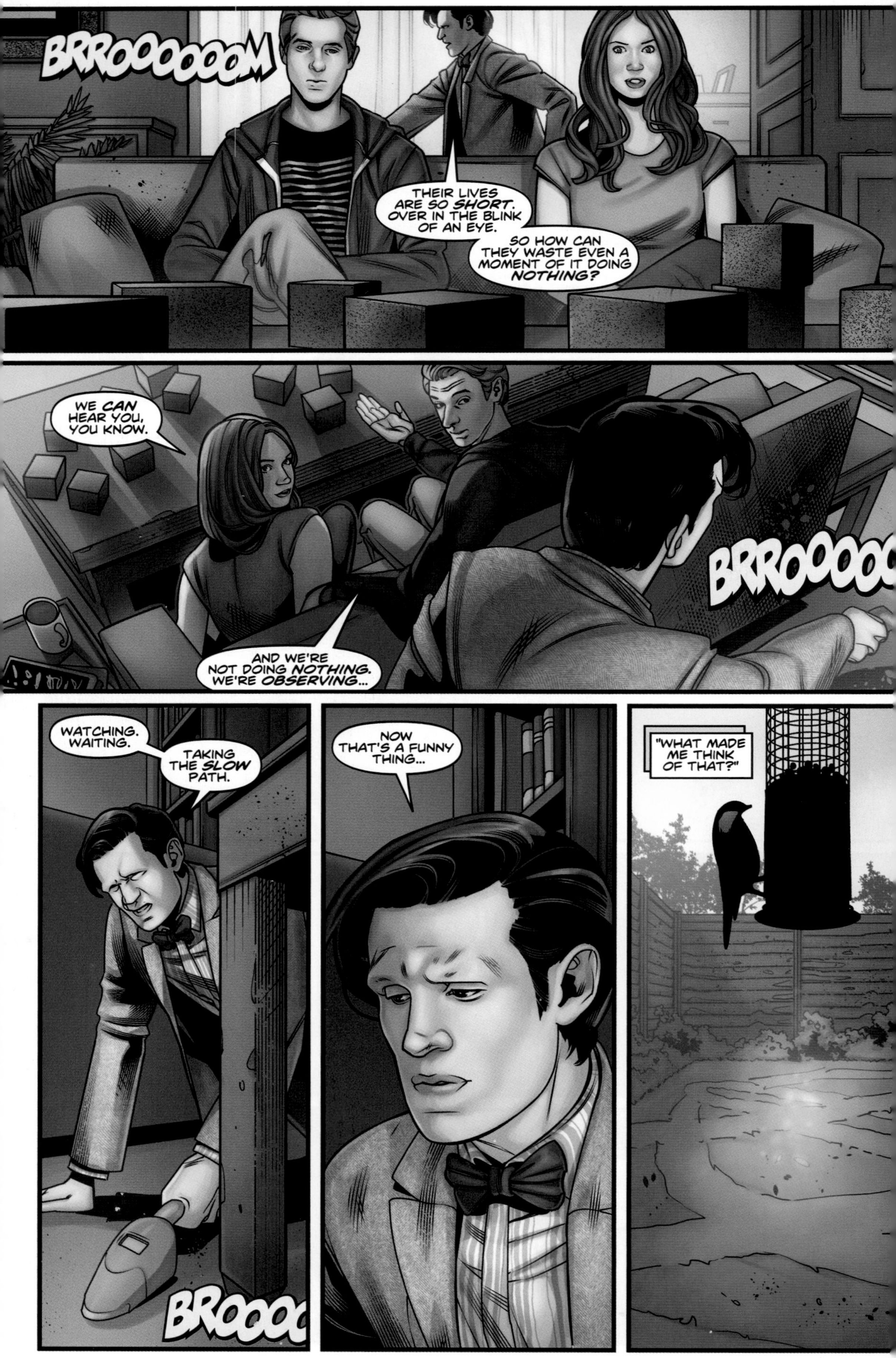
BRROOOOOOM
THEIR LIVES ARE SO SHORT. OVER IN THE BLINK OF AN EYE.
SO HOW CAN THEY WASTE EVEN A MOMENT OF IT DOING NOTHING?
WE CAN HEAR YOU, YOU KNOW.
BRROOOOO
AND WE'RE NOT DOING NOTHING. WE'RE OBSERVING...
WATCHING. WAITING.
TAKING THE SLOW PATH.
BROOOO
NOW THAT'S A FUNNY THING...
"WHAT MADE ME THINK OF THAT?"

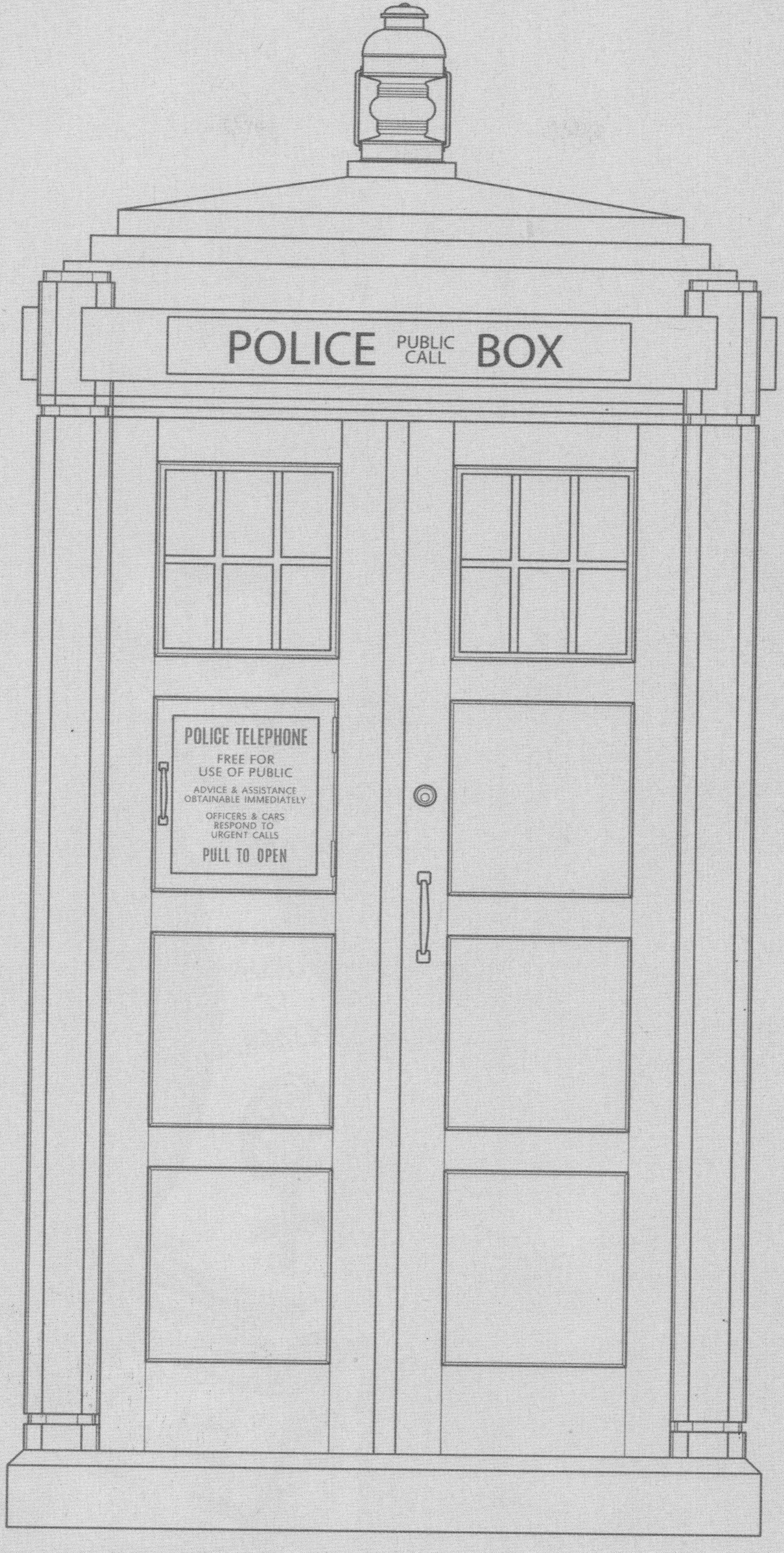
POLICE PUBLIC CALL BOX
POLICE TELEPHONE
FREE FOR USE OF PUBLIC
ADVICE & ASSISTANCE OBTAINABLE IMMEDIATELY
OFFICERS & CARS RESPOND TO URGENT CALLS
PULL TO OPEN

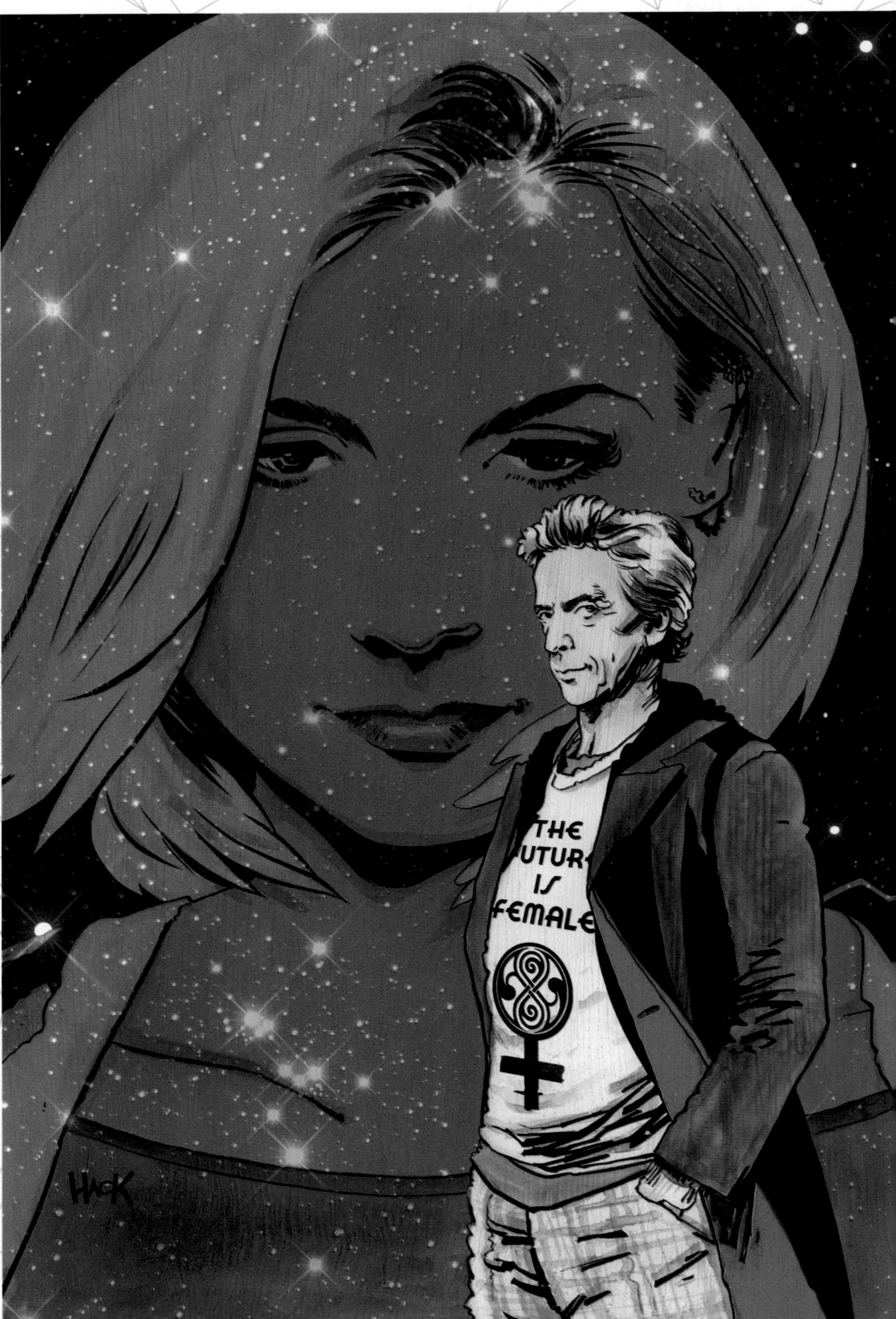
THE
UTUR
IS
FEMALE
HACK
Cover by Robert Hack

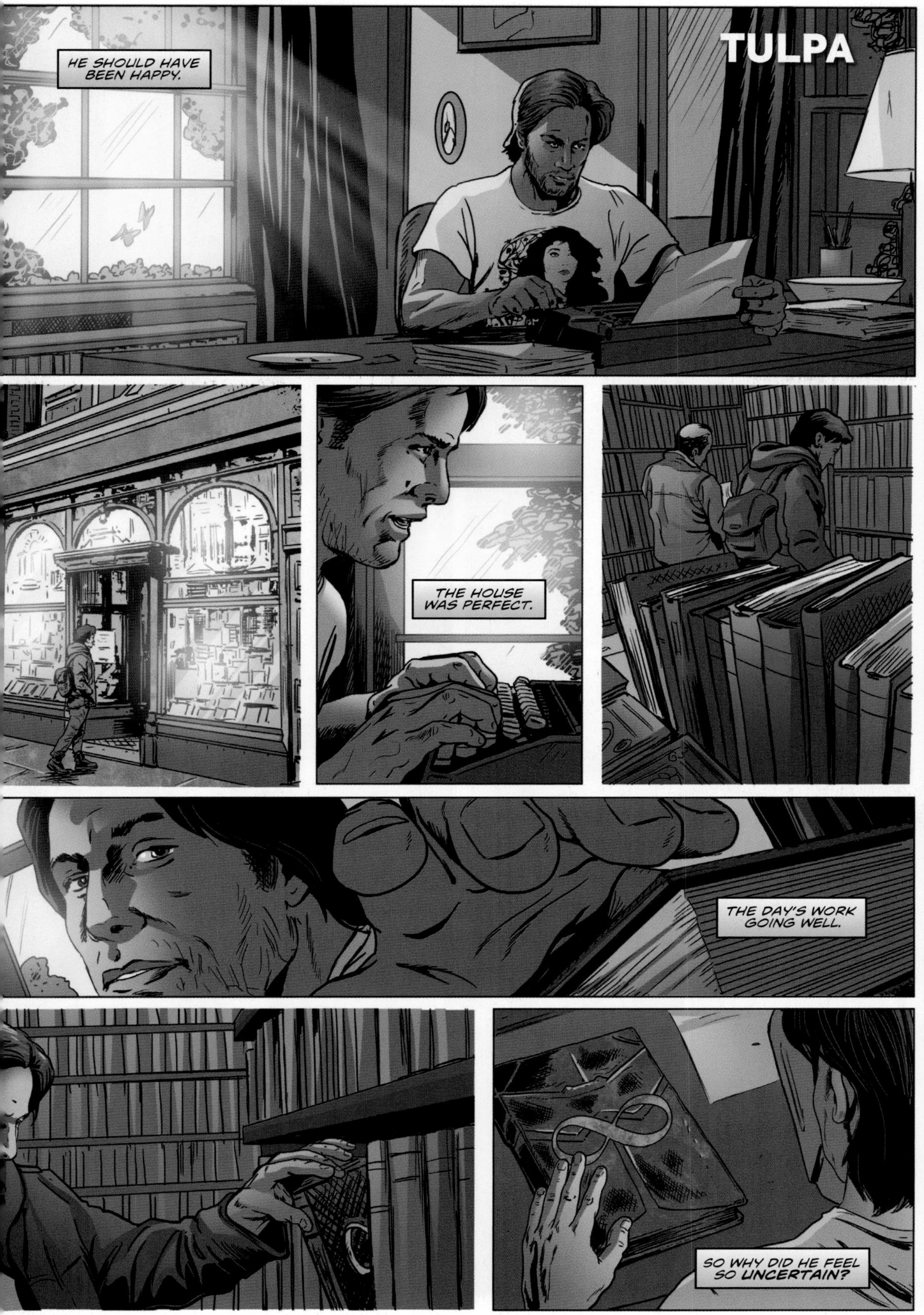
TULPA
HE SHOULD HAVE BEEN HAPPY.
THE HOUSE WAS PERFECT.
THE DAY'S WORK GOING WELL.
SO WHY DID HE FEEL SO UNCERTAIN?

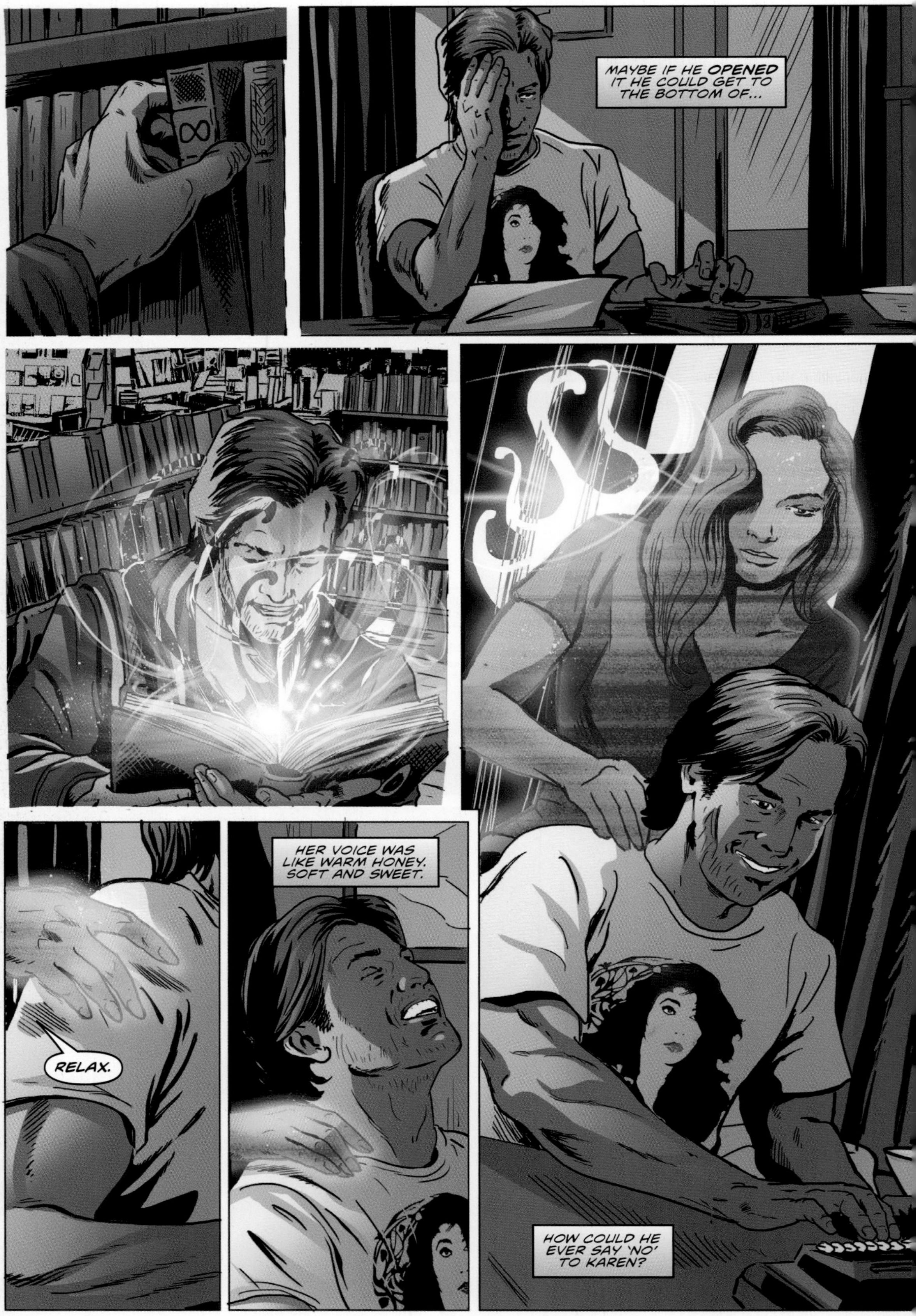
MAYBE IF HE OPENED IT HE COULD GET TO THE BOTTOM OF...
RELAX.
HER VOICE WAS LIKE WARM HONEY. SOFT AND SWEET.
HOW COULD HE EVER SAY 'NO' TO KAREN?

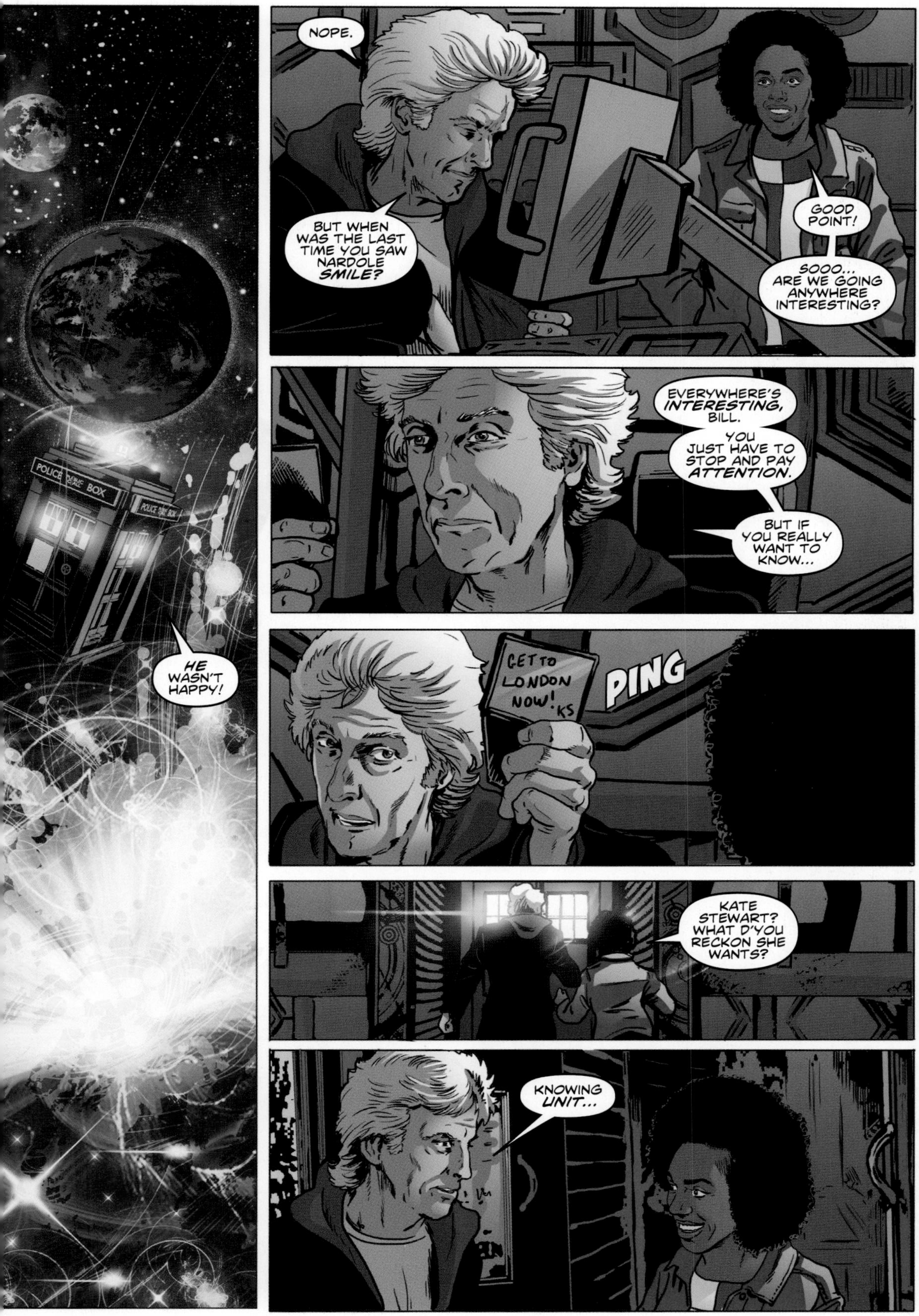
NOPE.
BUT WHEN WAS THE LAST TIME YOU SAW NARDOLE *SMILE?*
GOOD POINT!
SOOO... ARE WE GOING ANYWHERE INTERESTING?
EVERYWHERE'S *INTERESTING,* BILL.
YOU JUST HAVE TO STOP AND PAY *ATTENTION.*
BUT IF YOU REALLY WANT TO KNOW...
POLICE BOX
HE WASN'T HAPPY!
GET TO LONDON NOW! KS
PING
KATE STEWART? WHAT D'YOU RECKON SHE WANTS?
KNOWING *UNIT...*

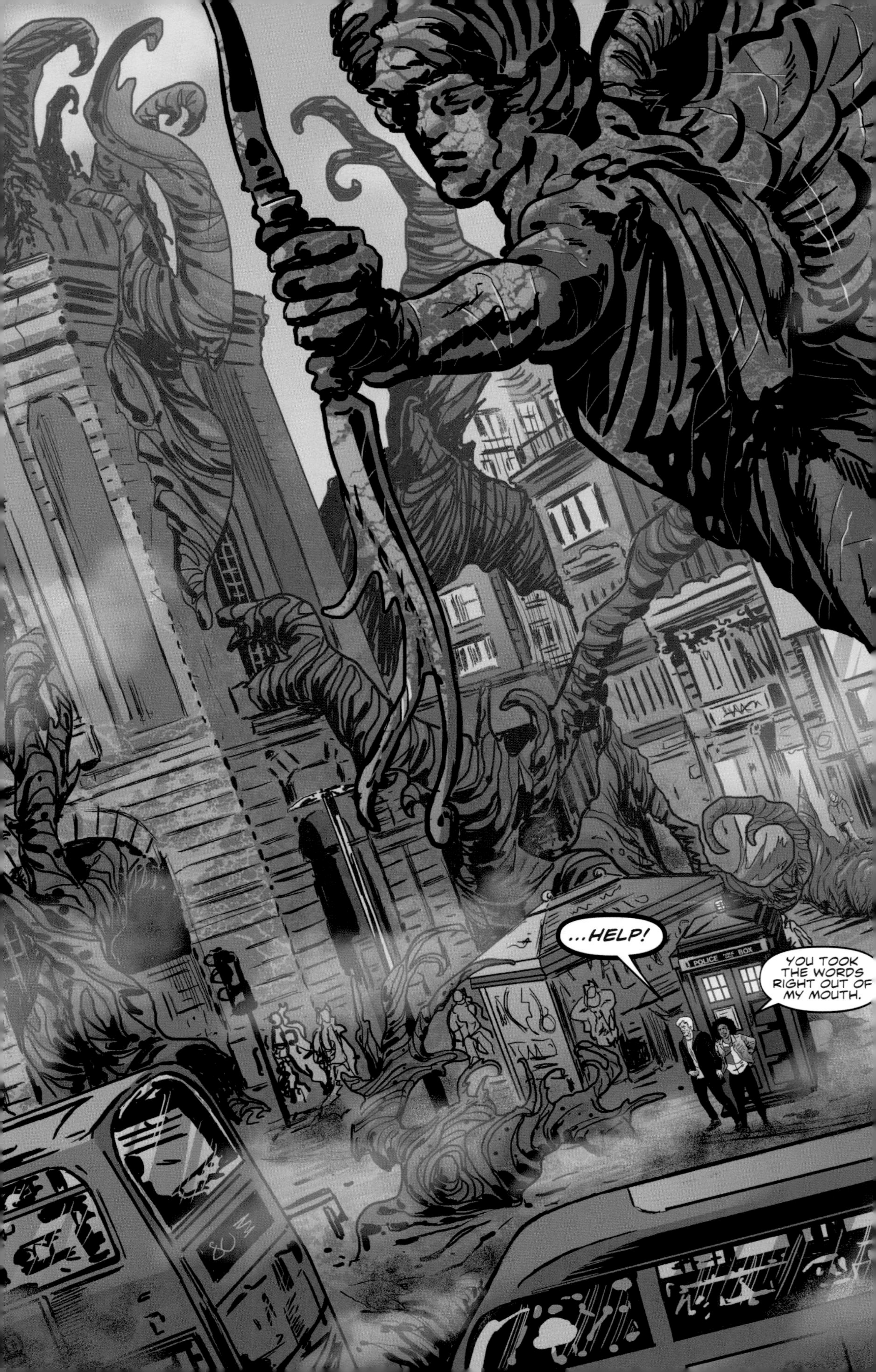
...HELP!
YOU TOOK THE WORDS RIGHT OUT OF MY MOUTH.

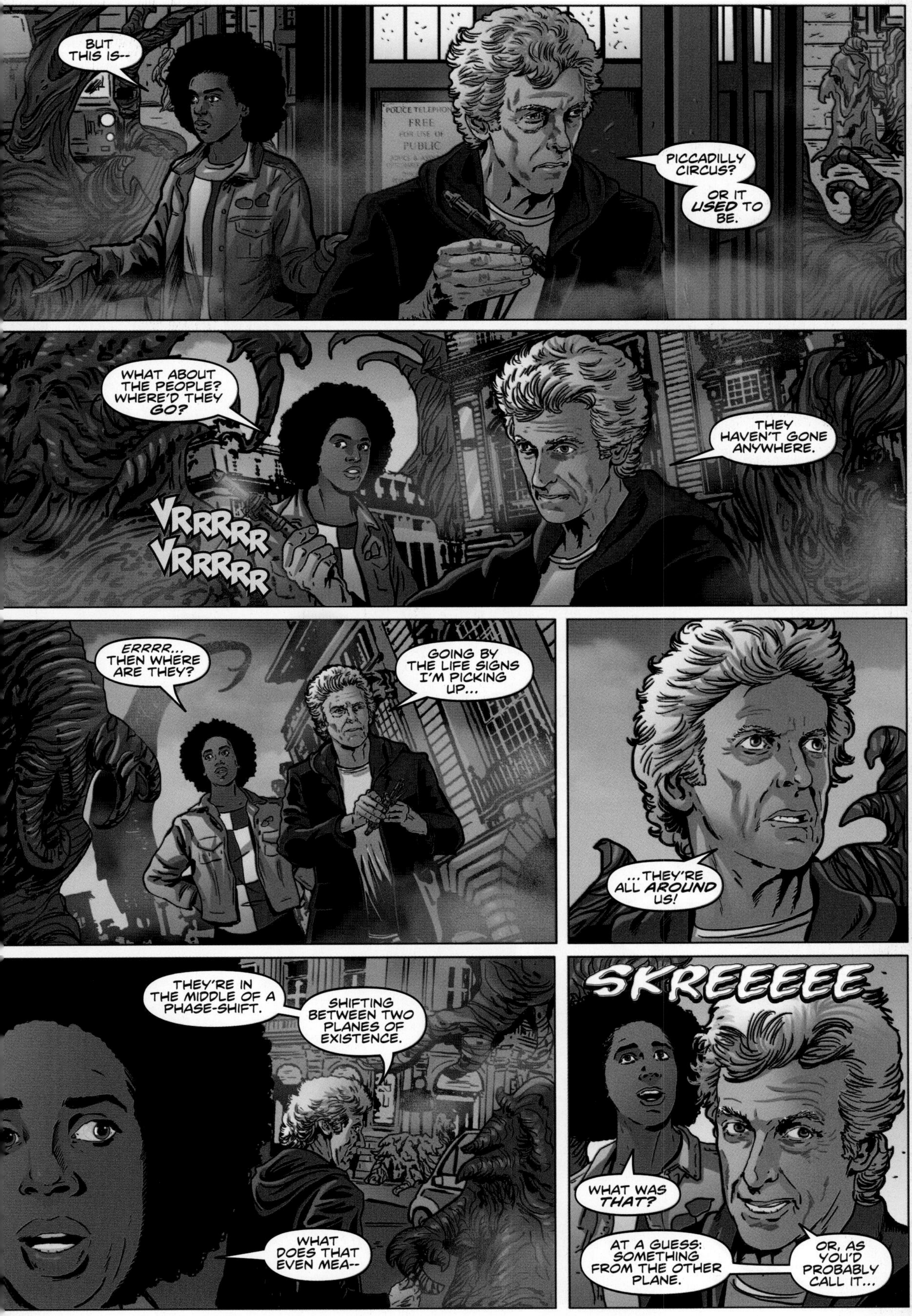
BUT THIS IS--
POLICE TELEPHONE FREE FOR USE OF PUBLIC
PICCADILLY CIRCUS?
OR IT USED TO BE.
WHAT ABOUT THE PEOPLE? WHERE'D THEY GO?
THEY HAVEN'T GONE ANYWHERE.
VRRRRR VRRRRR
ERRRR... THEN WHERE ARE THEY?
GOING BY THE LIFE SIGNS I'M PICKING UP...
...THEY'RE ALL AROUND US!
THEY'RE IN THE MIDDLE OF A PHASE-SHIFT.
SHIFTING BETWEEN TWO PLANES OF EXISTENCE.
WHAT DOES THAT EVEN MEA--
SKREEEEEE
WHAT WAS THAT?
AT A GUESS: SOMETHING FROM THE OTHER PLANE.
OR, AS YOU'D PROBABLY CALL IT...

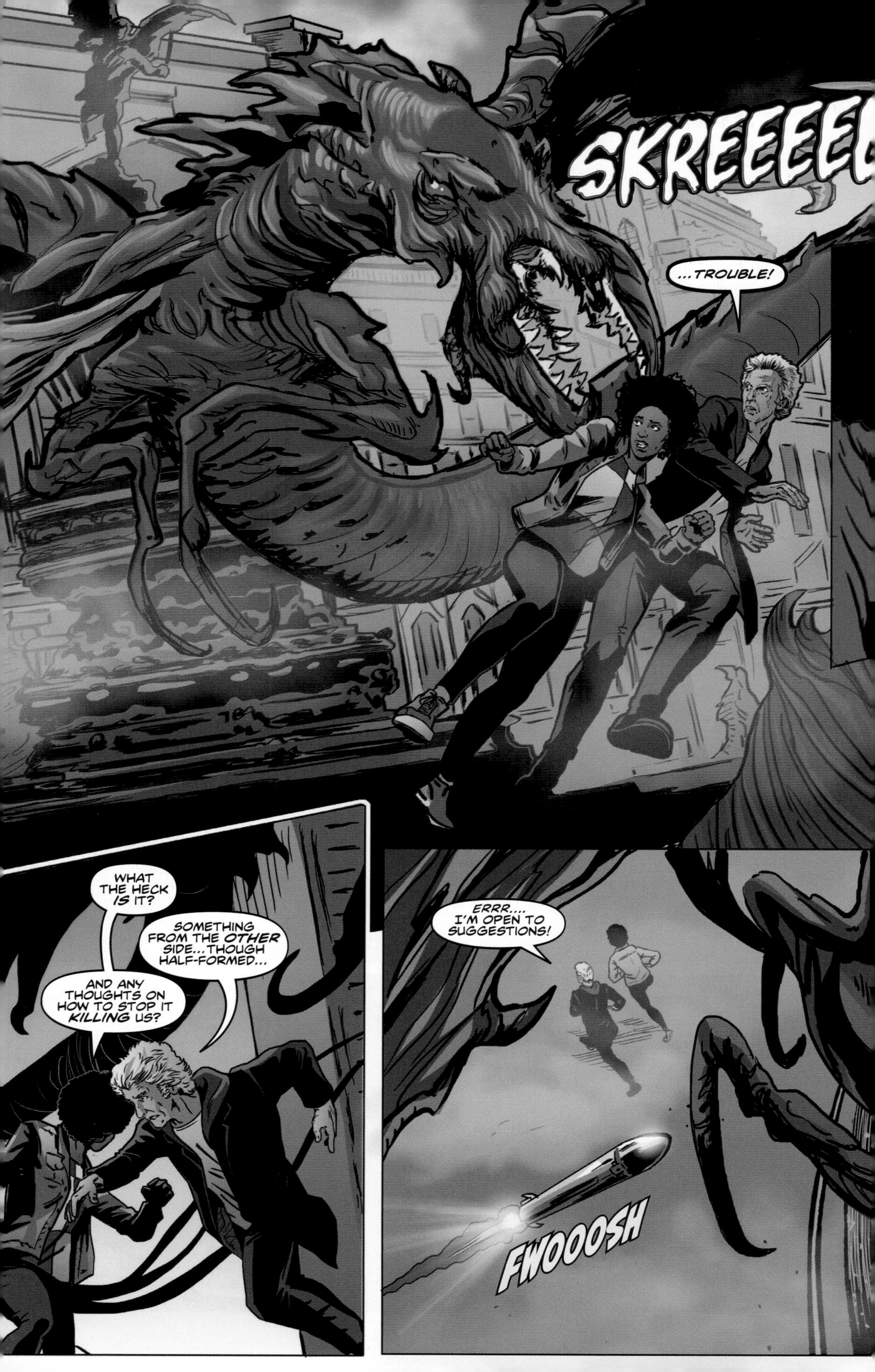

SKREEEEE
...TROUBLE!
WHAT THE HECK *IS* IT?
SOMETHING FROM THE *OTHER* SIDE... THOUGH HALF-FORMED...
AND ANY THOUGHTS ON HOW TO STOP IT *KILLING* US?
ERRR.... I'M OPEN TO SUGGESTIONS!
FWOOOSH

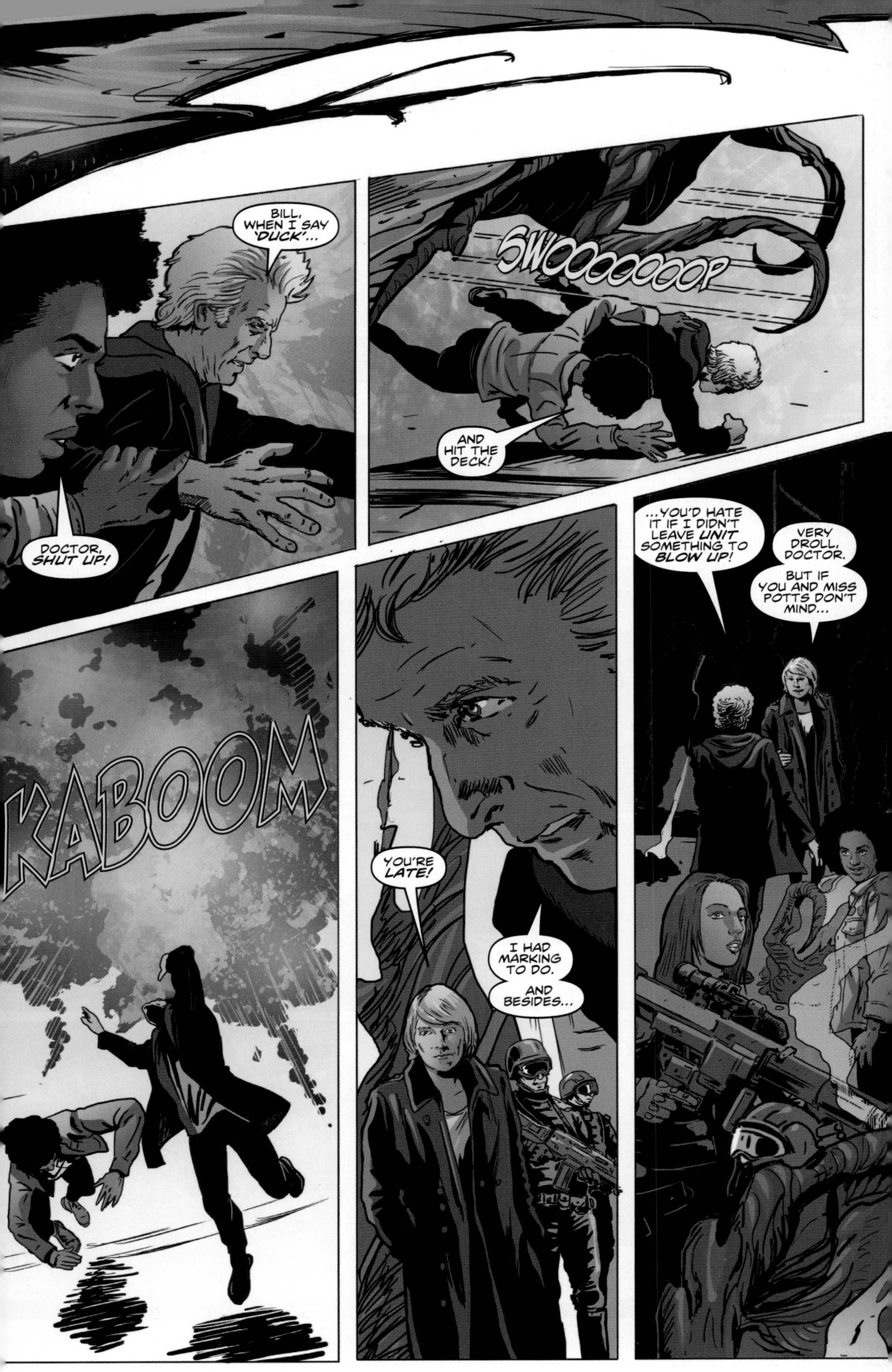

BILL, WHEN I SAY 'DUCK'...
DOCTOR, SHUT UP!
SWOOOOOOOOP
AND HIT THE DECK!
KABOOM
YOU'RE LATE!
I HAD MARKING TO DO.
AND BESIDES...
...YOU'D HATE IT IF I DIDN'T LEAVE UNIT SOMETHING TO BLOW UP!
VERY DROLL, DOCTOR.
BUT IF YOU AND MISS POTTS DON'T MIND...

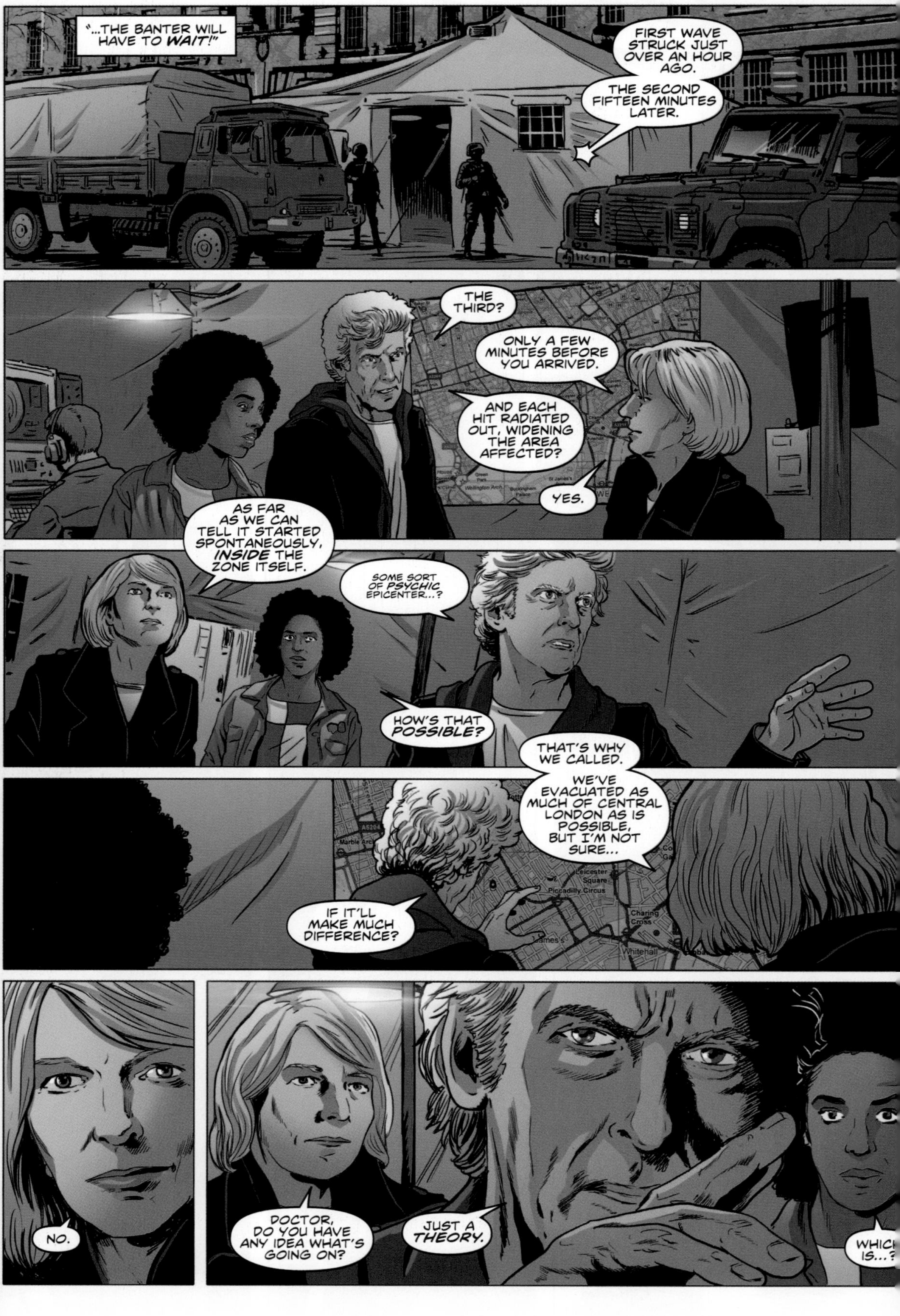
"...THE BANTER WILL HAVE TO WAIT!"
FIRST WAVE STRUCK JUST OVER AN HOUR AGO.
THE SECOND FIFTEEN MINUTES LATER.
THE THIRD?
ONLY A FEW MINUTES BEFORE YOU ARRIVED.
AND EACH HIT RADIATED OUT, WIDENING THE AREA AFFECTED?
YES.
AS FAR AS WE CAN TELL IT STARTED SPONTANEOUSLY, INSIDE THE ZONE ITSELF.
SOME SORT OF PSYCHIC EPICENTER...?
HOW'S THAT POSSIBLE?
THAT'S WHY WE CALLED.
WE'VE EVACUATED AS MUCH OF CENTRAL LONDON AS IS POSSIBLE, BUT I'M NOT SURE...
IF IT'LL MAKE MUCH DIFFERENCE?
NO.
DOCTOR, DO YOU HAVE ANY IDEA WHAT'S GOING ON?
JUST A THEORY.
WHICH IS...?

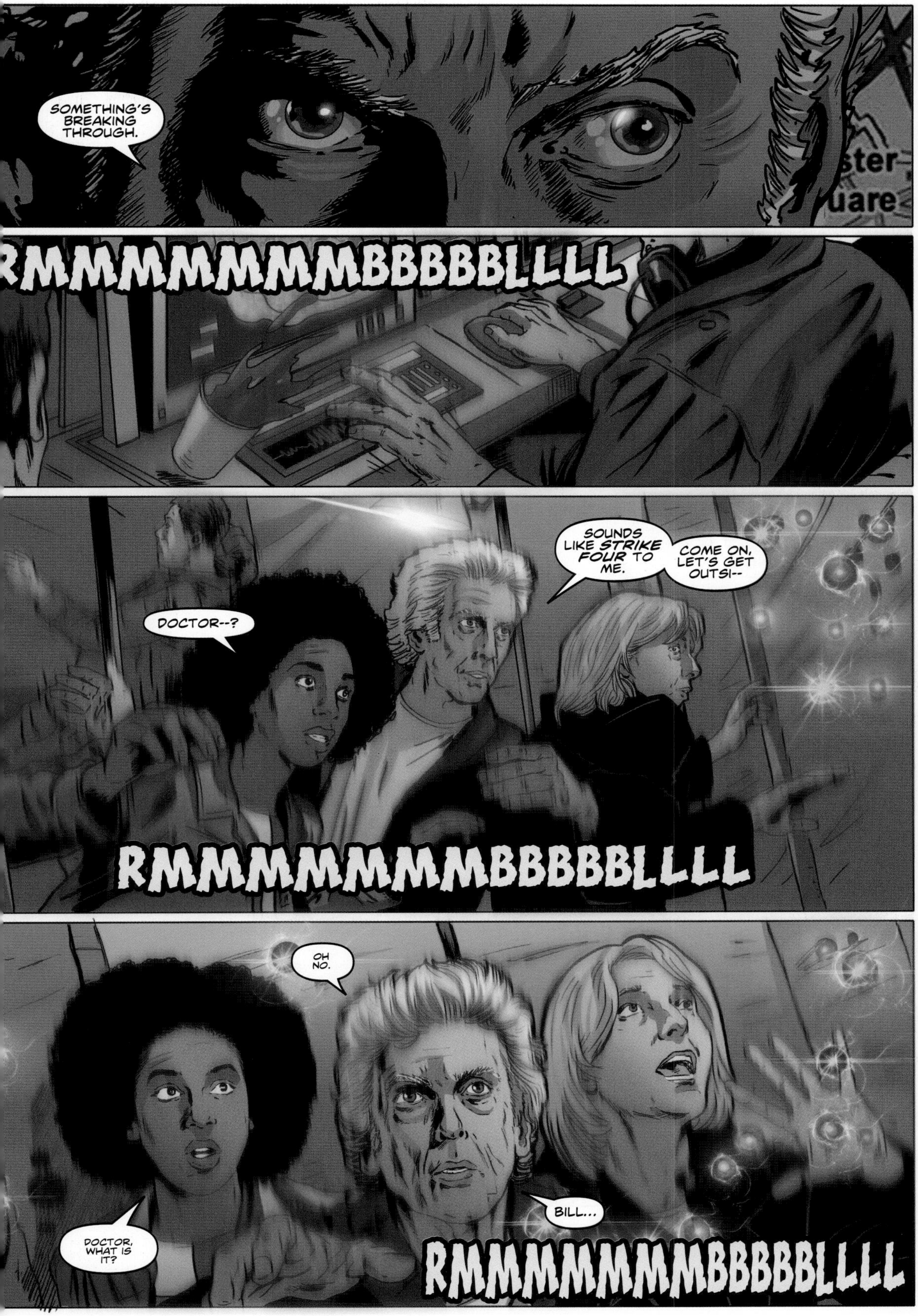
SOMETHING'S BREAKING THROUGH.
ster
uare
RMMMMMMMMBBBBBLLLL
DOCTOR--?
SOUNDS LIKE STRIKE FOUR TO ME.
COME ON, LET'S GET OUTSI--
RMMMMMMMMBBBBBLLLL
OH NO.
BILL...
DOCTOR, WHAT IS IT?
RMMMMMMMMBBBBBLLLL

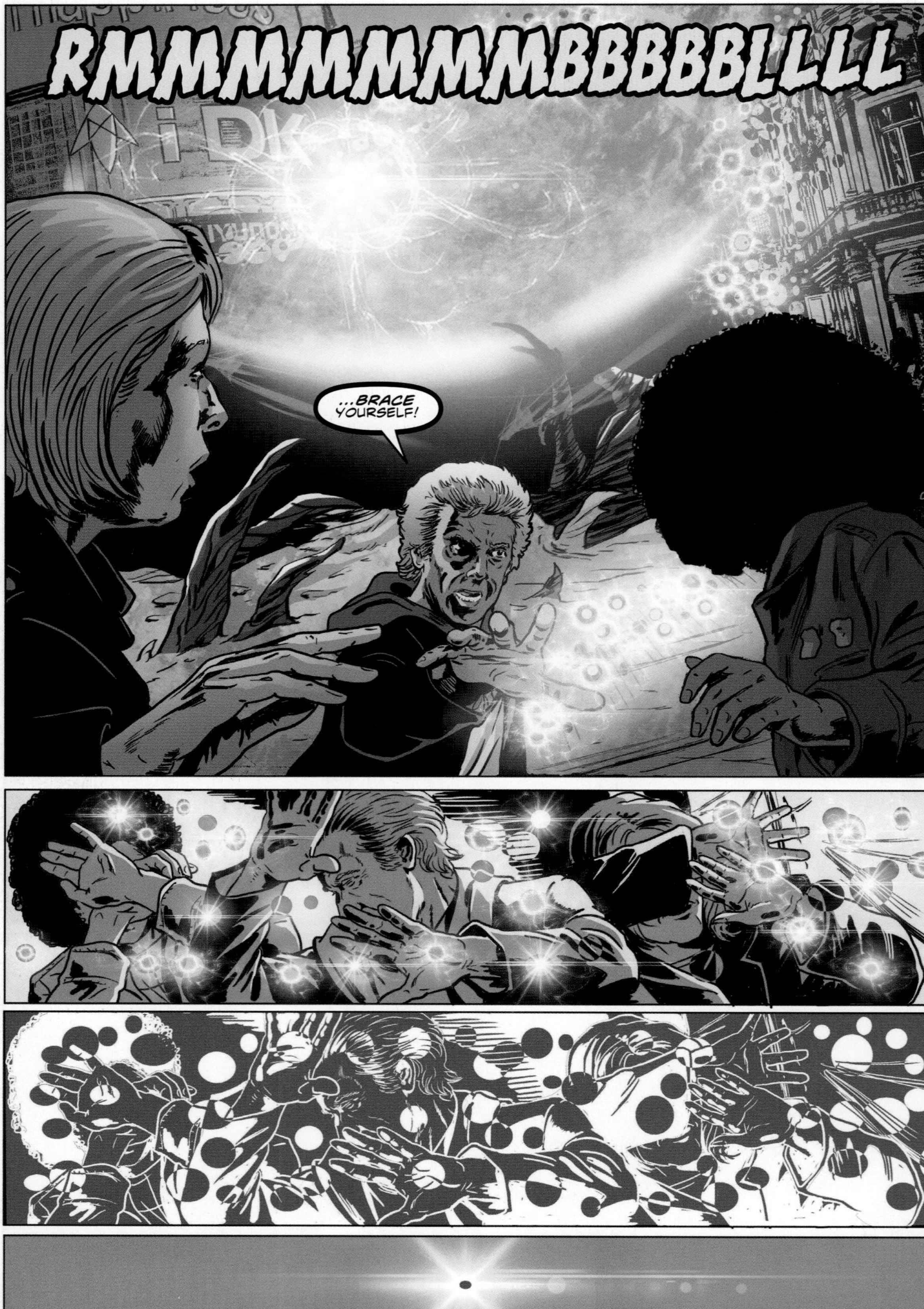
RMMMMMMMMBBBBBLLLL
...BRACE YOURSELF!

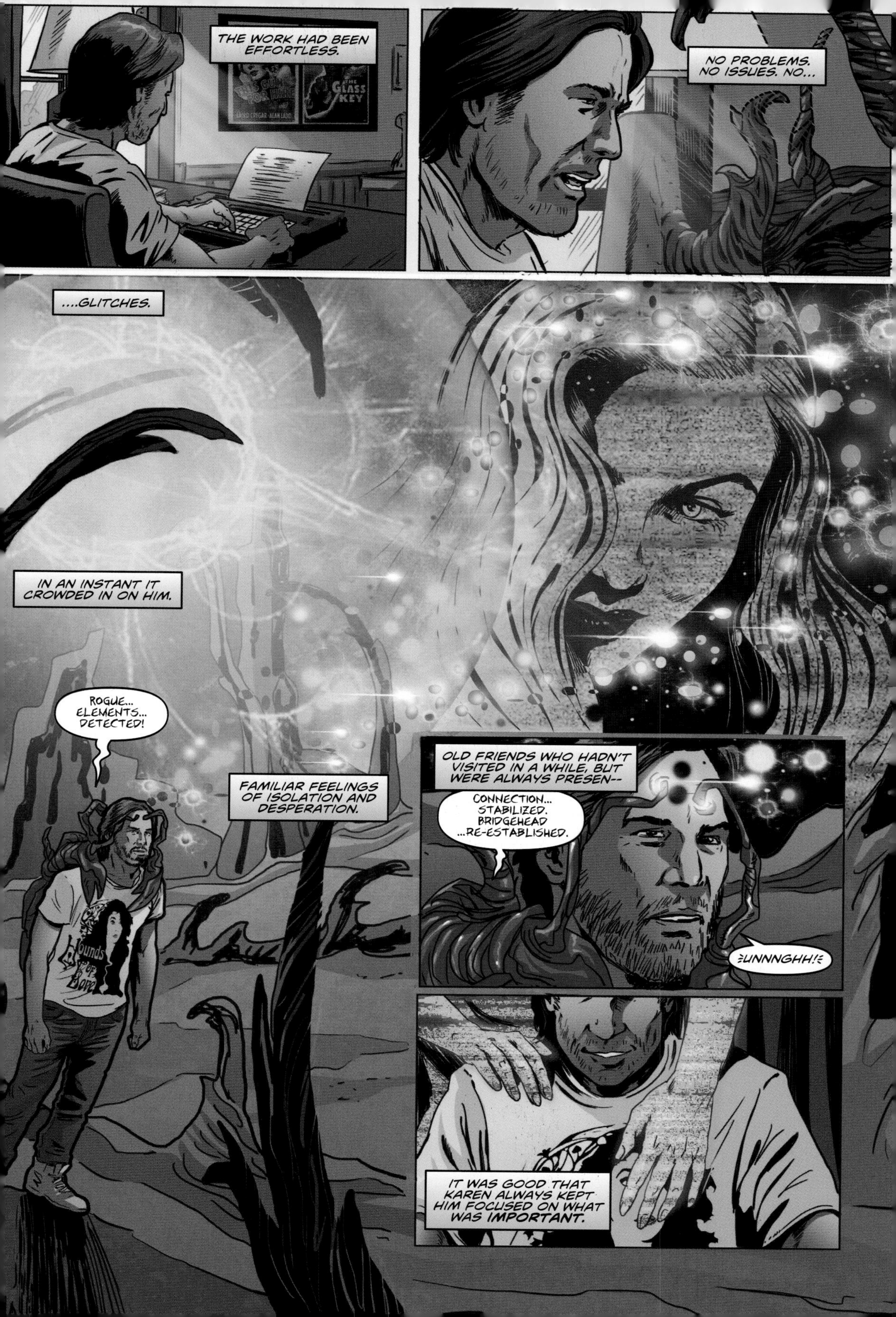
THE WORK HAD BEEN EFFORTLESS.
NO PROBLEMS. NO ISSUES. NO...
....GLITCHES.
IN AN INSTANT IT CROWDED IN ON HIM.
ROGUE... ELEMENTS... DETECTED!
FAMILIAR FEELINGS OF ISOLATION AND DESPERATION.
OLD FRIENDS WHO HADN'T VISITED IN A WHILE, BUT WERE ALWAYS PRESEN--
CONNECTION... STABILIZED. BRIDGEHEAD ...RE-ESTABLISHED.
UNNNGHH!
IT WAS GOOD THAT KAREN ALWAYS KEPT HIM FOCUSED ON WHAT WAS IMPORTANT.

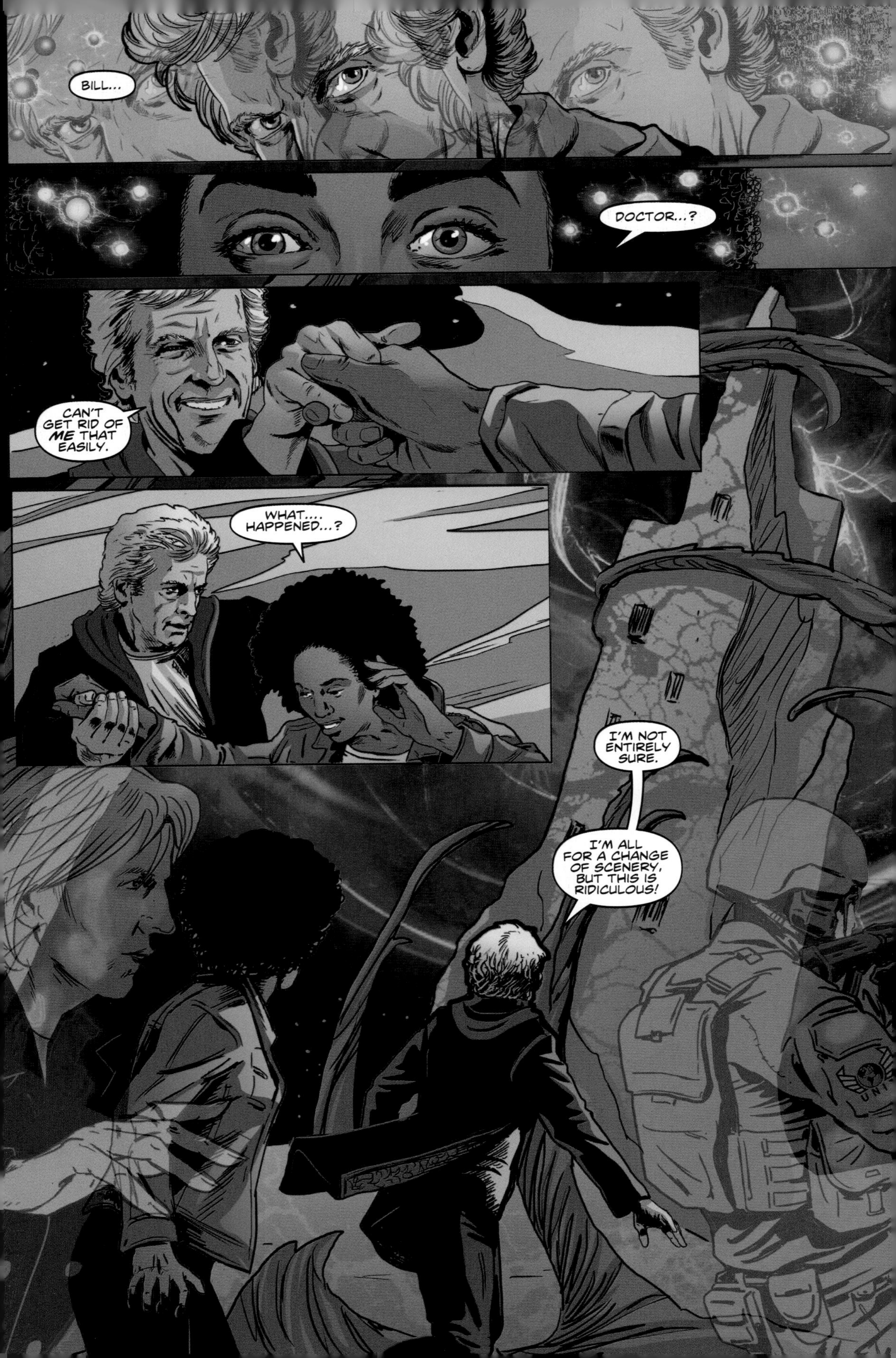
BILL...
DOCTOR...?
CAN'T GET RID OF *ME* THAT EASILY.
WHAT.... HAPPENED...?
I'M NOT ENTIRELY SURE.
I'M ALL FOR A CHANGE OF SCENERY, BUT THIS IS RIDICULOUS!

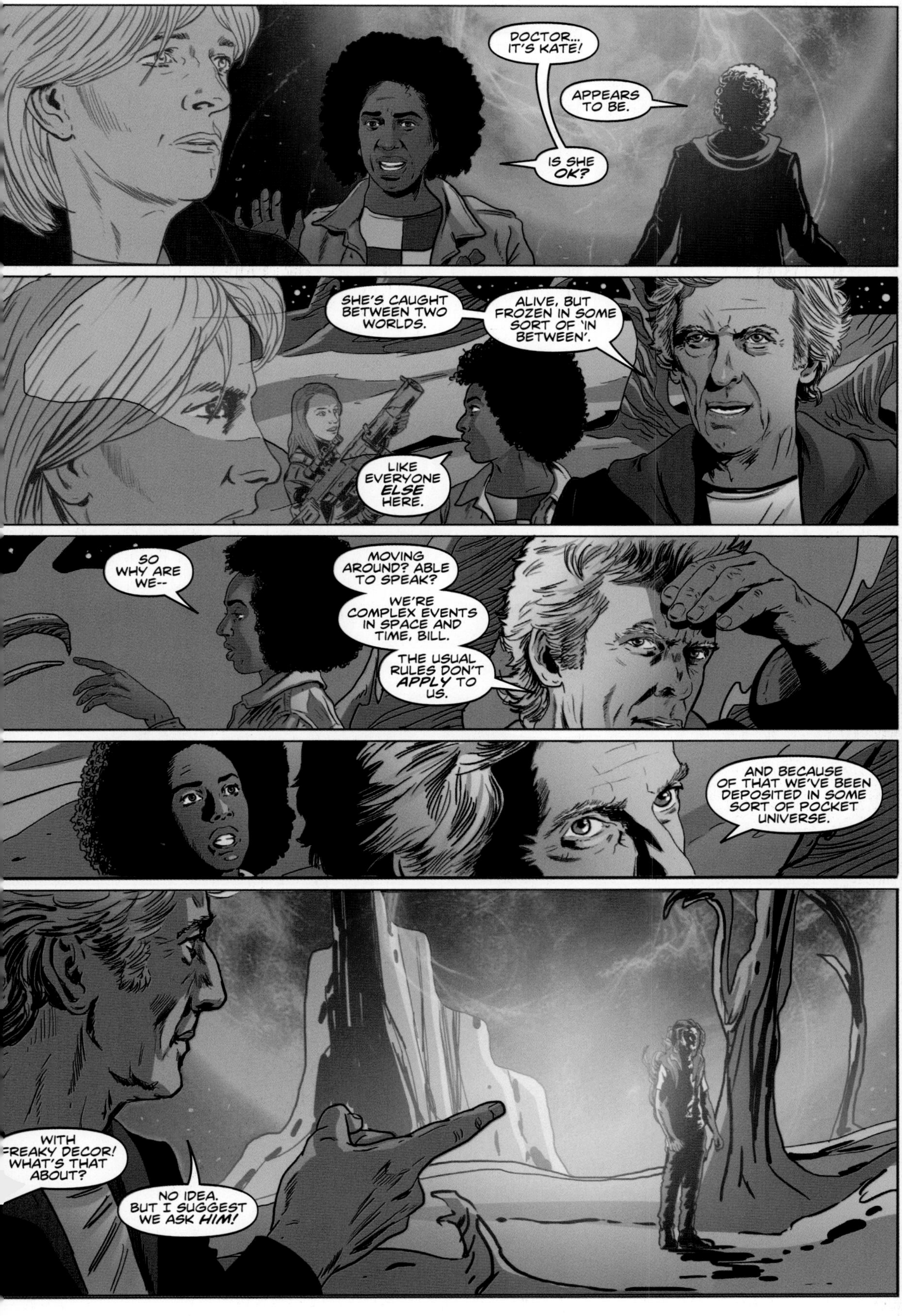
DOCTOR... IT'S KATE!
APPEARS TO BE.
IS SHE OK?
SHE'S CAUGHT BETWEEN TWO WORLDS.
ALIVE, BUT FROZEN IN SOME SORT OF 'IN BETWEEN'.
LIKE EVERYONE ELSE HERE.
SO WHY ARE WE--
MOVING AROUND? ABLE TO SPEAK?
WE'RE COMPLEX EVENTS IN SPACE AND TIME, BILL.
THE USUAL RULES DON'T APPLY TO US.
AND BECAUSE OF THAT WE'VE BEEN DEPOSITED IN SOME SORT OF POCKET UNIVERSE.
WITH FREAKY DECOR! WHAT'S THAT ABOUT?
NO IDEA. BUT I SUGGEST WE ASK HIM!

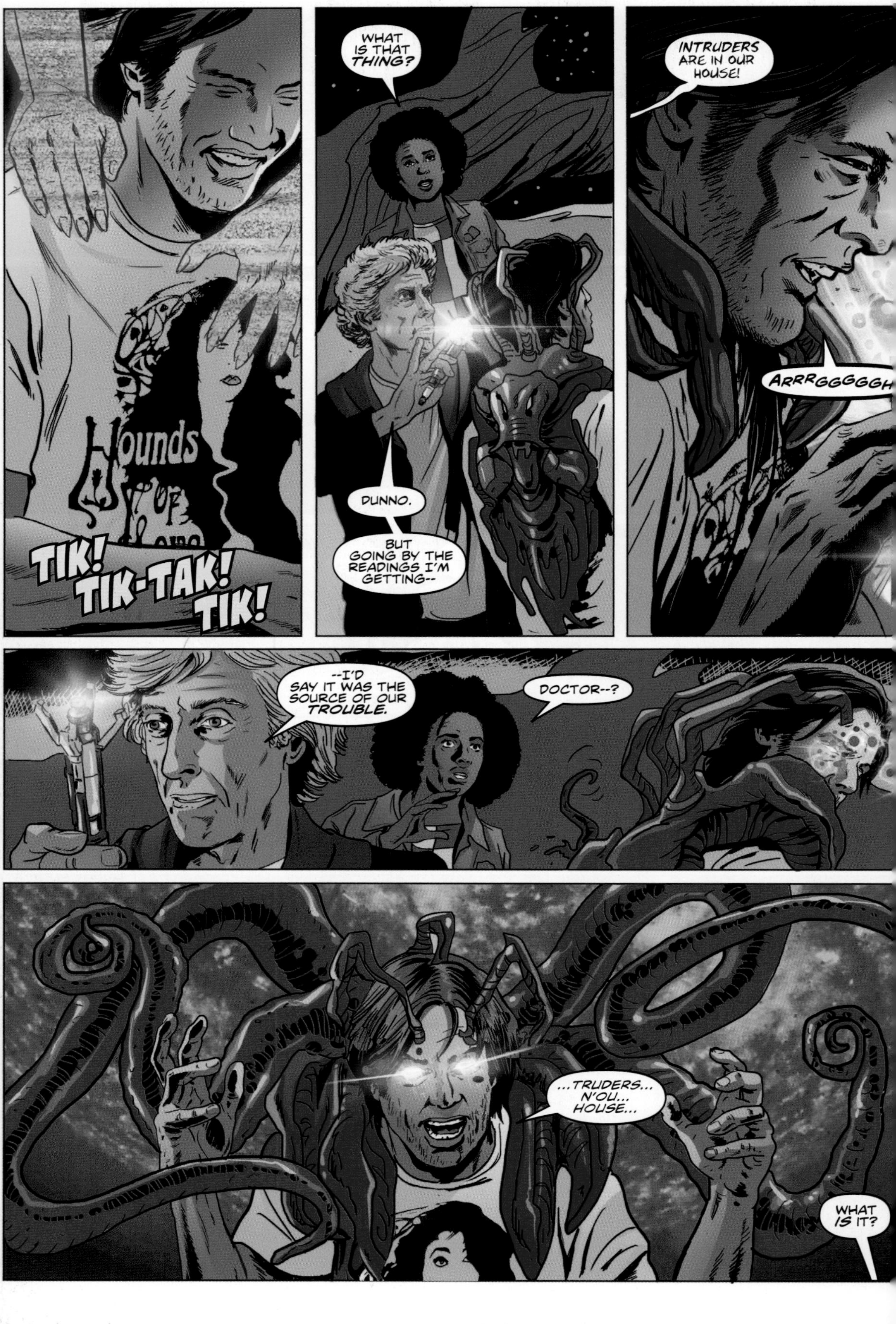
Hounds of
TIK! TIK-TAK! TIK!
WHAT IS THAT THING?
DUNNO.
BUT GOING BY THE READINGS I'M GETTING--
INTRUDERS ARE IN OUR HOUSE!
ARRRGGGGGH
--I'D SAY IT WAS THE SOURCE OF OUR TROUBLE.
DOCTOR--?
...TRUDERS... N'OU... HOUSE...
WHAT IS IT?

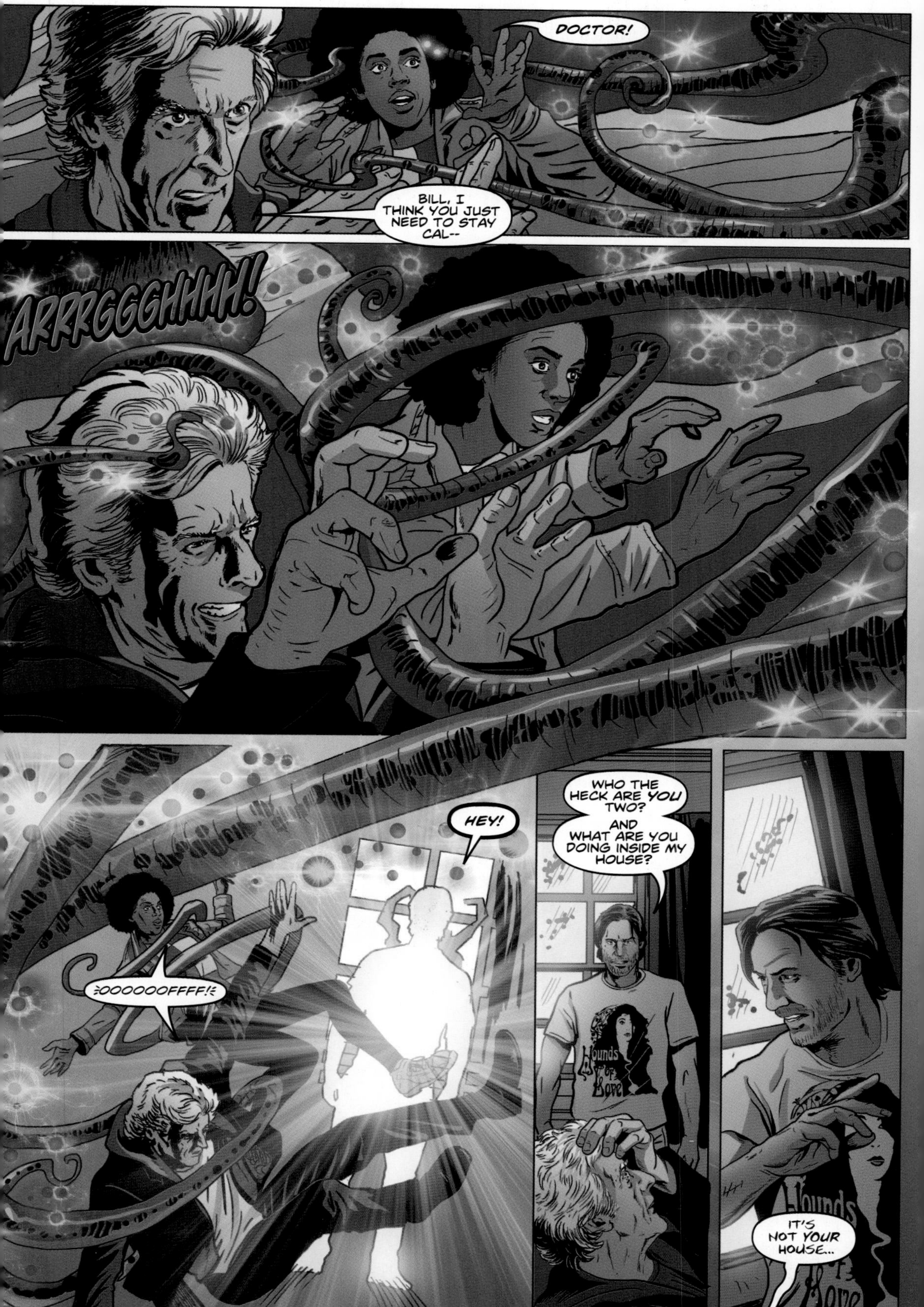
DOCTOR!
BILL, I THINK YOU JUST NEED TO STAY CAL--
ARRRGGGHHHH!
HEY!
OOOOOOFFFF!
WHO THE HECK ARE YOU TWO?
AND WHAT ARE YOU DOING INSIDE MY HOUSE?
Hounds of Love
IT'S NOT YOUR HOUSE...

...THIS IS THE HOUSE OF THE KAR-YN!

THE KAR-YN...?

BUT THAT'S IMPOSSIBLE.

KAREN...?!

WHO'S KAREN?

NOT KAR-EN..

...THE KAR-YN! IMAGINARIANS FROM THE PLANET KAR-IS.

YOU KNOW OF US?

THEY USED T TELL STORIE ABOUT YOU O GALLIFREY.

"THE ONES WHO COULD SCUL DREAMS"

AND THE ABILITY TO CARV WITH OUR MINDS WOULD BE OUR SALVATION.

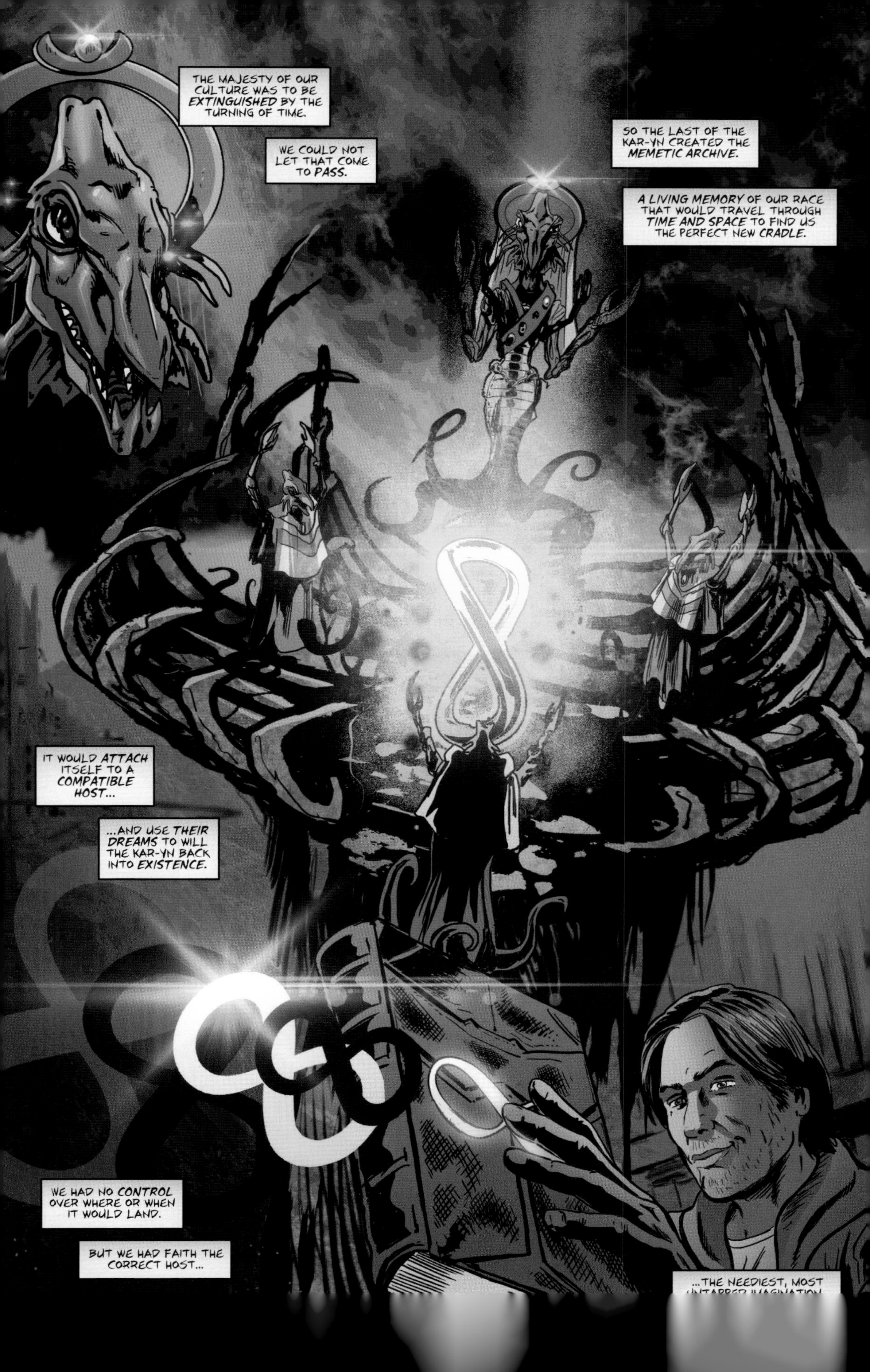

THE MAJESTY OF OUR CULTURE WAS TO BE EXTINGUISHED BY THE TURNING OF TIME.
WE COULD NOT LET THAT COME TO PASS.
SO THE LAST OF THE KAR-YN CREATED THE MEMETIC ARCHIVE.
A LIVING MEMORY OF OUR RACE THAT WOULD TRAVEL THROUGH TIME AND SPACE TO FIND US THE PERFECT NEW CRADLE.
IT WOULD ATTACH ITSELF TO A COMPATIBLE HOST...
...AND USE THEIR DREAMS TO WILL THE KAR-YN BACK INTO EXISTENCE.
WE HAD NO CONTROL OVER WHERE OR WHEN IT WOULD LAND.
BUT WE HAD FAITH THE CORRECT HOST...
...THE NEEDIEST, MOST

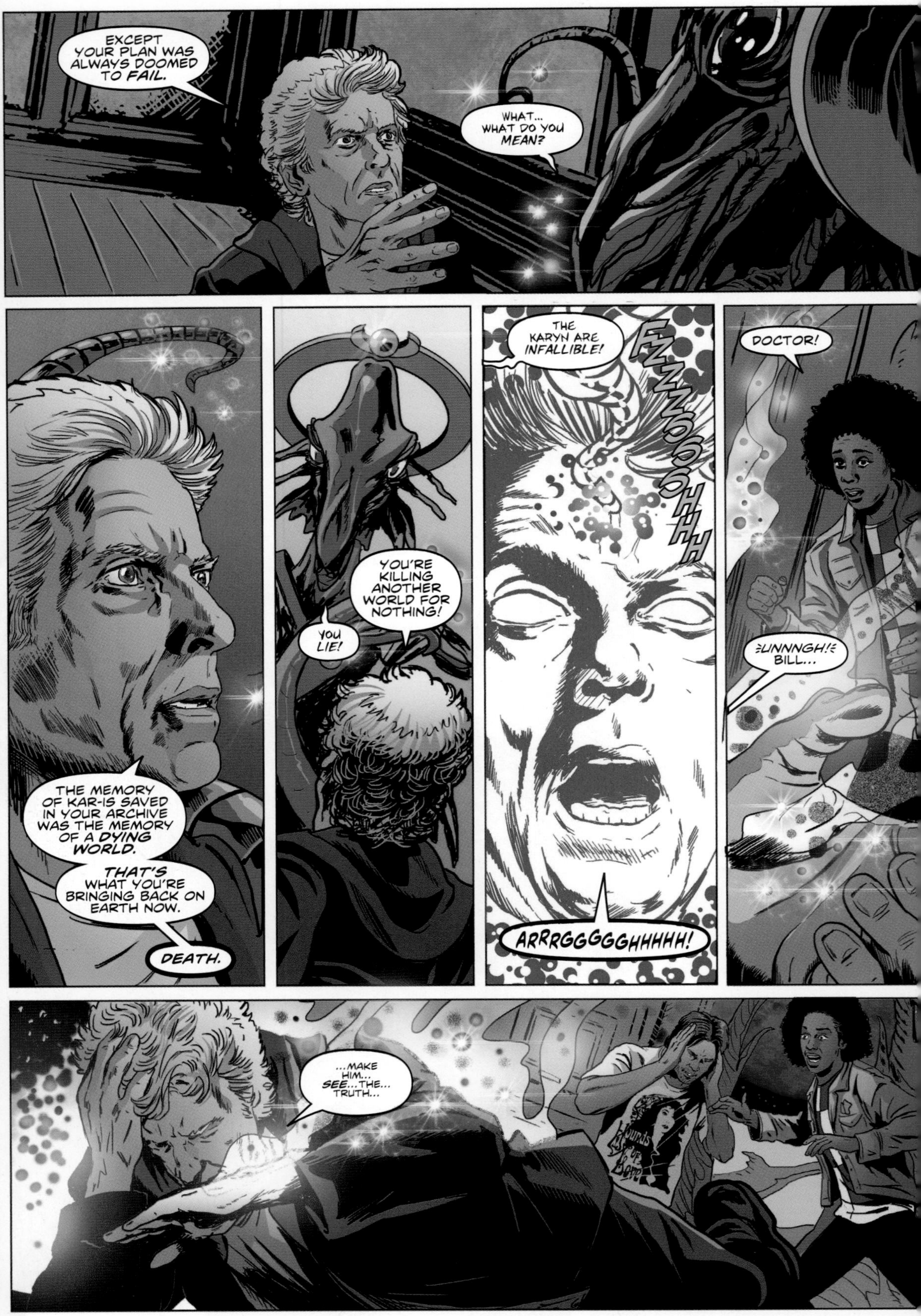
EXCEPT YOUR PLAN WAS ALWAYS DOOMED TO FAIL.
WHAT... WHAT DO YOU MEAN?
THE MEMORY OF KAR-IS SAVED IN YOUR ARCHIVE WAS THE MEMORY OF A DYING WORLD.
THAT'S WHAT YOU'RE BRINGING BACK ON EARTH NOW.
DEATH.
YOU'RE KILLING ANOTHER WORLD FOR NOTHING!
YOU LIE!
THE KARYN ARE INFALLIBLE!
FZZZZSSSHHHH
ARRRGGGGGHHHHH!
DOCTOR!
UNNNGH! BILL...
...MAKE HIM... SEE... THE... TRUTH...

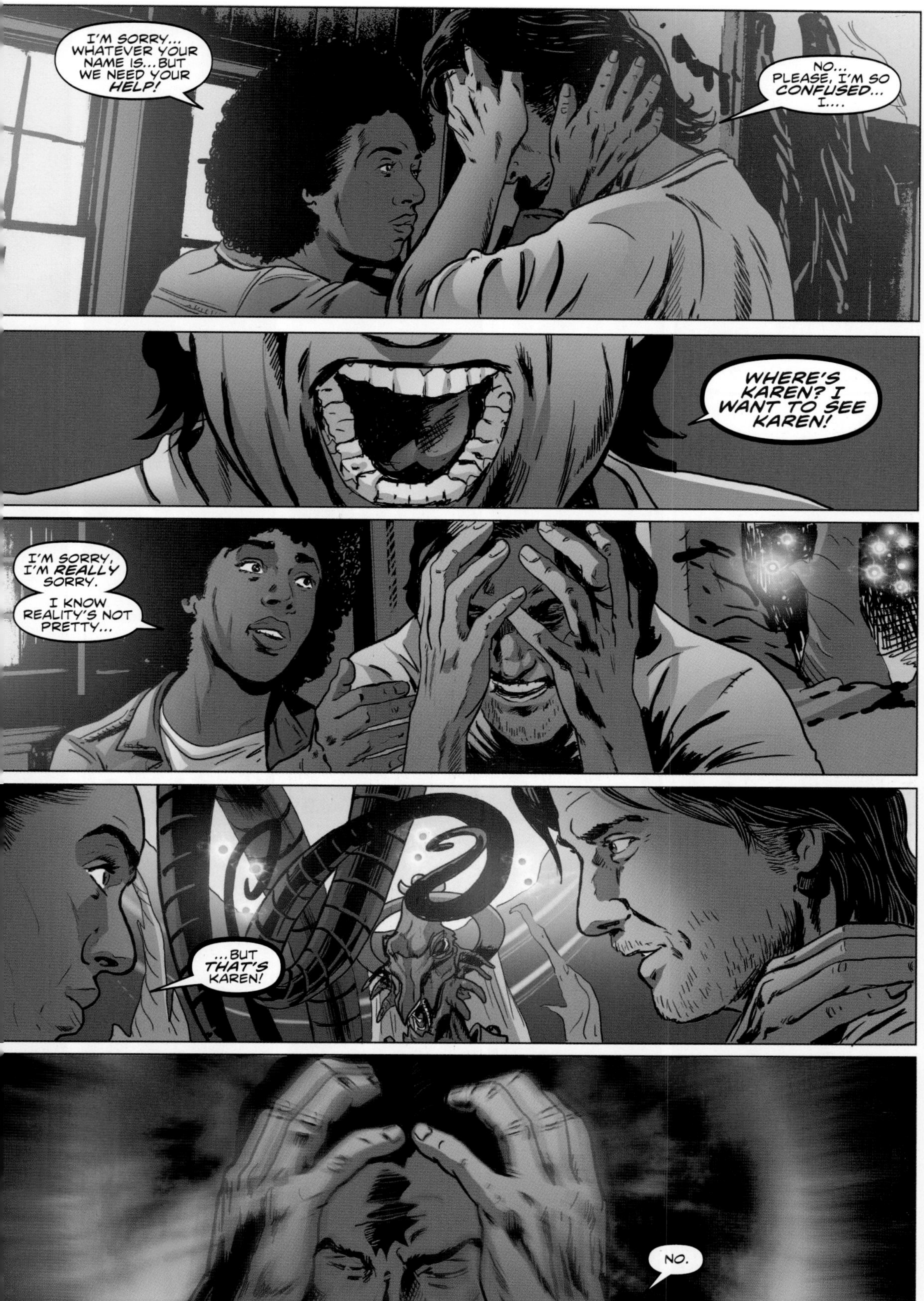
I'M SORRY... WHATEVER YOUR NAME IS...BUT WE NEED YOUR HELP!
NO... PLEASE, I'M SO CONFUSED... I....
WHERE'S KAREN? I WANT TO SEE KAREN!
I'M SORRY, I'M REALLY SORRY.
I KNOW REALITY'S NOT PRETTY...
...BUT THAT'S KAREN!
NO.

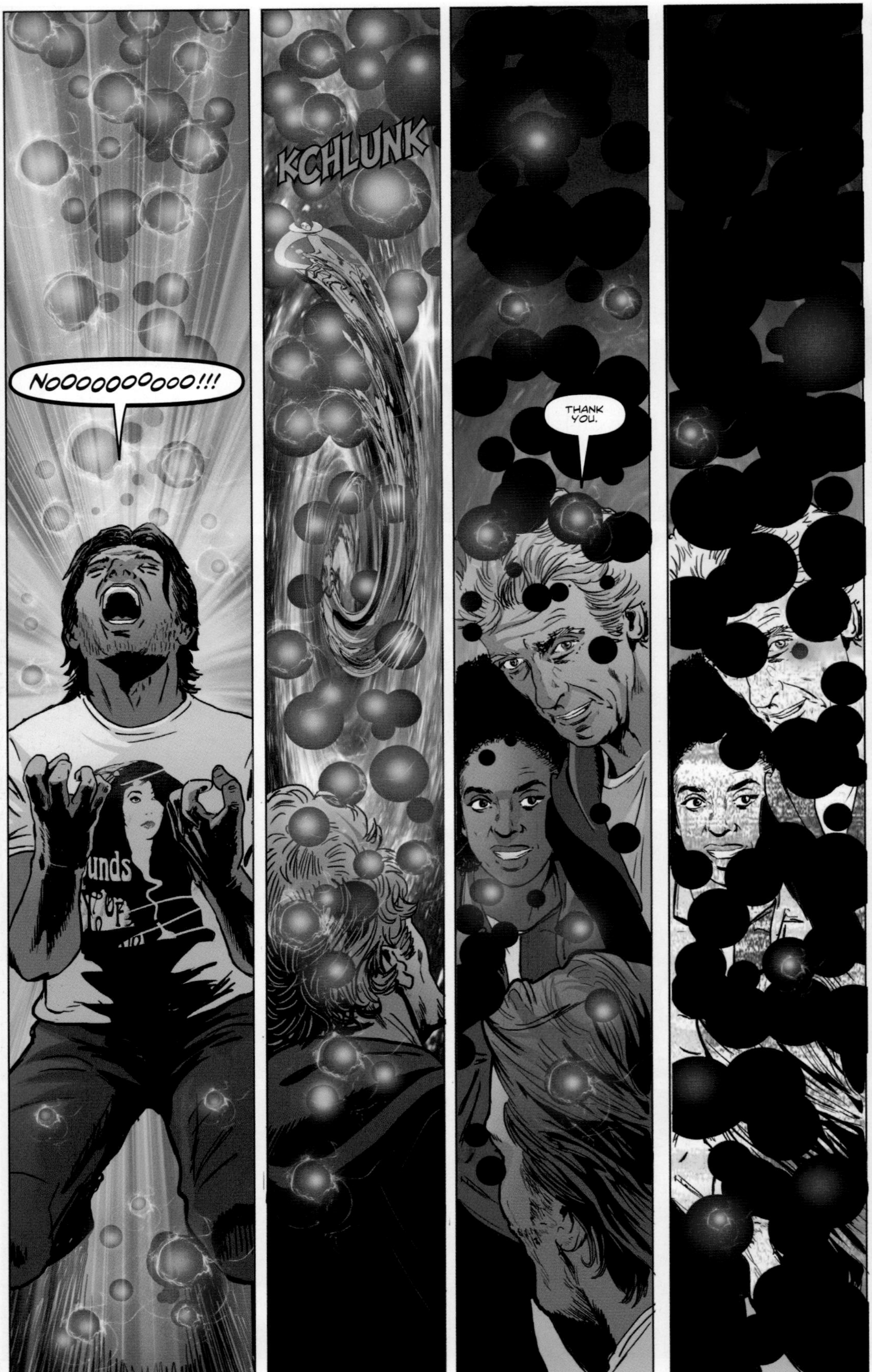

NOOOOOOOOOO!!!
KCHLUNK
THANK YOU.

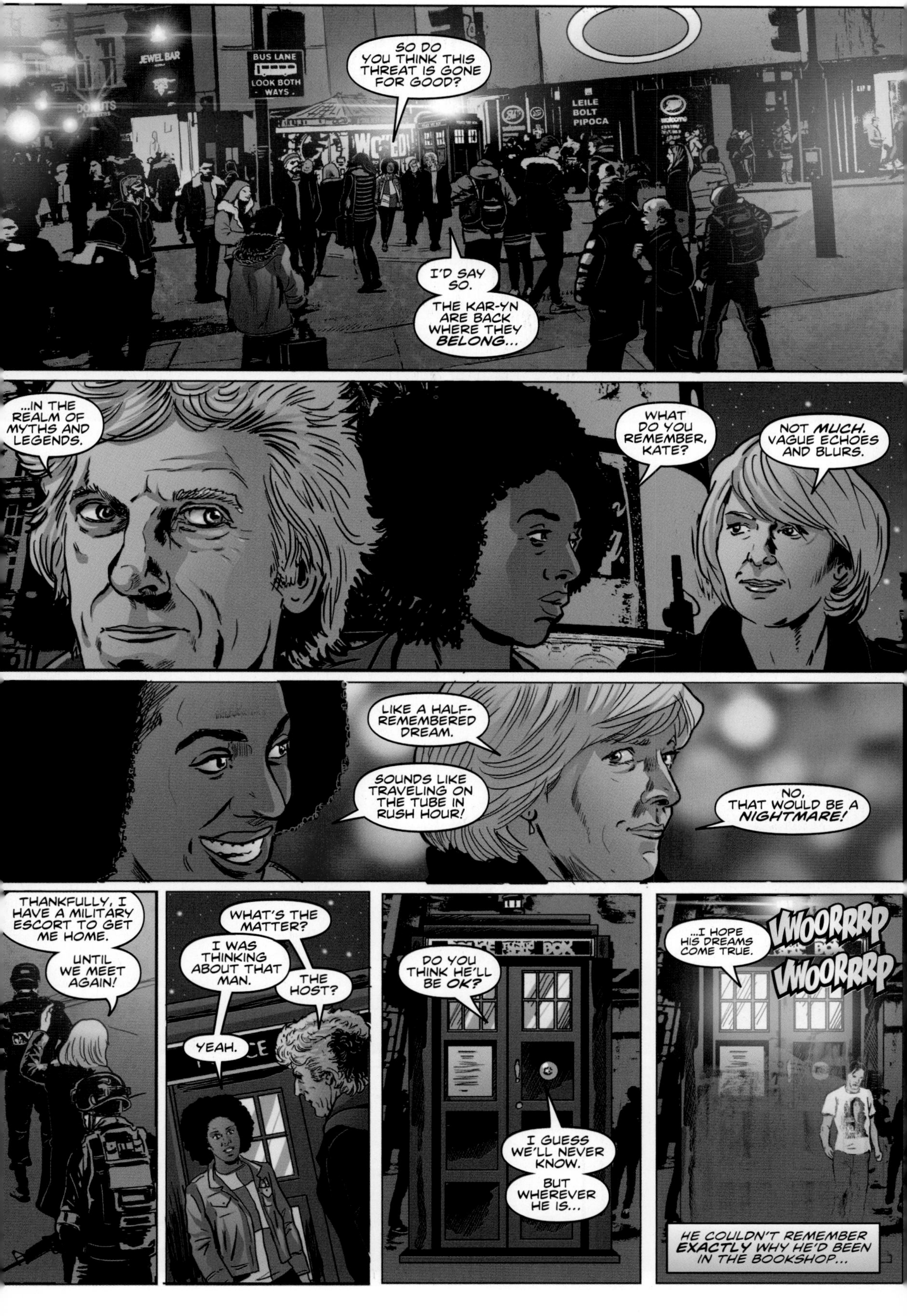

JEWEL BAR
BUS LANE
LOOK BOTH WAYS
LEILE BOLT PIPOCA
SO DO YOU THINK THIS THREAT IS GONE FOR GOOD?
I'D SAY SO.
THE KAR-YN ARE BACK WHERE THEY BELONG...
...IN THE REALM OF MYTHS AND LEGENDS.
WHAT DO YOU REMEMBER, KATE?
NOT MUCH. VAGUE ECHOES AND BLURS.
LIKE A HALF-REMEMBERED DREAM.
SOUNDS LIKE TRAVELING ON THE TUBE IN RUSH HOUR!
NO, THAT WOULD BE A NIGHTMARE!
THANKFULLY, I HAVE A MILITARY ESCORT TO GET ME HOME.
UNTIL WE MEET AGAIN!
WHAT'S THE MATTER?
I WAS THINKING ABOUT THAT MAN.
THE HOST?
YEAH.
DO YOU THINK HE'LL BE OK?
I GUESS WE'LL NEVER KNOW.
BUT WHEREVER HE IS...
...I HOPE HIS DREAMS COME TRUE.
VWOORRRP
VWOORRRP
HE COULDN'T REMEMBER EXACTLY WHY HE'D BEEN IN THE BOOKSHOP...

...BUT THE FEELING OF **SADNESS** THAT WASHED OVER HIM -- LIKE HE'D HAD SOMETHING AND **LOST** IT -- MEANT HE HAD TO LEAVE.

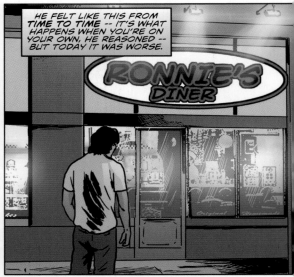

HE FELT LIKE THIS FROM **TIME TO TIME** -- IT'S WHAT HAPPENS WHEN YOU'RE ON YOUR OWN, HE REASONED -- BUT TODAY IT WAS WORSE.

RONNIE'S DINER

AT HIS AGE HE WAS PRETTY SURE THAT HIS DREAMS WOULD NEVER COME TRU--

SO, WHAT ARE YOU HAVING?

HER VOICE WAS LIKE WARM HONEY.

I'M NOT SURE WHAT YOU FANCY--

KAREN

THE DREAMING

SOFT AND SWEET.

--BUT THE SPECIALS TODAY ARE **REALLY** GOOD.

KAREN

WHAT DO YOU RECOMMEND?

WELL, IF YOU ASK ME...

HE WASN'T SURE WHY, BUT HE JUST HAD A FEELING...

...A FEELING THAT EVERYTHING WOULD BE **ALRIGHT**.

THE END... FOR NOW!

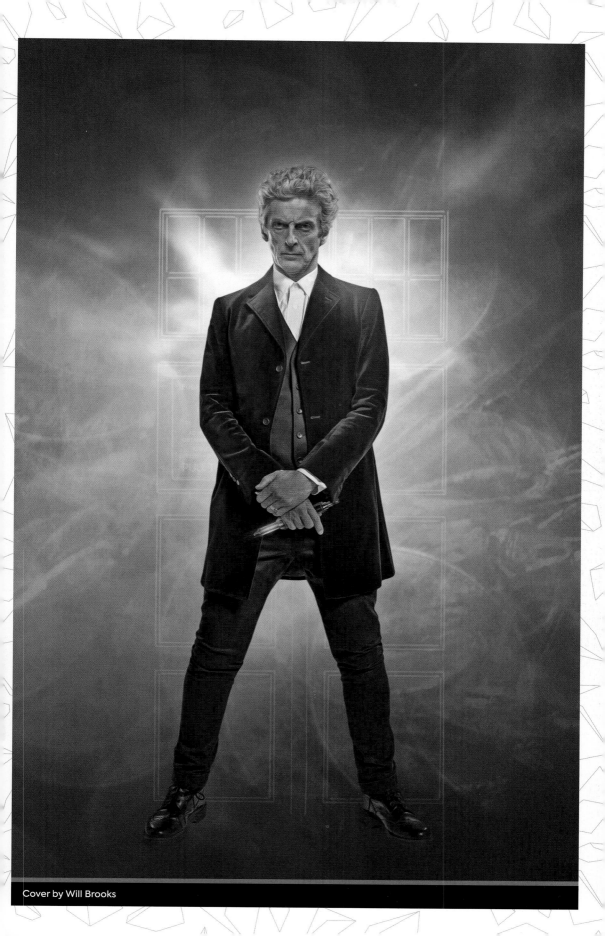

Cover by Will Brooks

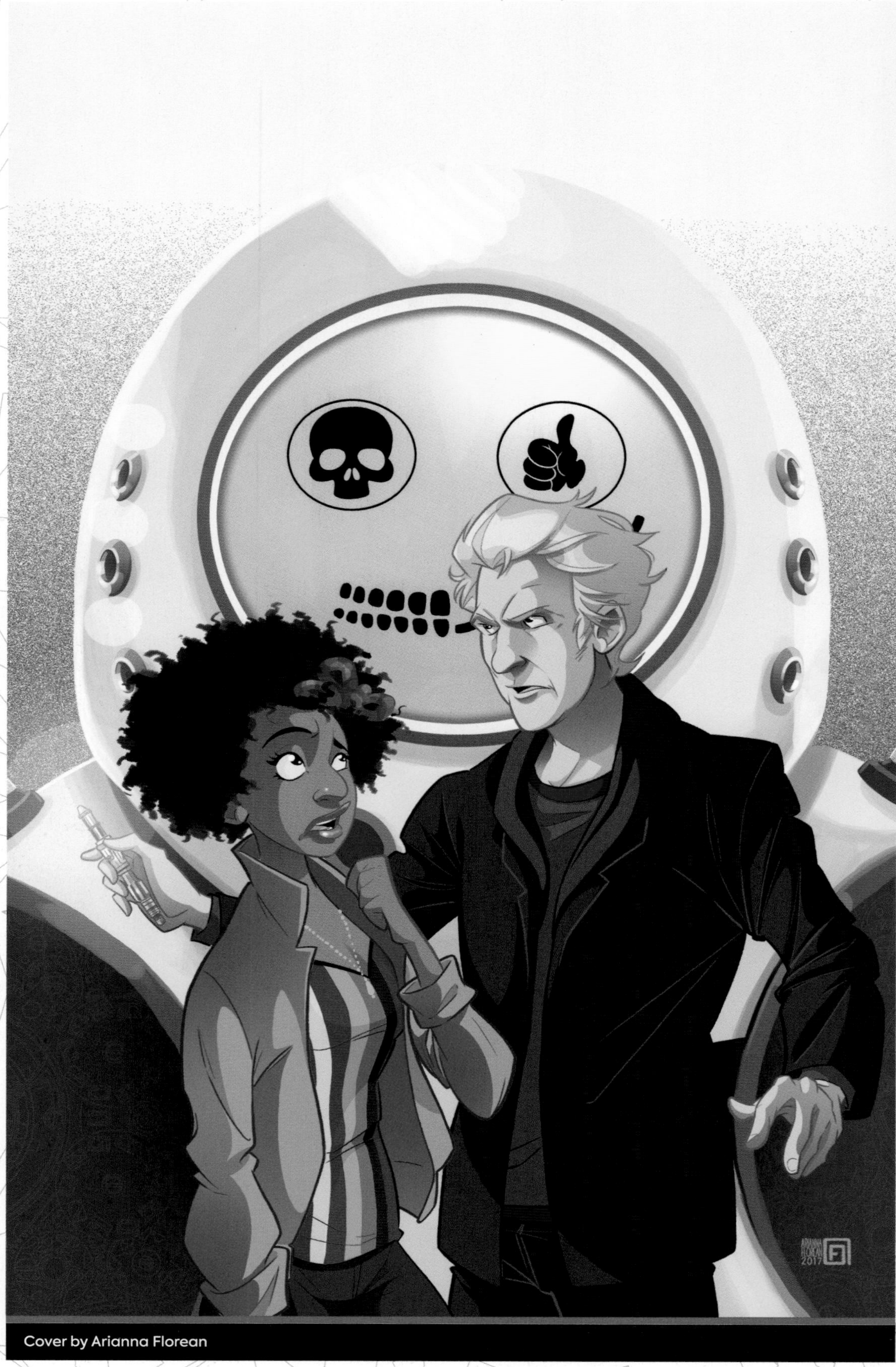
ARIANNA FLOREAN 2017

Cover by Arianna Florean

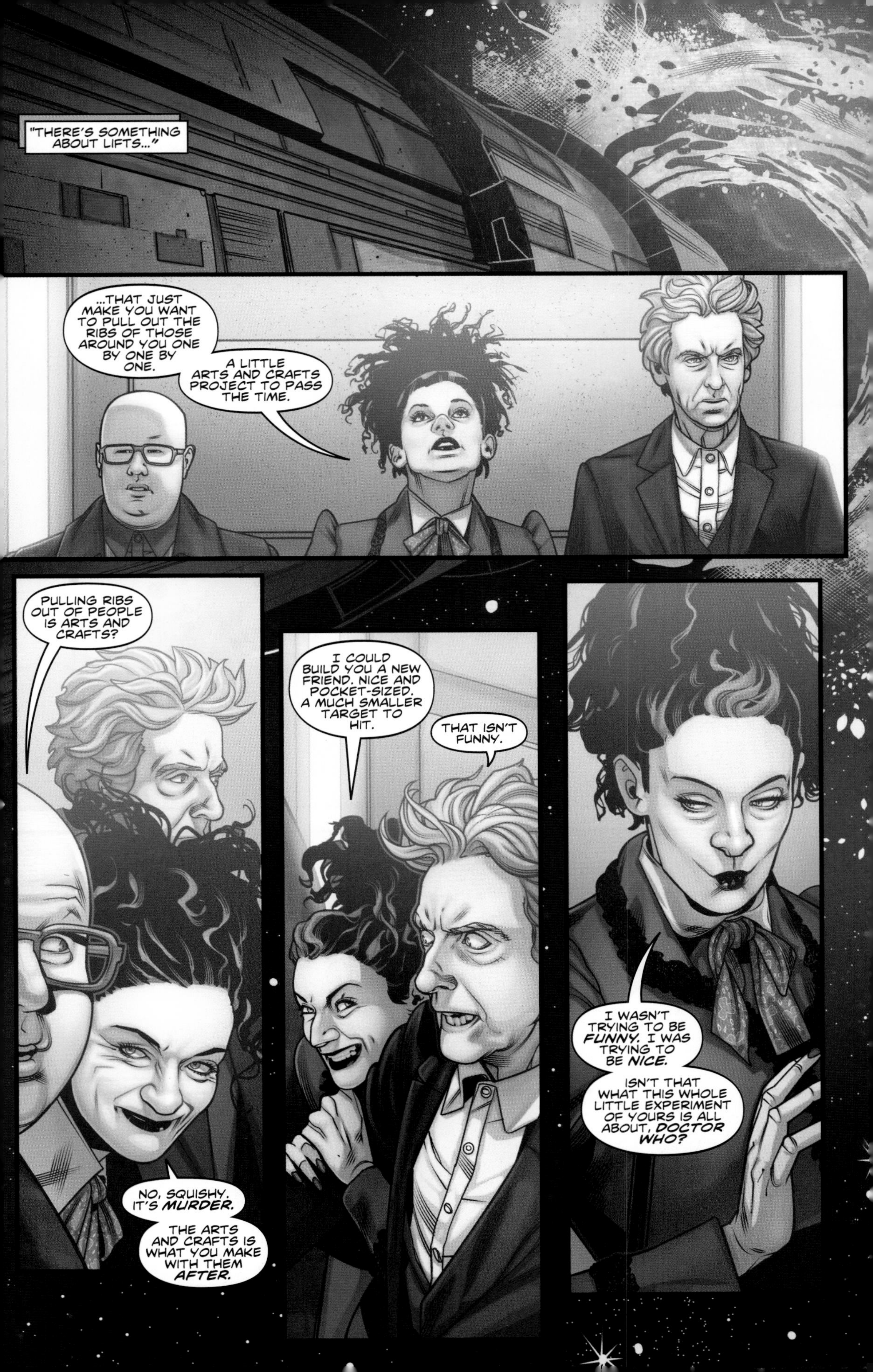
"THERE'S SOMETHING ABOUT LIFTS..."
...THAT JUST MAKE YOU WANT TO PULL OUT THE RIBS OF THOSE AROUND YOU ONE BY ONE BY ONE.
A LITTLE ARTS AND CRAFTS PROJECT TO PASS THE TIME.
PULLING RIBS OUT OF PEOPLE IS ARTS AND CRAFTS?
NO, SQUISHY. IT'S *MURDER.*
THE ARTS AND CRAFTS IS WHAT YOU MAKE WITH THEM *AFTER.*
I COULD BUILD YOU A NEW FRIEND. NICE AND POCKET-SIZED. A MUCH SMALLER TARGET TO HIT.
THAT ISN'T FUNNY.
I WASN'T TRYING TO BE *FUNNY.* I WAS TRYING TO BE *NICE.*
ISN'T THAT WHAT THIS WHOLE LITTLE EXPERIMENT OF YOURS IS ALL ABOUT, *DOCTOR WHO?*

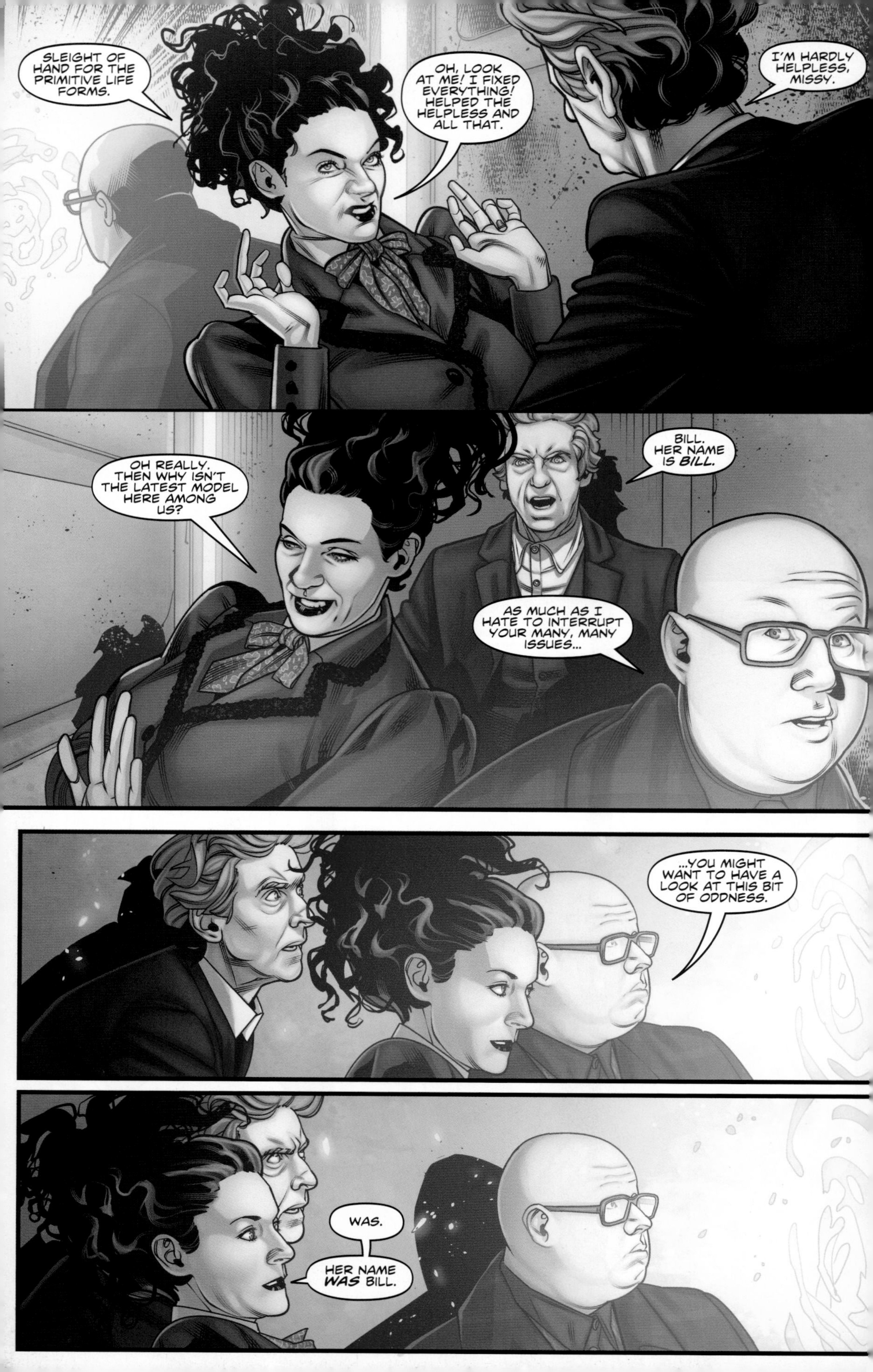
SLEIGHT OF HAND FOR THE PRIMITIVE LIFE FORMS.
OH, LOOK AT ME! I FIXED EVERYTHING! HELPED THE HELPLESS AND ALL THAT.
I'M HARDLY HELPLESS, MISSY.
OH REALLY. THEN WHY ISN'T THE LATEST MODEL HERE AMONG US?
BILL. HER NAME IS *BILL.*
AS MUCH AS I HATE TO INTERRUPT YOUR MANY, MANY ISSUES...
...YOU MIGHT WANT TO HAVE A LOOK AT THIS BIT OF ODDNESS.
WAS.
HER NAME **WAS** BILL.

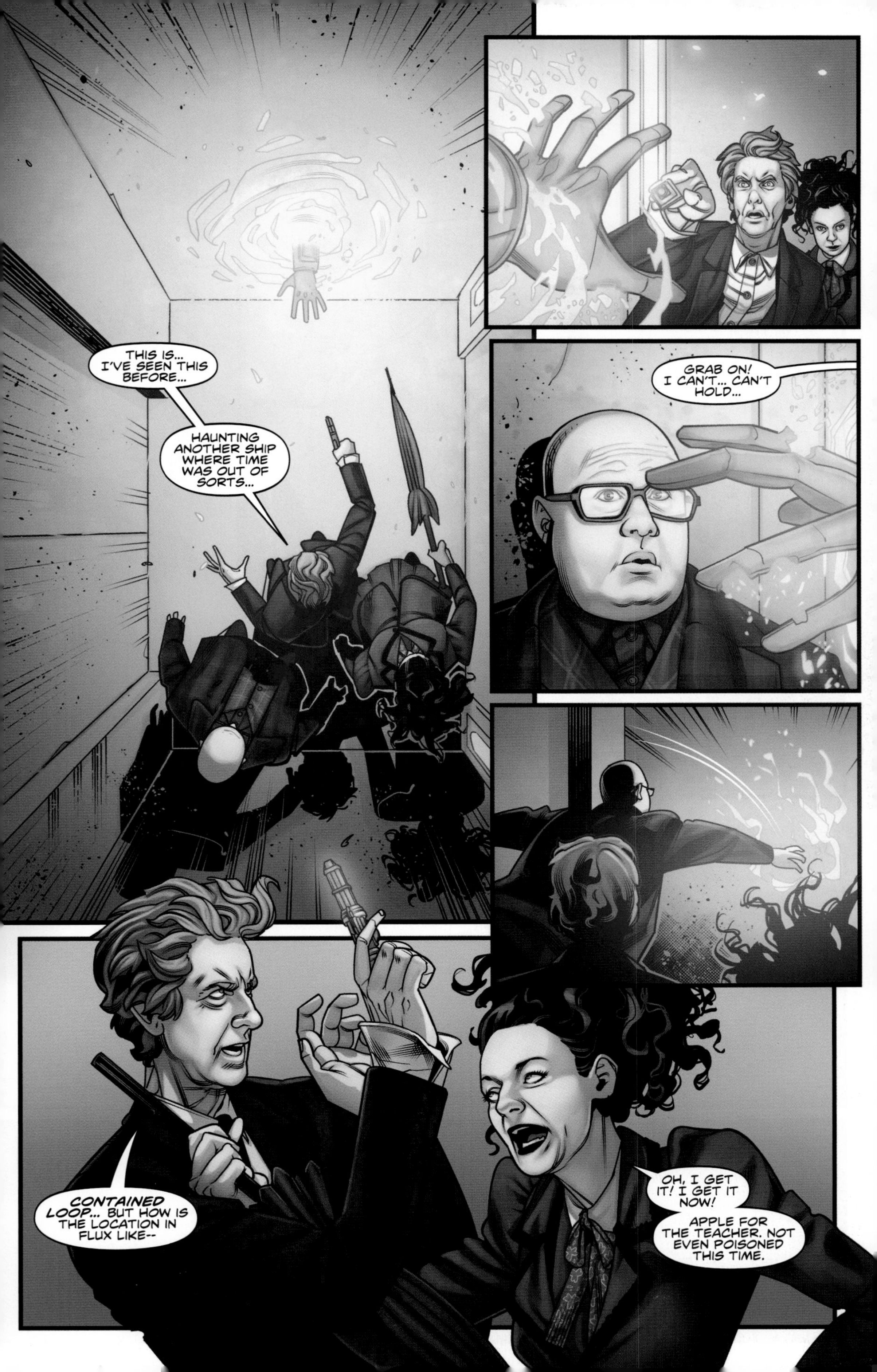
THIS IS... I'VE SEEN THIS BEFORE...
HAUNTING ANOTHER SHIP WHERE TIME WAS OUT OF SORTS...
GRAB ON! I CAN'T... CAN'T HOLD...
CONTAINED LOOP... BUT HOW IS THE LOCATION IN FLUX LIKE--
OH, I GET IT! I GET IT NOW!
APPLE FOR THE TEACHER. NOT EVEN POISONED THIS TIME.

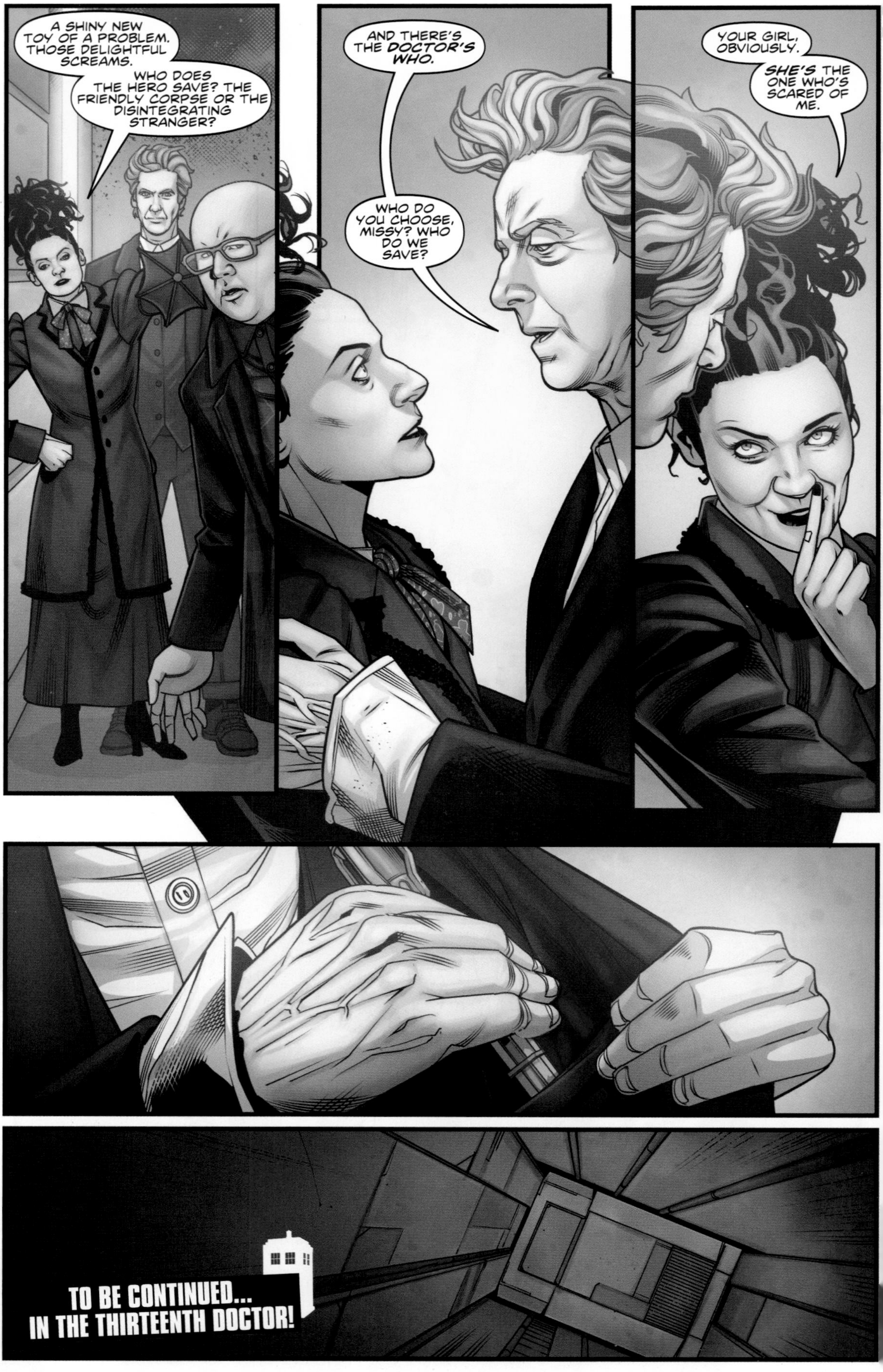
A SHINY NEW TOY OF A PROBLEM. THOSE DELIGHTFUL SCREAMS.
WHO DOES THE HERO SAVE? THE FRIENDLY CORPSE OR THE DISINTEGRATING STRANGER?
AND THERE'S THE DOCTOR'S WHO.
WHO DO YOU CHOOSE, MISSY? WHO DO WE SAVE?
YOUR GIRL, OBVIOUSLY.
SHE'S THE ONE WHO'S SCARED OF ME.
TO BE CONTINUED... IN THE THIRTEENTH DOCTOR!

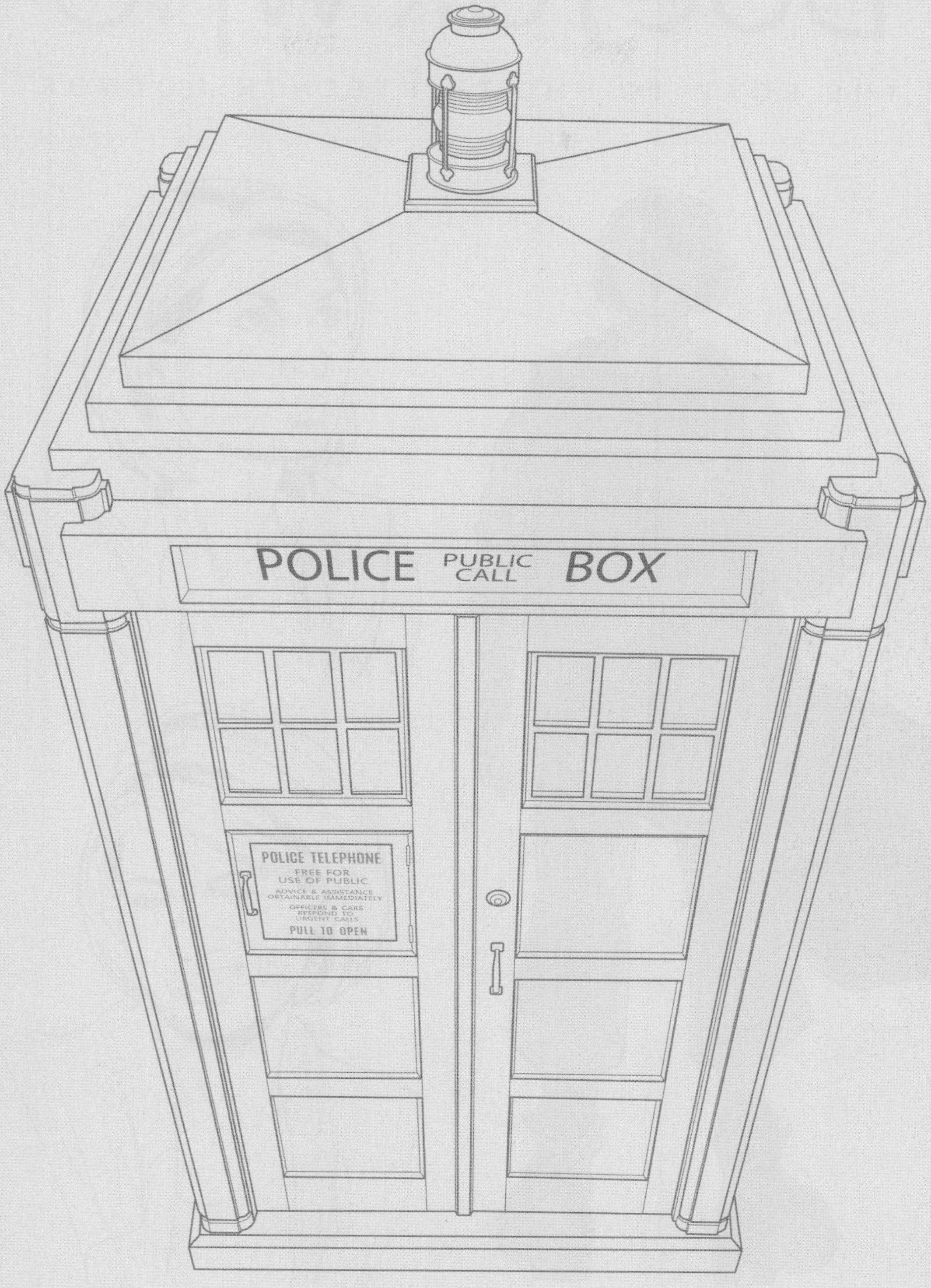
POLICE PUBLIC CALL BOX
POLICE TELEPHONE
FREE FOR USE OF PUBLIC
ADVICE & ASSISTANCE OBTAINABLE IMMEDIATELY
OFFICERS & CARS RESPOND TO URGENT CALLS
PULL TO OPEN

BBC

DOCTOR WHO

THE ROAD TO THE THIRTEENTH DOCTOR

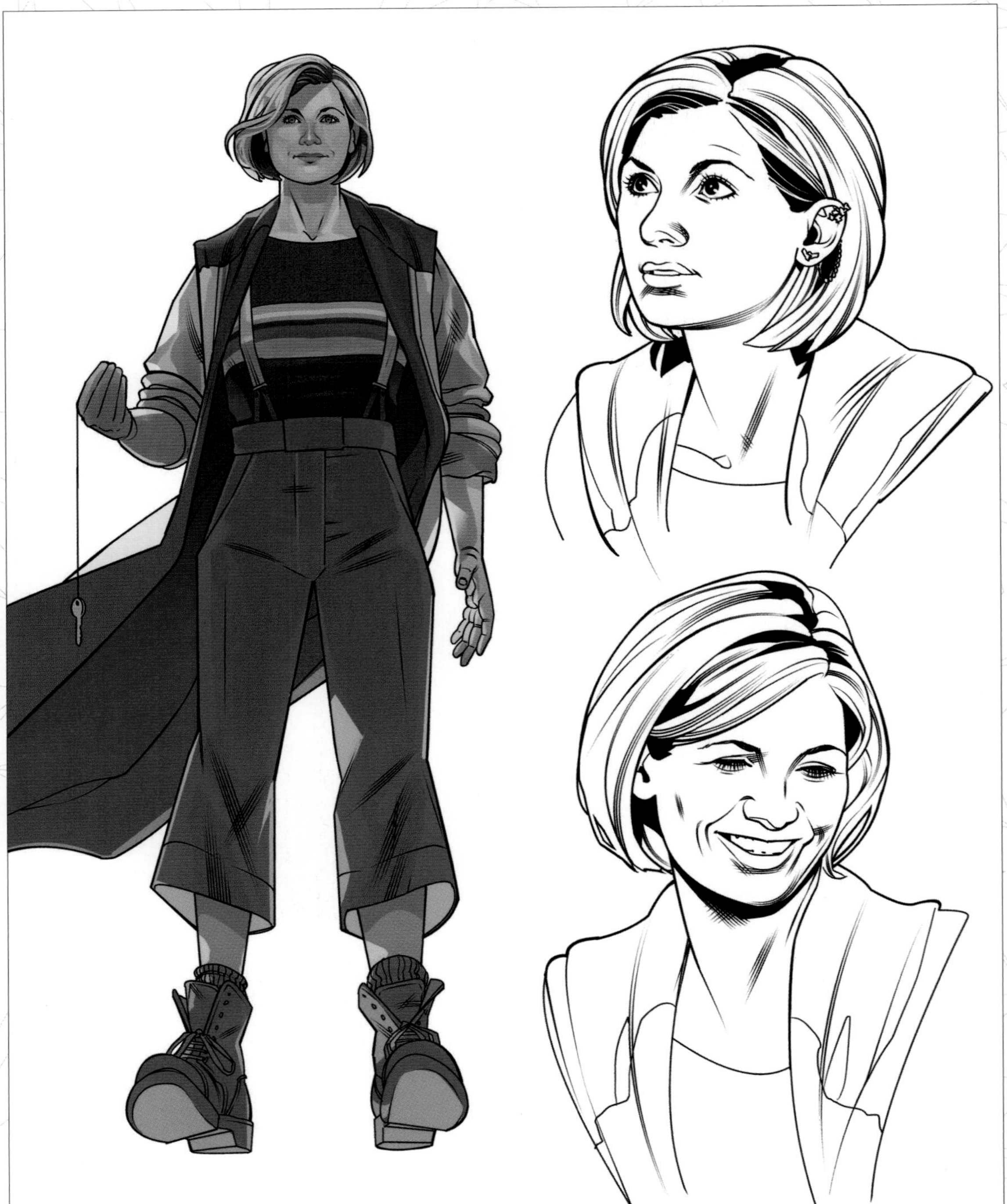

THE THIRTEENTH DOCTOR • RACHAEL STOTT

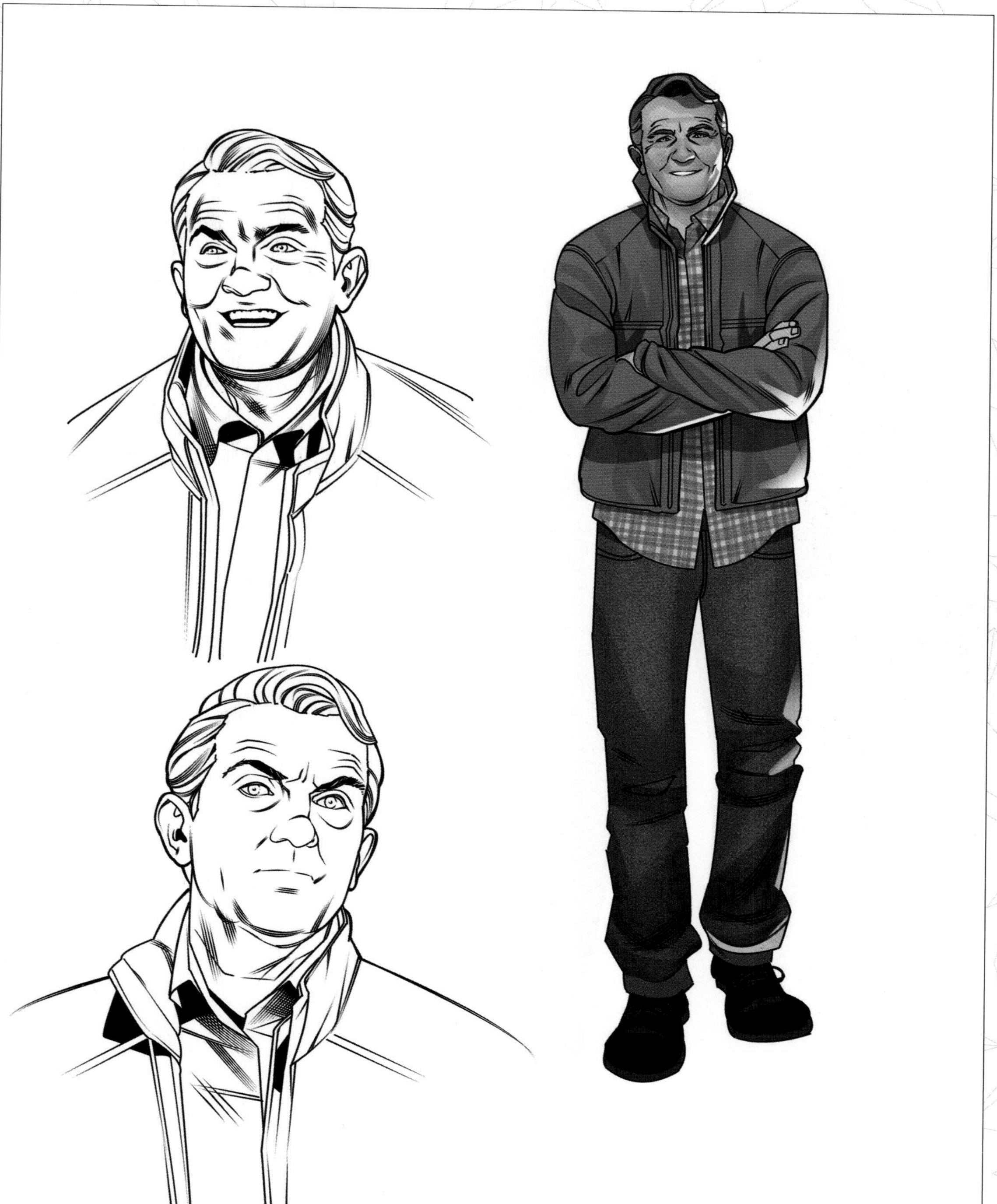

GRAHAM • RACHAEL STOTT

BBC

DOCTOR WHO

THE ROAD TO THE THIRTEENTH DOCTOR

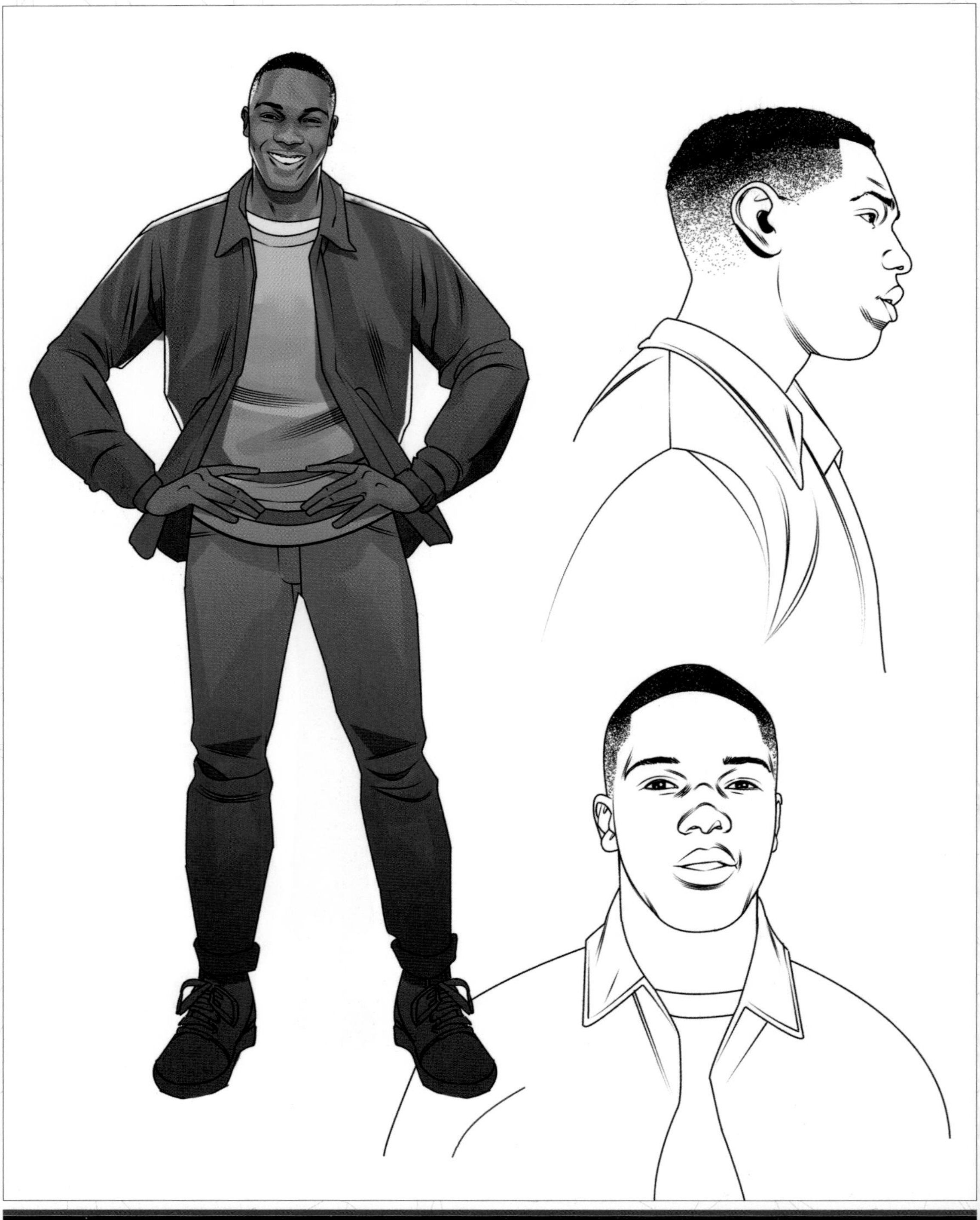

RYAN • RACHAEL STOTT

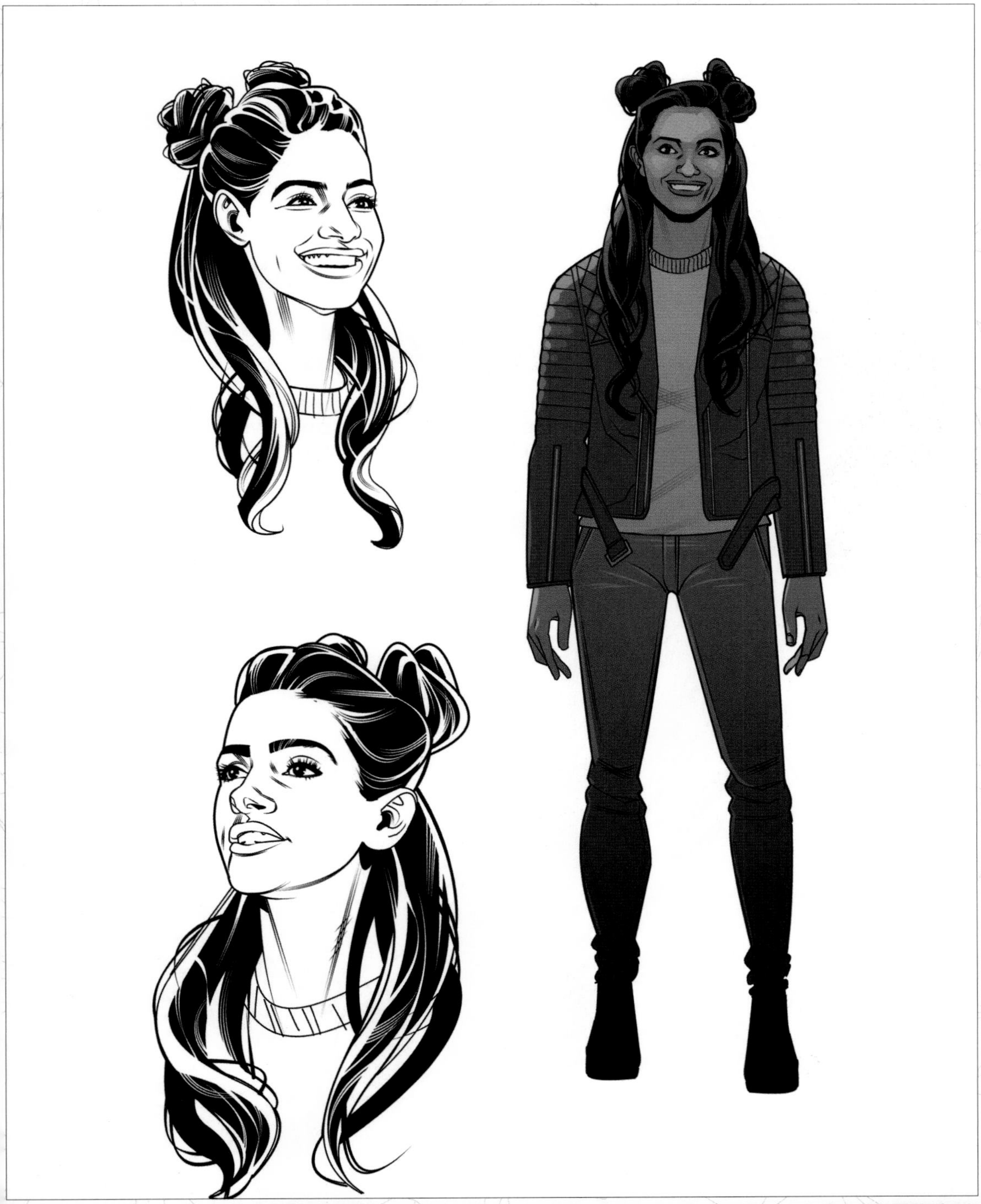

YASMIN • RACHAEL STOTT

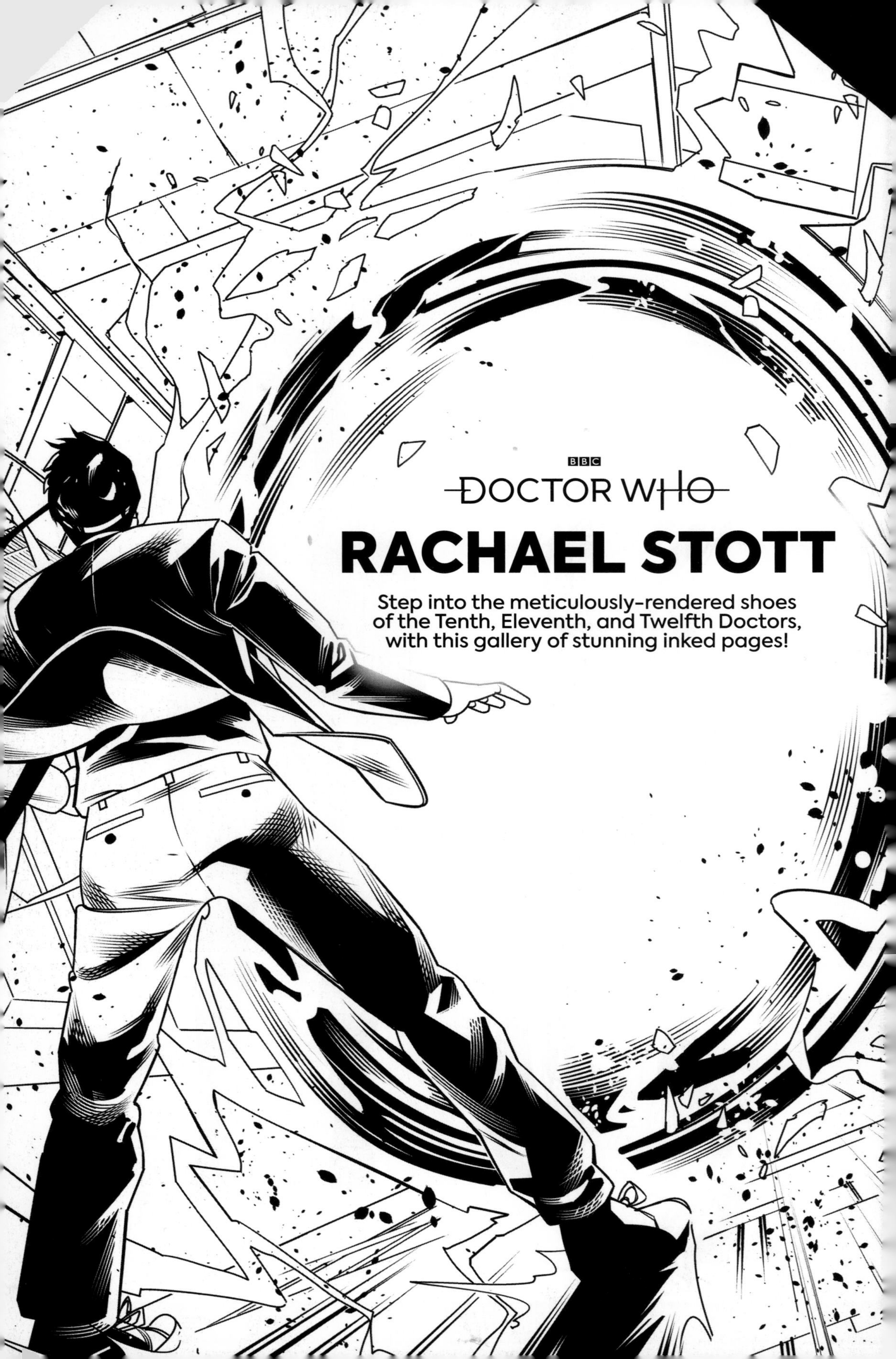

BBC DOCTOR WHO

RACHAEL STOTT

Step into the meticulously-rendered shoes of the Tenth, Eleventh, and Twelfth Doctors, with this gallery of stunning inked pages!

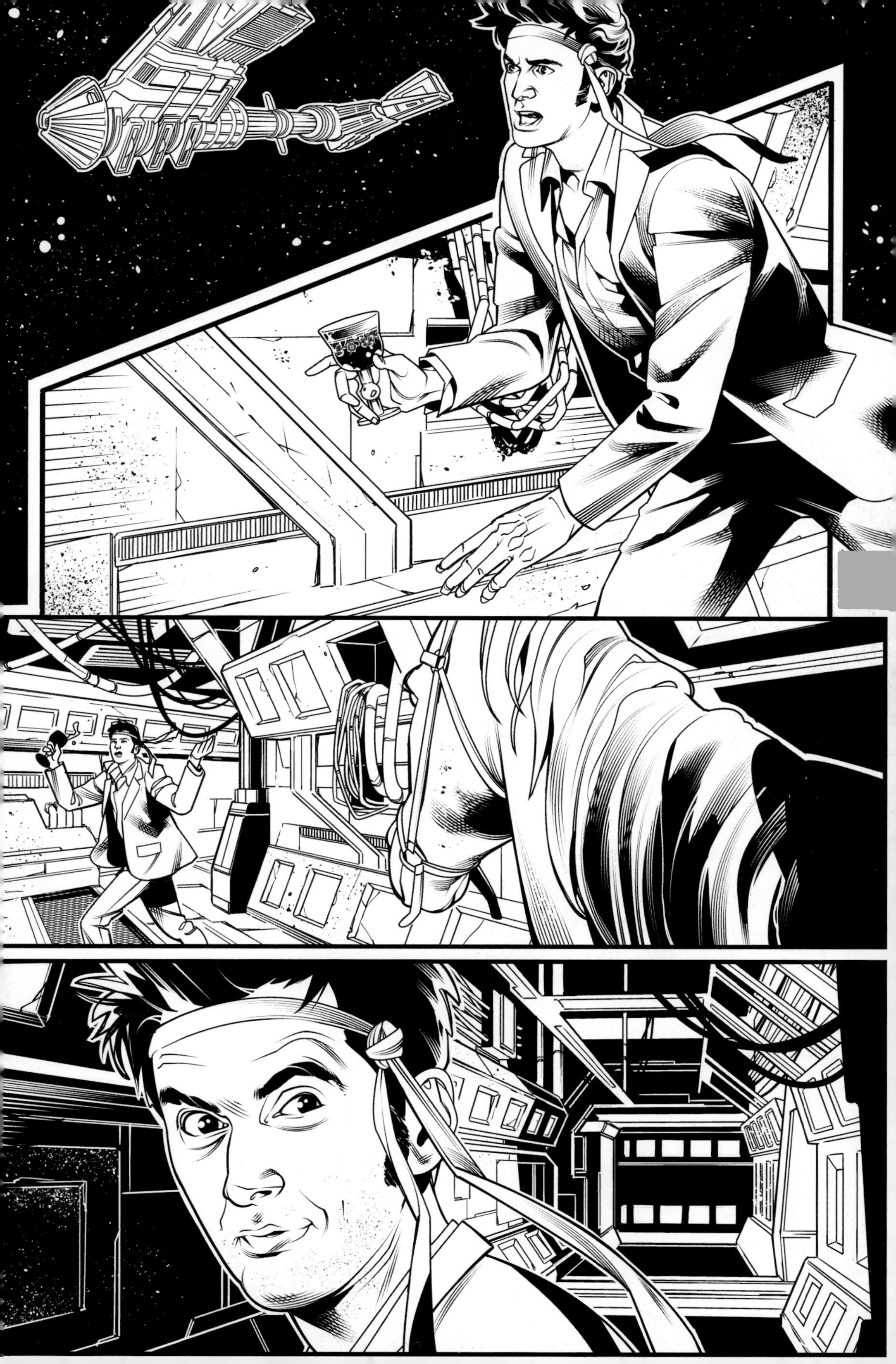

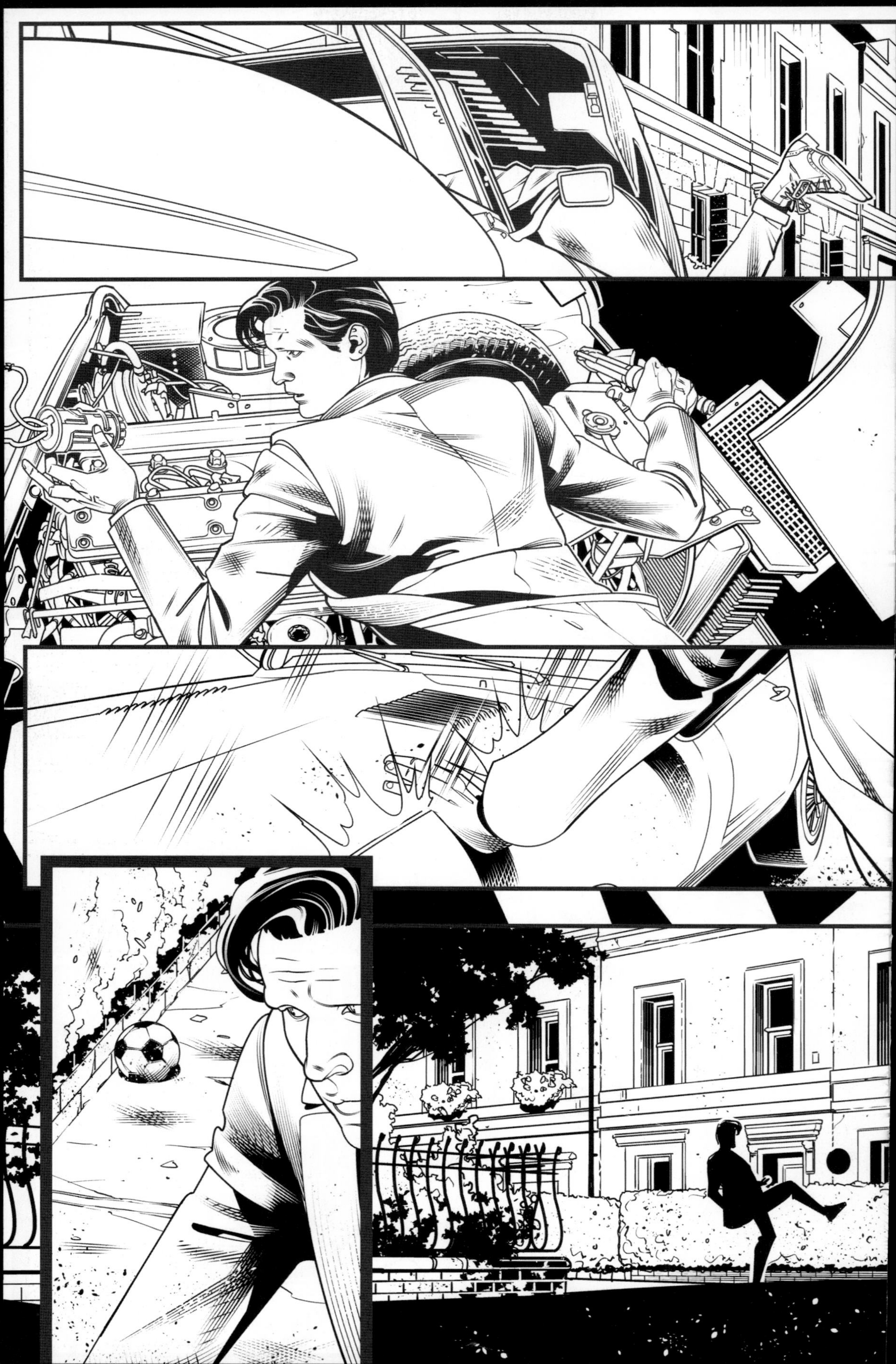

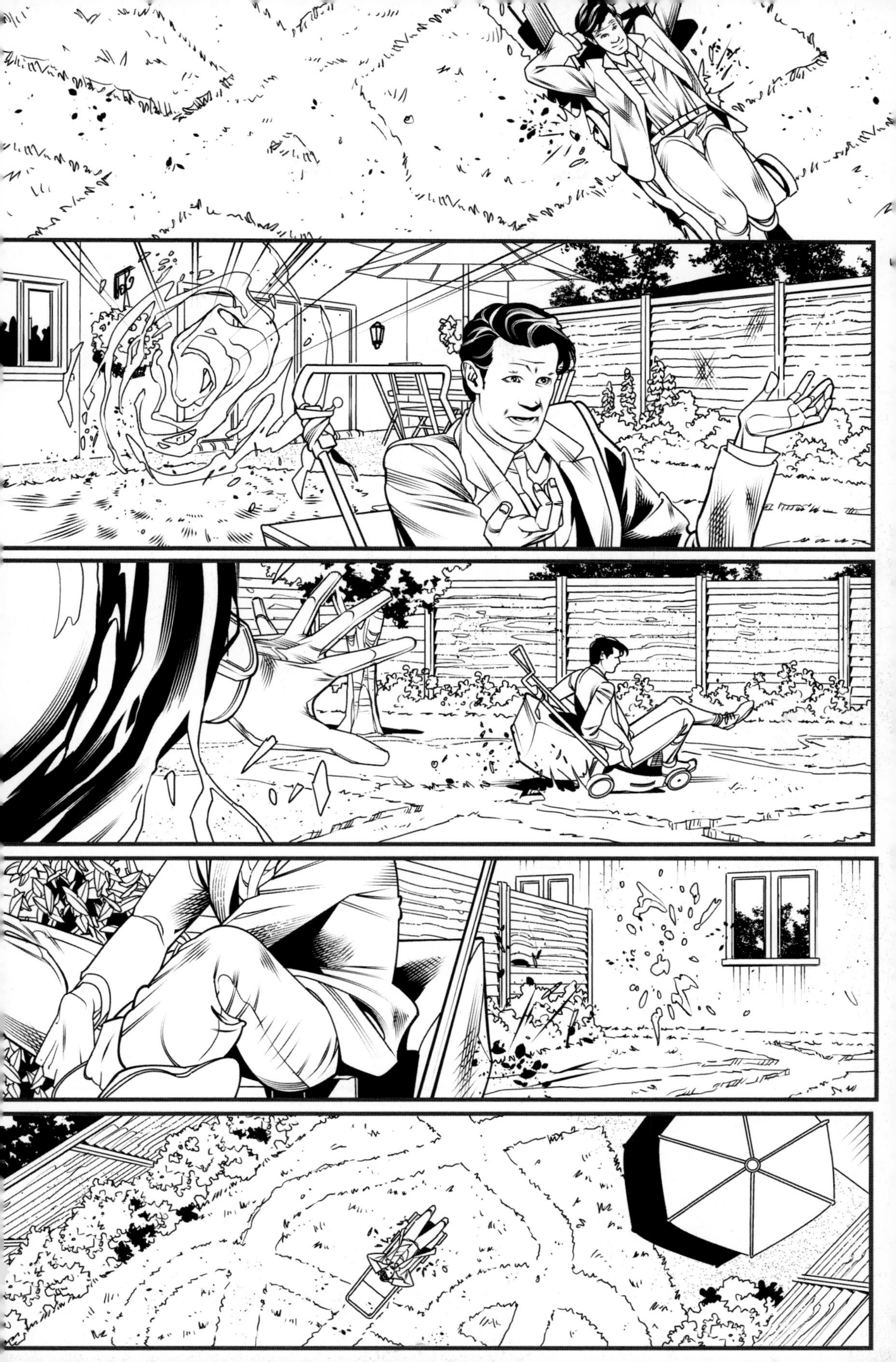

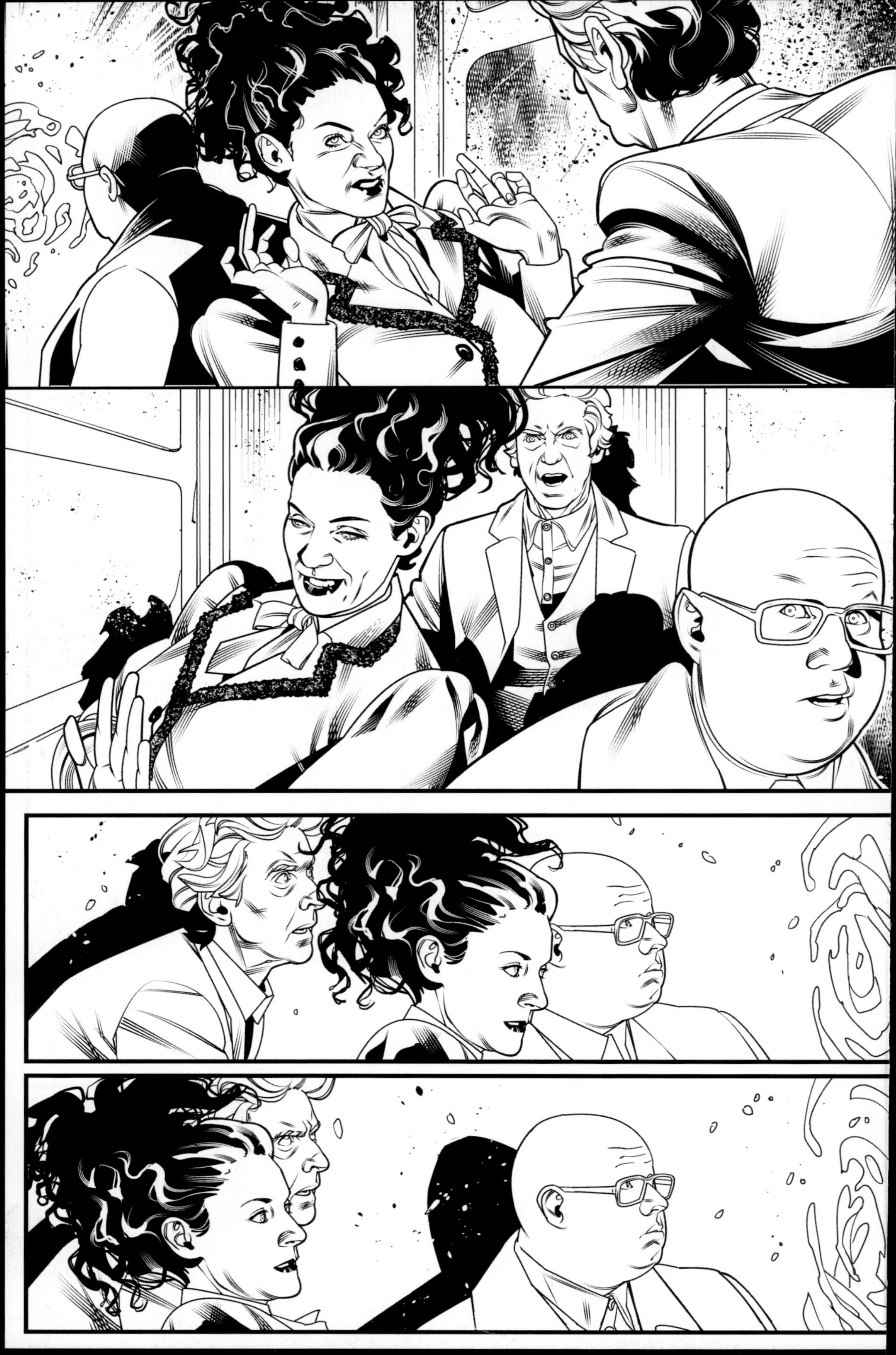

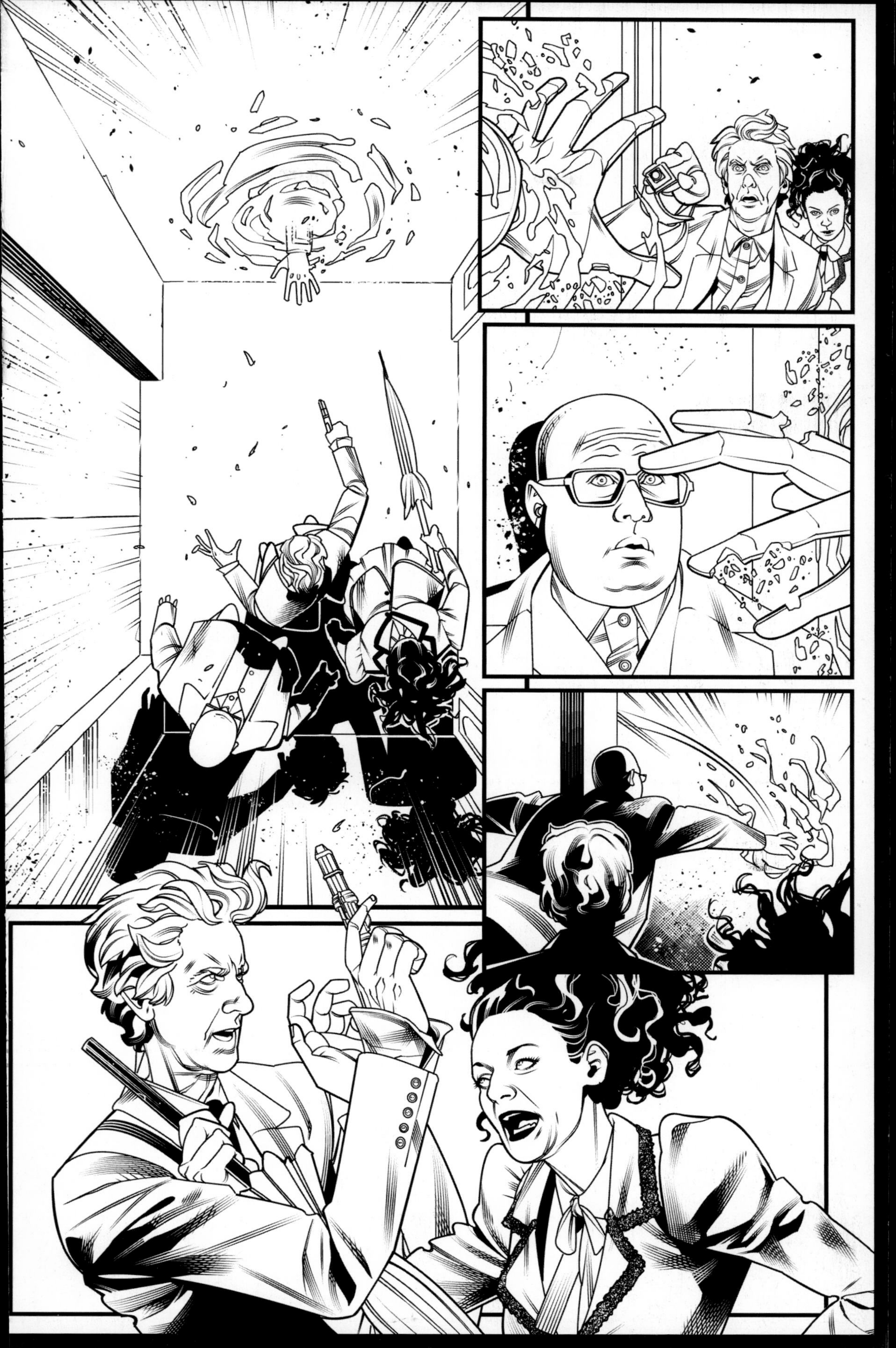

BBC
DOCTOR WHO

READER'S GUIDE

With so many amazing *Doctor Who* collections already on the shelves, it c be difficult to know where to start. That's where this handy guide comes ir And don't be overwhelmed – every collection is designed to be welcomin whatever your knowledge of *Doctor Who*.

THE TWELFTH DOCTOR

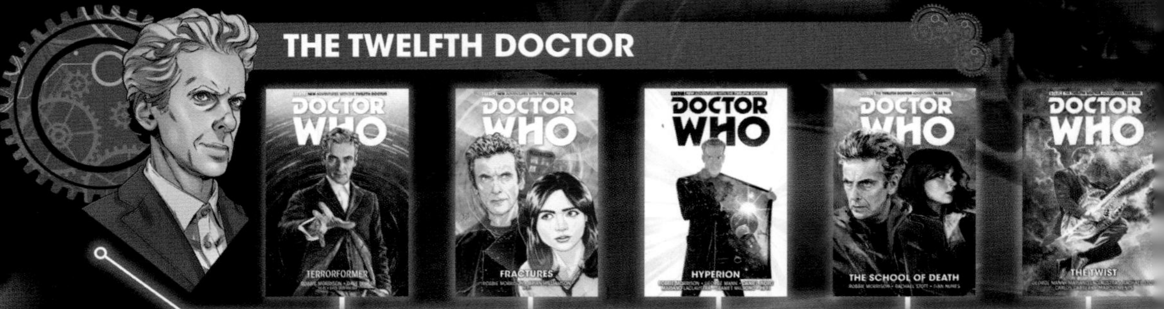
DOCTOR WHO
TERRORFORMER
DOCTOR WHO
FRACTURES
DOCTOR WHO
HYPERION
DOCTOR WHO
THE SCHOOL OF DEATH
DOCTOR WHO
THE TWIST

VOL. 1: TERRORFORMER

VOL. 2: FRACTURES

VOL. 3: HYPERION

YEAR TWO BEGINS! VOL. 4: SCHOOL OF DEATH

VOL. 5: THE TWIST

THE ELEVENTH DOCTOR

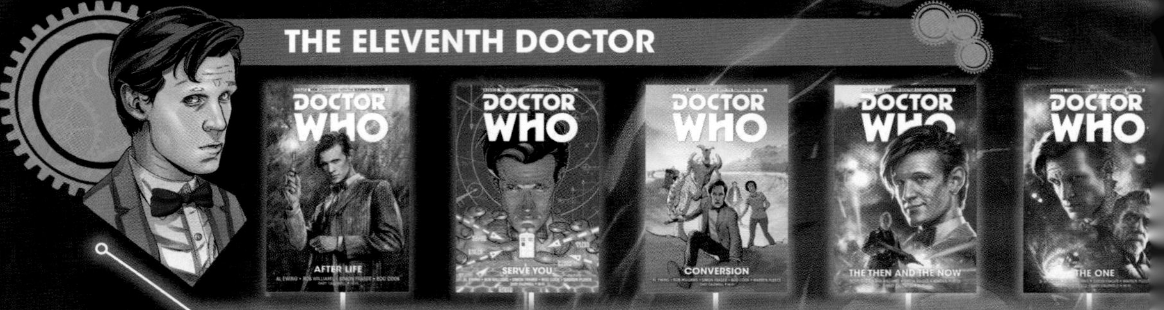
DOCTOR WHO
AFTER LIFE
DOCTOR WHO
SERVE YOU
DOCTOR WHO
CONVERSION
DOCTOR WHO
THE THEN AND THE NOW
DOCTOR WHO
THE ONE

VOL. 1: AFTER LIFE

VOL. 2: SERVE YOU

VOL. 3: CONVERSION

YEAR TWO BEGINS! VOL. 4: THE THEN AND THE NOW

VOL. 5: THE ONE

THE TENTH DOCTOR

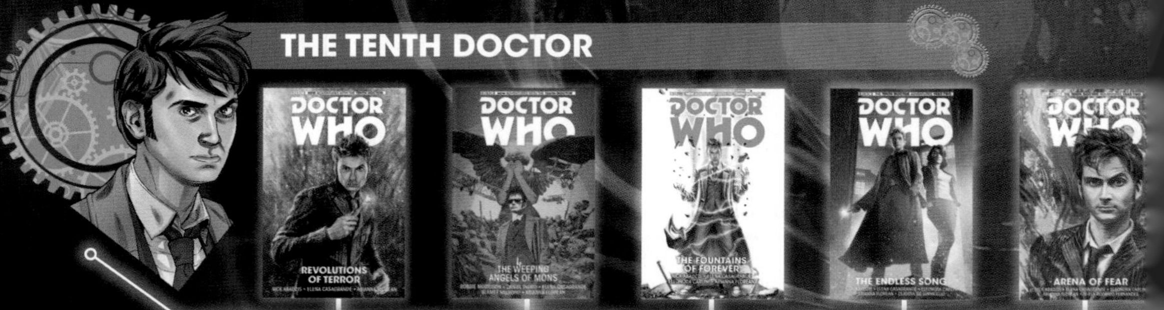
DOCTOR WHO
REVOLUTIONS OF TERROR
DOCTOR WHO
THE WEEPING ANGELS OF MONS
DOCTOR WHO
THE FOUNTAINS OF FOREVER
DOCTOR WHO
THE ENDLESS SONG
DOCTOR WHO
ARENA OF FEAR

VOL. 1: REVOLUTIONS OF TERROR

VOL. 2: THE WEEPING ANGELS OF MONS

VOL. 3: THE FOUNTAINS OF FOREVER

YEAR TWO BEGINS! VOL. 4: THE ENDLESS SONG

VOL. 5: ARENA OF FEAR

THE NINTH DOCTOR

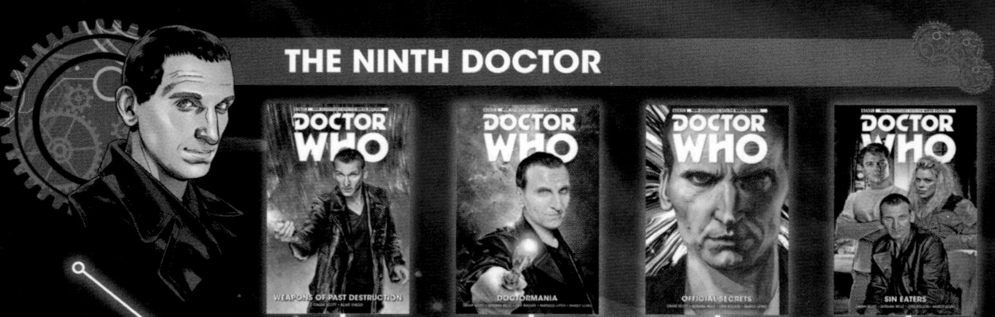
DOCTOR WHO
WEAPONS OF PAST DESTRUCTION
DOCTOR WHO
DOCTORMANIA
DOCTOR WHO
OFFICIAL SECRETS
DOCTOR WHO
SIN EATERS

VOL. 1: WEAPONS OF PAST DESTRUCTION

VOL. 2: DOCTORMANIA

VOL. 3: OFFICIAL SECRETS

VOL. 4: SIN EATERS

:h comic series is entirely self-contained and focused on one Doctor, so you can follow one, two, or all
'our favorite Doctors, as you wish! The series are arranged in TV season-like Years, collected into roughly
ee collections per Year. Feel free to start at Volume 1 of any series, or jump straight to the volumes
elled in blue! Each book, and every comic, features a catch-up and character guide at the beginning,
king it easy to jump on board – and each comic series has a very different flavor, representative of that
:tor's era on screen. If in doubt, set the TARDIS Randomizer and dive in wherever you land!

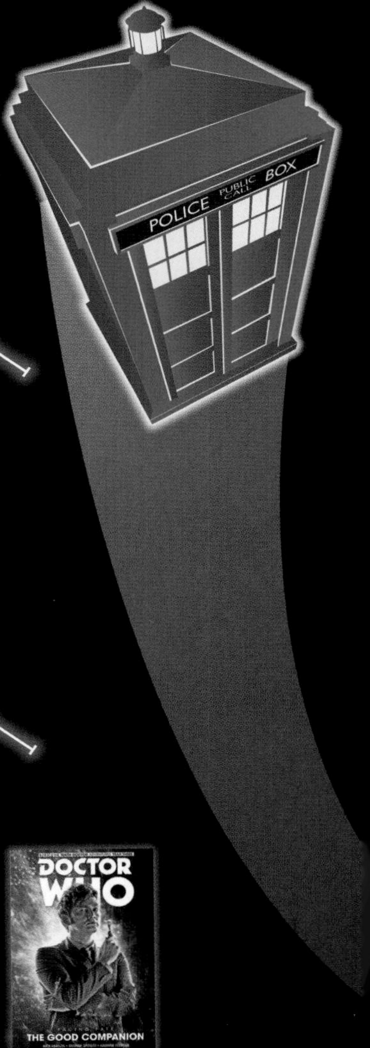

POLICE PUBLIC CALL BOX

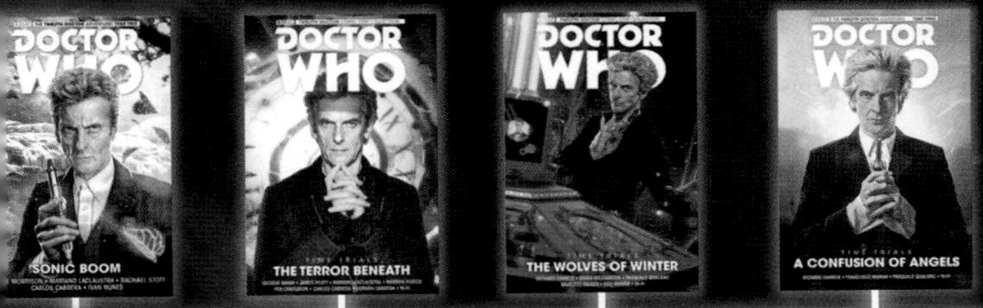

DOCTOR WHO
SONIC BOOM
DOCTOR WHO
THE TERROR BENEATH
DOCTOR WHO
THE WOLVES OF WINTER
DOCTOR WHO
A CONFUSION OF ANGELS

VOL. 6: SONIC BOOM

YEAR THREE BEGINS! TIME TRIALS VOL. 1: THE TERROR BENEATH

TIME TRIALS VOL. 2: THE WOLVES OF WINTER

TIME TRIALS VOL. 3: A CONFUSION OF ANGELS

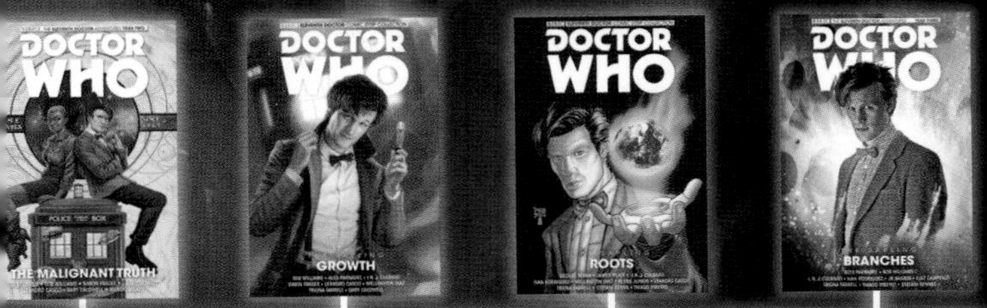

DOCTOR WHO
THE MALIGNANT TRUTH
DOCTOR WHO
GROWTH
DOCTOR WHO
ROOTS
DOCTOR WHO
BRANCHES

VOL. 6: MALIGNANT TRUTH

YEAR THREE BEGINS! THE SAPLING VOL. 1: GROWTH

THE SAPLING VOL. 2: ROOTS

THE SAPLING VOL. 3: BRANCHES

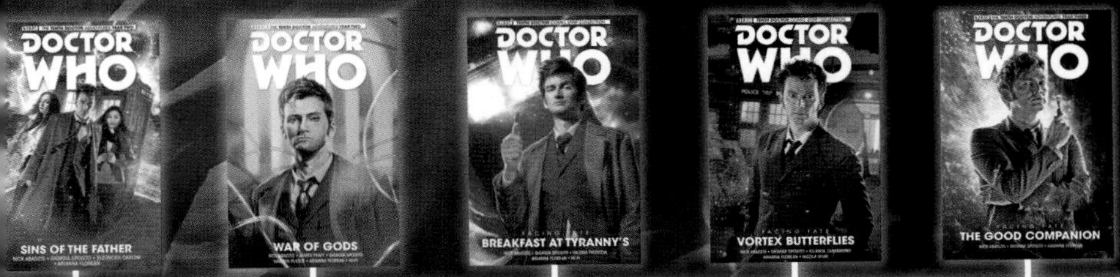

DOCTOR WHO
SINS OF THE FATHER
DOCTOR WHO
WAR OF GODS
DOCTOR WHO
BREAKFAST AT TYRANNY'S
DOCTOR WHO
VORTEX BUTTERFLIES
DOCTOR WHO
THE GOOD COMPANION

VOL. 6: NS OF THE FATHER

VOL. 7: WAR OF GODS

YEAR THREE BEGINS! FACING FATE VOL. 1: BREAKFAST AT TYRANNY'S

FACING FATE VOL. 2: VORTEX BUTTERFLIES

FACING FATE VOL. 3: THE GOOD COMPANION

CLASSIC DOCTORS

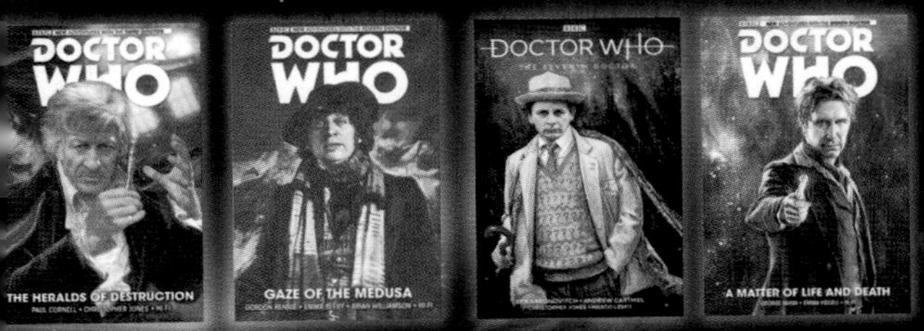

DOCTOR WHO
THE HERALDS OF DESTRUCTION
DOCTOR WHO
GAZE OF THE MEDUSA
DOCTOR WHO
DOCTOR WHO
A MATTER OF LIFE AND DEATH

THIRD DOCTOR: THE HERALDS OF

FOURTH DOCTOR: GAZE OF THE

SEVENTH DOCTOR: OPERATION

EIGHTH DOCTOR: A MATTER OF LIFE

MULTI-DOCTOR EVENTS

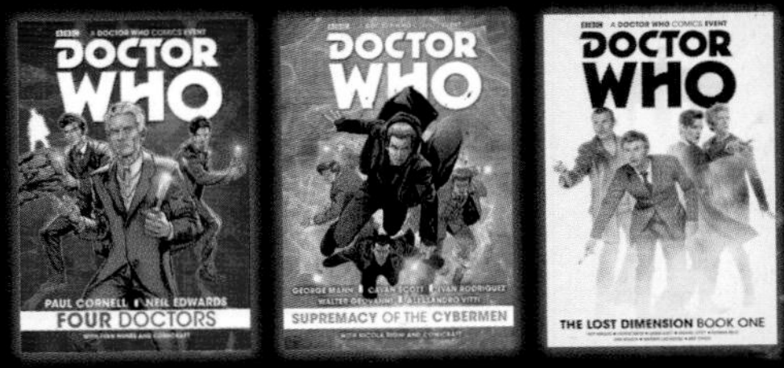

DOCTOR WHO
PAUL CORNELL NEIL EDWARDS
FOUR DOCTORS
DOCTOR WHO
SUPREMACY OF THE CYBERMEN
DOCTOR WHO
THE LOST DIMENSION BOOK ONE

FOUR DOCTORS

SUPREMACY OF THE CYBERMEN

THE LOST DIMENSION

BBC

DOCTOR WHO

THE THIRTEENTH DOCTOR VOLUME 0

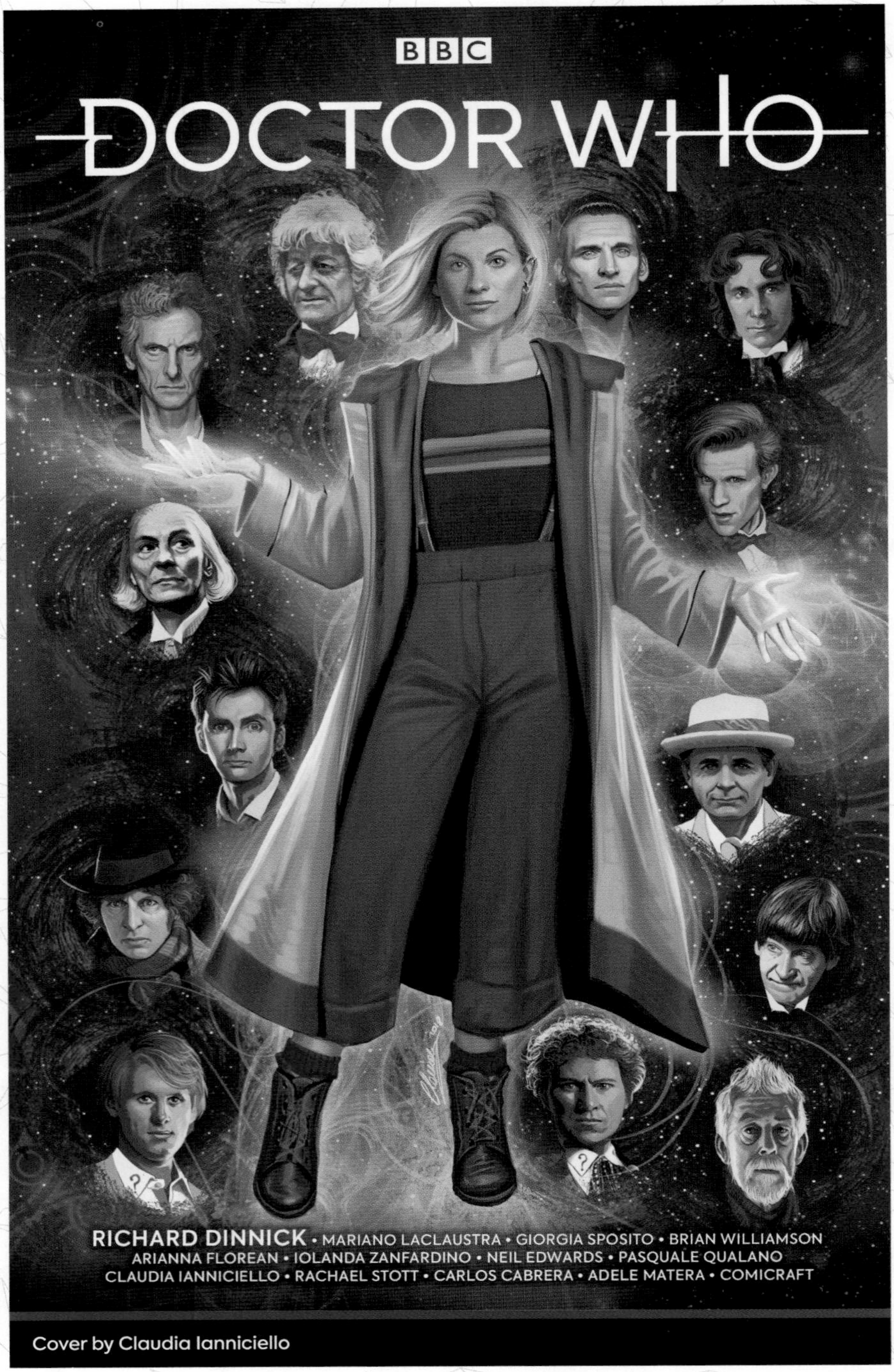

BBC
DOCTOR WHO
RICHARD DINNICK • MARIANO LACLAUSTRA • GIORGIA SPOSITO • BRIAN WILLIAMSON
ARIANNA FLOREAN • IOLANDA ZANFARDINO • NEIL EDWARDS • PASQUALE QUALANO
CLAUDIA IANNICIELLO • RACHAEL STOTT • CARLOS CABRERA • ADELE MATERA • COMICRAFT

Cover by Claudia Ianniciello

FROM RICHARD DINNICK • MARIANO LACLAUSTRA • GIORGIA SPOSITO
BRIAN WILLIAMSON • ARIANNA FLOREAN • IOLANDA ZANFARDINO

The Many Lives of Doctor Who

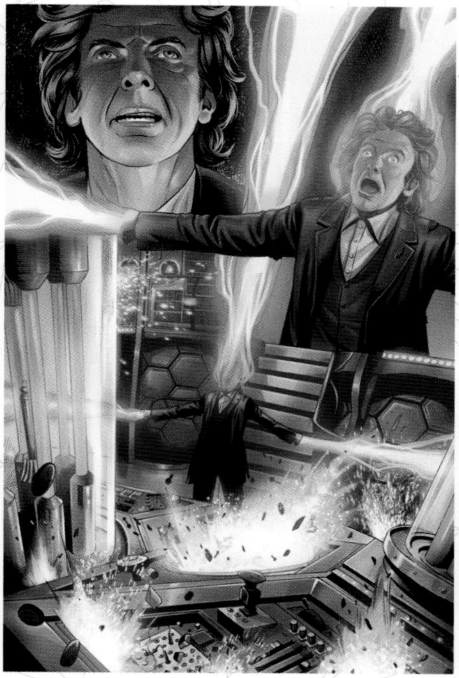

As the Twelfth Doctor regenerates into the Thirteenth, they flash back across their many lives and multiple incarnations – revealing brand-new stories from every era and face of the Doctor to date!

Written by **Richard Dinnick** (*The Twelfth Doctor*) and illustrated by a fantastic selection of mind-blowing artistic talents, this is the perfect introduction to *Doctor Who* for new readers, and the ultimate celebration of the series for long-term fans!

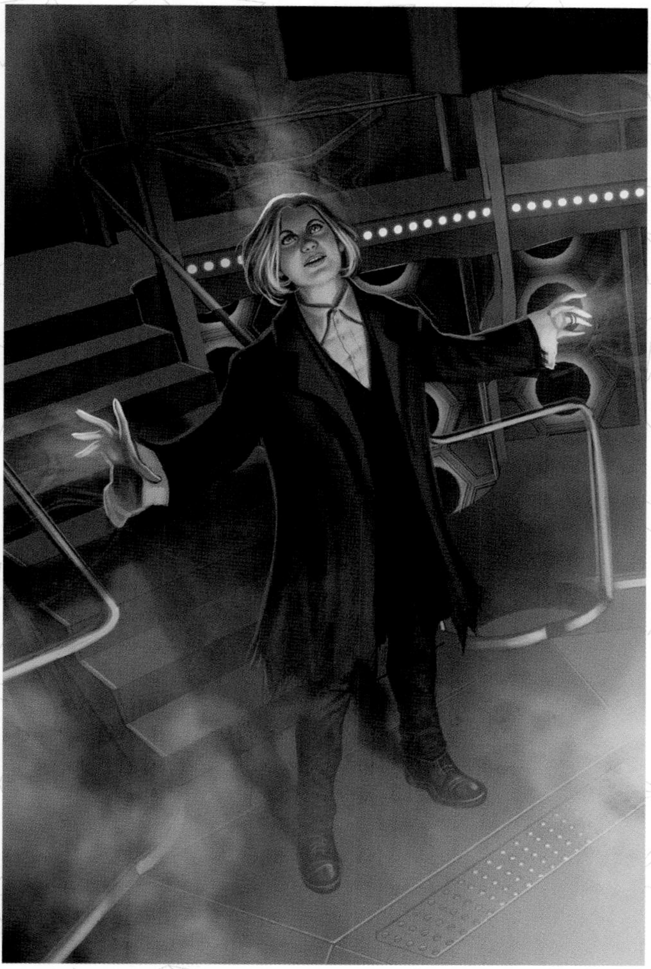

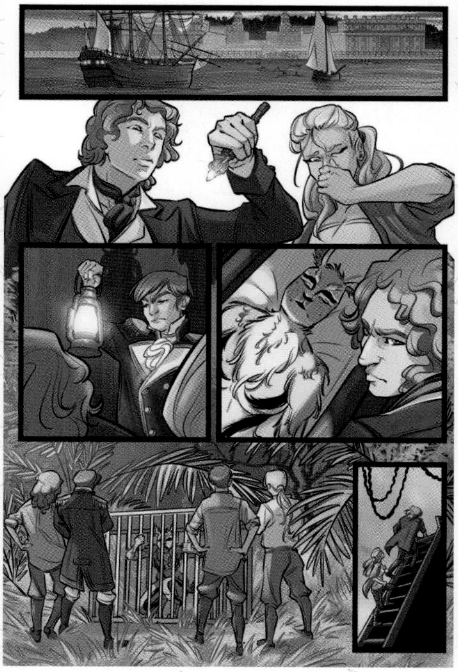

NEIL EDWARDS • PASQUALE QUALANO • CLAUDIA IANNICIELLO
RACHAEL STOTT • CARLOS CABRERA • ADELE MATERA • DIJJO LIMA

JODY HOUSER • RACHAEL STOTT • ENRICA EREN ANGIOLINI

Cover by Babs Tarr

FROM JODY HOUSER • RACHAEL STOTT • ENRICA EREN ANGIOLINI

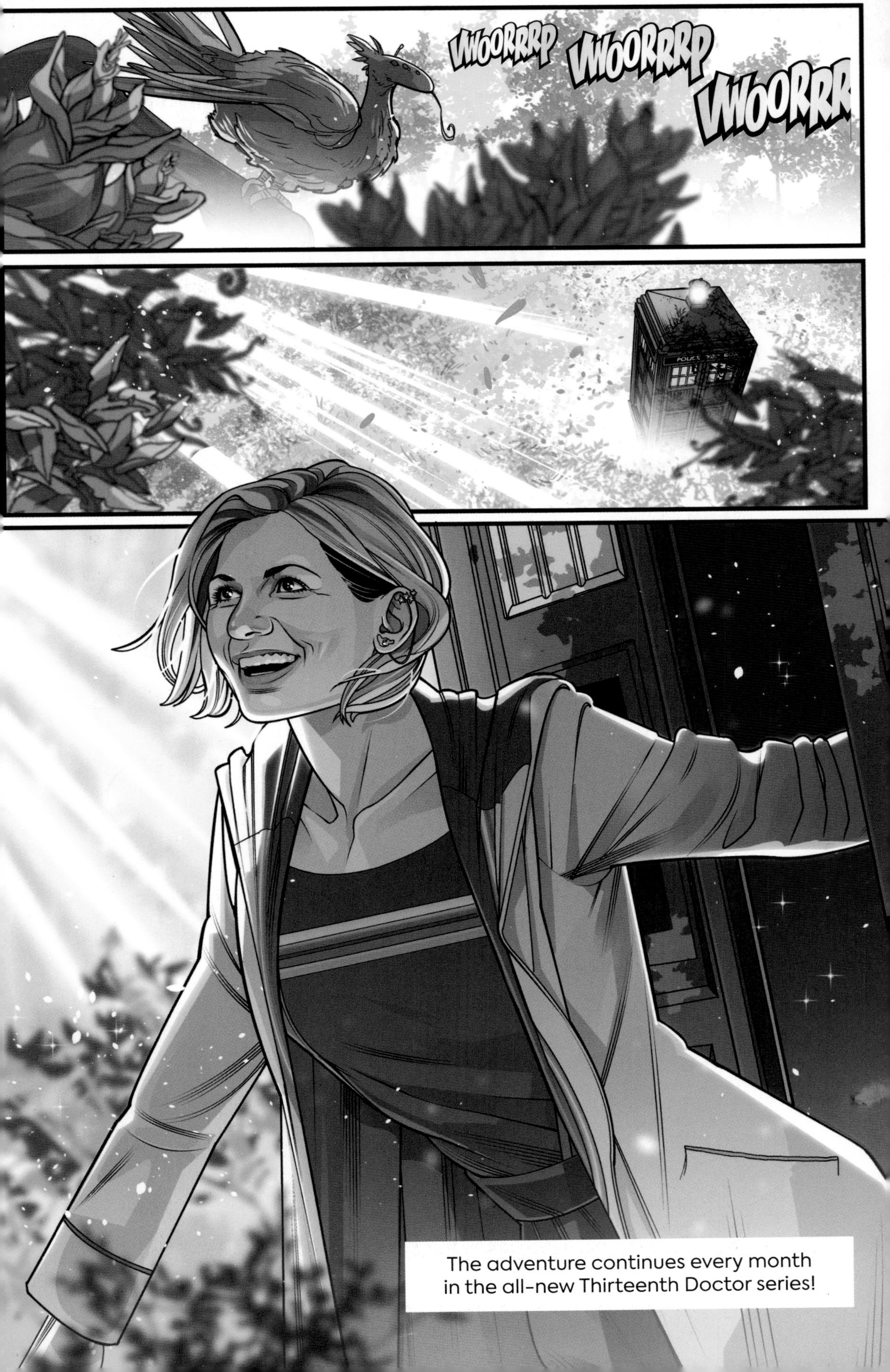
VWOORRRP
VWOORRRP
VWOORRR
The adventure continues every month in the all-new Thirteenth Doctor series!

BBC

DOCTOR WHO

THE ROAD TO THE THIRTEENTH DOCTOR

Biographies

James Peaty
is a prolific British writer and director who has worked on some of comics' most famous titles, such as *2000AD, Supergirl*, and *Doctor Who*.

Iolanda Zanfardino
is a brilliant rising star artist from Italy who has worked on interior art for *Doctor Who*, and on numerous covers, including *Sea of Thieves*. She is currently working on her own graphic novel, *The Magnetic Collection*, which she has both written and drawn.

Pasquale Qualano
is an Italian artist whose beautiful work can be seen in a myriad of titles such as *She-Hulk, DC Bombshells*, and *Batman 66* along with work for publishers including Titan Comics, Zenescope, IDW, and Red Giant Entertainment. In addition to his work in comics and sculpture, Pasquale teaches art at the School of Comics in Salerno.

Brian Williamson
is a veteran British artist whose highly detailed linework has contributed to many great titles including *Doctor Who: The Fourth Doctor, Torchwood, Batman*, and *Spider-Man*, to name but a few. Brian has also written several comics stories, including for *Torchwood* magazine.

Dijjo Lima
is an amazing colorist and designer from Brazil. His stunning colors have brought a huge variety of titles to life, including; *X-Men Blue, Spider-Man, Aquaman, Superman, Assassin's Creed: Origins*, and *Torchwood*. He is a 2018 Ringo Award nominee, for Best Colorist.

Jody Houser
is an extremely talented and prolific writer of comics, perhaps best known for her work on *Faith* for Valiant, and *Mother Panic* for the Young Animal imprint at DC Comics. She has also written *Star Wars: Rogue One, Star Wars: Age of Republic, Amazing Spider-Man: Renew Your Vows*, and *Spider-Girls* for Marvel, *The X-Files: Origins* and *Orphan Black* for IDW, and *Stranger Things, StarCraft*, and *Halo* for Dark Horse.

Rachael Stott
is a tremendous British artist who has worked on some of the most high-profile titles in comics, including *Star Trek, Planet of the Apes, Ghostbusters*, and *Doctor Who*. She has also worked on comics covers for titles like *Archie Comics*. A past winner of the Best Newcomer Award at the British Comics Awards, Rachael continues to enjoy critical acclaim for her brilliant work.

Enrica Eren Angiolini
is a fantastic colorist and illustrator from Italy. Enrica's rich colors go from strength to strength, as demonstrated by her work on *Warhammer 40,000, Shades of Magic: The Steel Prince*, and her cover work for Titan Comics, Dark Horse, and Aspen Comics.

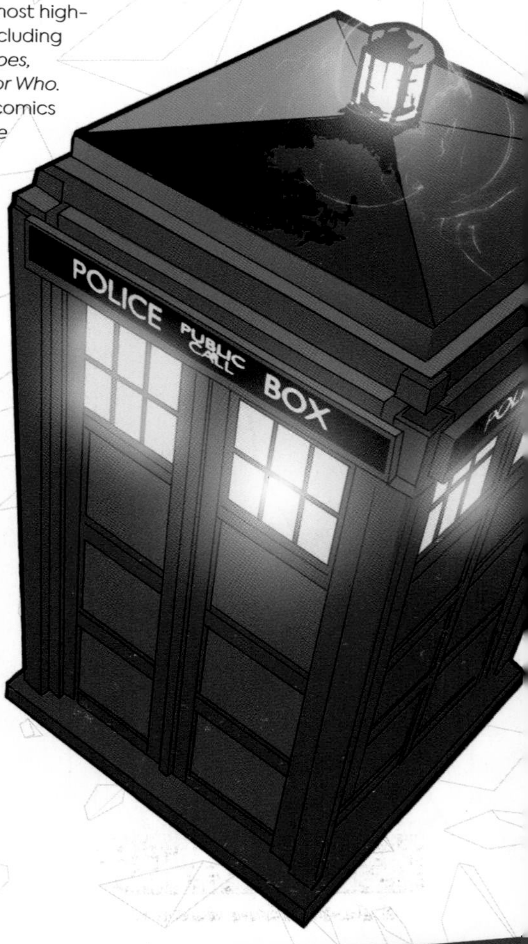
POLICE PUBLIC CALL BOX